ROSE REISMAN'S
Enlightened
HOME
COOKING

ROSE REISMAN'S
Enlightened
HOME
COOKING

Robert
ROSE

Rose Reisman's Enlightened Home Cooking

Copyright © 1996 Rose Reisman

The National Breast Cancer Fund does not represent or warrant that the use of the recipes contained in this book will either reduce the risk of developing breast cancer or improve the prognosis for those who have been treated for breast cancer. Any questions regarding the impact of diet and health should be directed to your physician. The National Breast Cancer Fund specifically disclaims any liability, loss or risk, personal or otherwise, which is incurred as a consequence, directly or indirectly, of the use and application of any of the contents of this book.

Y-ME National Breast Cancer Organization does not represent or warrant that the use of the recipes contained in this book will either reduce the risk of developing breast cancer or improve the prognosis for those who have been treated for breast cancer. Any questions regarding the impact of diet and health should be directed to your physician. Y-ME National Breast Cancer Organization specifically disclaims any liability, loss or risk, personal or otherwise, which is incurred as a consequence, directly or indirectly, of the use and application of any of the contents of this book.

For complete cataloguing data, see page 6.

DESIGN AND PAGE COMPOSITION:	MATTHEWS COMMUNICATIONS DESIGN
PHOTOGRAPHY:	MARK T. SHAPIRO
ART DIRECTION/FOOD PHOTOGRAPHY:	SHARON MATTHEWS
FOOD STYLIST:	KATE BUSH
MANAGING EDITOR:	PETER MATTHEWS
COPY EDITOR:	WENDY THOMAS
INDEXER:	BARBARA SCHON
COLOR SCANS & FILM:	POINTONE GRAPHICS

Cover photo: Roasted Chicken with Apricot Orange Glaze and Couscous Stuffing (page 116)

Distributed in the U.S. by:
Firefly Books (U.S.) Inc.
P.O. Box 1338
Ellicott Station
Buffalo, NY 14205

Distributed in Canada by:
Stoddart Publishing Co. Ltd.
34 Lesmill Road
North York, Ontario
M3B 2T6

ORDER LINES
Tel: (416) 499-8412
Fax: (416) 499-8313

ORDER LINES
Tel: (416) 445-3333
Fax: (416) 445-5967

Published by: Robert Rose Inc. • 156 Duncan Mill Road, Suite 12
Toronto, Ontario, Canada M3B 2N2   Tel: (416) 449-3535

Printed in Canada

234567 BP 99 98 97 96

CONTENTS

CATALOGUING INFORMATION

IN THE U.S.

Canadian Cataloguing in Publication Data

Reisman, Rose, 1953–

    Rose Reisman's enlightened home cooking

Published as a fund raising project of the Y-ME
National Breast Cancer Organization

Includes index.

ISBN 1-896503-16-0

1. Cookery   2. Low-fat diet – Recipes.
3. Low-calorie diet – Recipes. 4. Nutrition.
I. Title.   II. Title: Enlightened home cooking.

RM237.7.R45 1996a   641.5'638   C95-932641-3

IN CANADA

Canadian Cataloguing in Publication Data

Reisman, Rose, 1953–

    Rose Reisman's enlightened home cooking

Published as a fund raising project of the
National Breast Cancer Fund

Includes index.

ISBN 1-896503-12-8

1. Cookery   2. Low-fat diet – Recipes.
3. Low-calorie diet – Recipes. 4. Nutrition.
I. Title.   II. Title: Enlightened home cooking.

RM237.7.R45 1996   641.5'638   C95-932640-5

To the ones I love

my husband Sam

my precious children
Natalie, David, Laura and Adam

They make *ALL* the difference.

ACKNOWLEDGEMENTS

My special thanks to the group of talented professionals with whom I've had the opportunity to work once again. They made my job "a piece of cake"!

Bob Dees, my mentor and friend — and now, as president of our new company, Robert Rose Inc., my new business partner.

Matthews Communications Design, with a special thanks to Peter and Sharon Matthews, who now seem to be working daily on my behalf — with books, logos, brochures, food product labels, and more. Peter, who directed the editorial, production, and pre-press work; and Sharon, for her expert page and cover design, photo art direction, and for her incredible patience.

Mark Shapiro, who continues to do work beyond the call of duty. With his brilliant, meticulous food photography, and generous gifts of photographs — a true friend of the family.

Helen Chambers and Lorraine Fullum-Bouchard, from A.D. Harvey Nutrition Consultants, for providing a comprehensive nutritional analysis of each recipe, as well as an excellent and informative introduction on family nutrition.

Dr. Roy Clark, Chair of the National Breast Cancer Fund, for his support and involvement in this new fund raising agency, and for his informative foreword on breast cancer.

Kate Bush, an outstanding food stylist, for her detailed and excellent work — and for her patience in contending with my kitchen during the photo shoot.

Shelley Vlahantones, the food props coordinator, whose creativity helped to establish the new and exciting look of our photographs. Also to the fine suppliers of products that appear in the food shots: The Compleat Kitchen; DeVerre; Main Course; and Urban Mode.

Dianne Hargrave, the best publicist an author could want, who daily handles her demanding job with such remarkable skill and efficiency.

Lesleigh Landry, my assistant testing chef, for her professional skills and growing appreciation of "enlightened" cooking. Also to Irene and Tanja, who assist in food preparation on a daily basis in my hectic home.

Stoddart Publishing, who now distributes my books across Canada, for their extraordinary efforts on my behalf.

Firefly Books, my U.S. distributor, who has worked so hard to get my books everywhere.

Helen Silverstein, my events promoter, whose talents have resulted in the most successful fund-raising events of my career.

And finally, a very special thanks to my lifetime friend, Kathy, who has always been by my side — not only to taste my recipes (and truthfully comment on each), but also just to be there as my "best buddy."

It has always been my privilege to be involved in a career where I can make a real difference in people's lives. And now, with over 500,000 books in print, I know that my "enlightened" recipes are having a significant effect on the way people eat — bringing a healthier, yet ultimately enjoyable style to mealtimes across North America.

I believe that *Rose Reisman's Enlightened Home Cooking* is a breakthrough for busy families preparing meals at home. Here I've focused on recipes that are healthy, easy to make, and offer uncompromising appeal to the palate of every family member. And for the very first time, I've included a special section created exclusively for young and teenaged children who, I believe, deserve a lot better than they're getting from fast-food restaurants and prepackaged foods. With "secretly healthy" dishes like **Creamy Baked Beefaroni**, **Turkey Macaroni Chili** and **Triple Chocolate Brownies**, you can make mealtimes with your kids a satisfying experience instead of a stress-filled battleground.

Most importantly, you may be able to make a tangible difference in the lifelong health prospects of your children. How? Dr. Michael Pollak, an oncologist at the Montreal Jewish General Hospital once told me that if he could do something to influence the diet of one age group, it would be children between 5 and 15 years of age. He pointed out that ongoing research suggests that an optimal diet for children in this category may have lifelong benefits for them, particularly with respect to the future risk of breast cancer.

Still, even the lightest, healthiest meals have to taste great. And in this book — with complete sections on appetizers, soups, salads, fish, chicken, meat, pasta and grains, vegetables and desserts — I've tested my new recipes over and over again to make sure each dish is a taste sensation.

With this book I've tried to include meals for just about any situation at home. Having some friends over for dinner? Try **Linguini with Pecan Oriental Sauce and Salmon** or **Chicken Breast Stuffed with Brie Cheese**. Just the kids? They'll love **Crunchy Baked Macaroni Cheese Casserole** and **Peanut Butter Chocolate Muffins**. Need something quick? Enjoy **Hoisin Burgers** or **Pork Fajitas with Sweet Pepper, Coriander and Cheese**. Busy schedule and you need something to keep over the next few days? Try **Ratatouille Meat Loaf Casserole with Cheese Topping** or **Chicken with Rice, Green Olives and Tomato Sauce**.

All of these wonderful recipes can be prepared in under 30 minutes with ingredients that are available at local supermarkets. All are nutritionally analyzed and provide informative tips and make-ahead suggestions. I promise you, these recipes will become as essential to your family as they have to mine.

This book, like my last two, will also make a difference in the fight against breast cancer. I am very proud that a portion of the proceeds from the sale of my last two books have helped to raise nearly $500,000 across North America for this cause. It amazes me the difference the purchase of a cookbook can make. And now, in association with the National Breast Cancer Fund (NBCF), sales of this book will contribute directly to research into the causes and prevention of breast cancer.

Finally, I just can't resist telling you about my new line of *Enlightened*™ food products. Developed in response to all those people who have asked me about where they can find high-quality, nutritionally sensible packaged foods, my *Enlightened*™ sauces and marinades provide a deliciously different alternative to what you normally find in supermarkets. They're all handmade with fresh ingredients, no preservatives, and feature complete nutritional analysis. In fact, these products are about as close as you can get to what I make in my own kitchen, adjusted only to provide maximum shelf life. So watch out for my *Enlightened*™ **Chunky Marinara Sauce with Sun Dried Tomatoes and Black Olives, Pasta Sauce with Mushrooms and Cheese, Hoisin Garlic Marinade, Oriental Cashew Sauce, Chocolate Fudge Sauce** and **Butterscotch Sauce.** They should be appearing in the coming year.

So here you have it — an approach to eating that takes the traditionally restrictive idea of "light" food out of the closet (or should I say pantry) and transforms it into something sublime — better, richer and more satisfying than the alternatives. These recipes, my latest creations, give you the freedom to prepare sensible, healthy meals without apology or sacrifice because there is no compromise in taste.

So enjoy my new Enlightened cooking. You'll stay light for life.

Rose Reisman

Public awareness of breast cancer has grown significantly in recent years. This in itself has been a positive development. But with the media's focus on a few gloomy statistics — for example, that one in nine women will experience the disease in her lifetime — the subject of breast cancer is often treated with an inordinate degree of pessimism.

The reality is that much progress is being made — in diagnosis, in treatment, and in understanding risk reduction. Radical surgery and radiation, for example, are rapidly becoming a thing of the past in early disease. With techniques such as mammography, it is now possible to identify breast cancer much sooner (hence the apparent increase in the incidence of the disease in women over 55). In such cases, more localized procedures, combined with hormone and drug therapies, are achieving excellent results.

Here's another statistic that often doesn't make the headlines: Breast cancer has one of the best survival rates of any type of cancer. With early detection, this rate is between 85 and 90 percent at 5 years. In fact, the average woman's chances of succumbing to breast cancer by the age of 75 are less than 3%. Even in high-risk groups, the probability is unlikely to exceed 10%.

And what about prevention? Although the precise causes of breast cancer continue to elude researchers, a number of potential risk factors are being identified. For example, there does appear to be an association between a high-fat diet, excessive weight gain and the incidence of breast cancer. And while this link is difficult to establish with certainty (although a number of studies into it are now underway), it still makes sense to follow a low-fat diet. Not only will it help you to avoid the consequences of excessive weight gain (and possible increase in breast cancer risk), but it will certainly help your heart (studies *have* proven this).

Rose Reisman's Enlightened Home Cooking provides a collection of recipes that combine sensible eating with great taste. And when you buy this book, you will be making a donation to Y-ME National Breast Cancer Organization in the U.S. and to the National Breast Cancer Fund in Canada.

R.M. Clark MB, BS, FRCR, FRCPC
Chairman, National Breast Cancer Fund

Sharon Green
Executive Director, Y-ME

FAMILY NUTRITION

When the world-famous Cordon Bleu cooking school introduced a "light" cooking class in 1995, it represented a major move away from the traditional high-fat style. Today, the school's La Lean Cuisine à la Francaise offers an introduction to healthy, balanced meal preparation, using techniques that can be applied to everyday cooking. This is a trend that has been gaining momentum in kitchens all over the world and is exactly what you will find in *Rose Reisman's Enlightened Home Cooking*.

The book features a wide range of recipes that the whole family will enjoy and you'll find it most helpful in the planning of family meals. In this era of hectic schedules, the family meal emerges as one of the few constants in a sea of variables. And it is here that children gain eating habits that, in most cases, will stay with them for the rest of their lives.

INTRODUCING NEW FOODS

Government food guides in the U.S. and Canada emphasize the importance of including a wide variety of foods in our diet. Children need to be encouraged to enjoy new foods in order to have this variety. They acquire their preferences by observing their parents. If new foods are presented as pleasurable experiences, children will respond accordingly. However, their level of curiosity will vary from day to day, so don't expect 100% acceptance. It has been shown that children may need to taste a new food eight to 10 times before they will accept it as a regular part of their diet.

It also helps to introduce new dishes in tasting-size portions, and to serve them along with old favorites. No matter how much time, effort or expense was involved in its preparation, don't pressure the child to eat a new food. Patience is the best recipe.

AVOIDING "CLEAN PLATE" SYNDROME

It is an accepted practice to feed babies on demand, but children are expected to eat at predetermined times. It is now believed that they also have internal cues that govern their hunger (as well as their satiety) and if left to their own management, will eat only what their body requires. Many adults continue to live according to their parents' exortations to "clean your plate" or "think of all the starving children in..." and they pass this on to their own children. This removes the control from the child and they learn to eat according to external cues instead of internal cues, which could be the beginning of a weight management problem.

BALANCING CARBOHYDRATES, PROTEIN AND FATS

To help you make good use of the nutrient analysis included with these recipes, the chart below will serve as a guide for your daily intake of carbohydrates, protein, and fat. The current recommendation for a healthy individual is that no more than 30% of calories should be derived from fat, although some authorities believe it should be lower. This refers to total daily caloric intake, not just the percentage of fats per meal or food item. Keep in mind that balance is the goal: By planning meals, the occasional higher-fat food can be included in a healthy diet when balanced with lower-fat foods for the rest of the day or week.

Daily caloric intake	Carbohydrates *55% of total calories* (g)	Protein *15% of total calories* (g)	Total fat *30% of total calories* (g)	Saturated fat *10% of total calories* (g)
1500	206	56	50	17
1800	248	68	60	20
2000	275	75	67	22

ARE "LOW FAT" FOODS RIGHT FOR CHILDREN?

This question frequently surfaces when, for various reasons, parents wish to reduce their fat intake, while their children have no apparent need for a similarly low-fat diet. There is nothing wrong with moderate consumption of higher-fat foods, and these can easily be served to children in the form of between-meal snacks, while the family meal focuses on low-fat dishes. Many children need the concentrated source of energy that higher-fat foods provide.

SOURCES OF FAT

One teaspoon of foods such as oil, butter, margarine or regular mayonnaise contains 4 to 5 grams of fat. These are visible fats and are relatively easy to control. But other sources of fats are less visible. These include: whole or partially skimmed dairy products such as milk, cheese and yogurt; meats, fish and poultry; many cookies, crackers and desserts;

and, of course, fried foods. The control of invisible fats requires more knowledge of the fat content of the foods consumed, so a full nutritional analysis is given with the recipes in this book.

While the quantity of fat used in cooking is important, so is the type of fat used. In testing the recipes for this book, when a vegetable oil was called for, we used canola oil. This is a good all-purpose oil which contains very little saturated fat and has a large percentage of monounsaturated fat. Olive oil was used for certain recipes where its special flavor enhances the overall enjoyment of a particular pasta dish. Olive oil and canola oil have similar chemical properties. Because they are in a liquid state, they do not contain trans-fatty acids. (Trans-fatty acids are formed when liquid oils are processed into solid fats and are believed to behave in a manner similar to saturated fats.)

REDUCE FAT, NOT TASTE

Why we enjoy the taste of fats is an area of great interest. Is it the taste, texture or smell? Is it a biological preference or a learned preference? Whatever it is, we do know that fat in food provides many sensory pleasures and for that reason when one reduces the fat used in cooking, substitutions must be made. In this book you will find many examples of effective "taste compensation." But let's say that you have some old favorite recipes for which you'd like to reduce the fat? Here is a brief summary of low-fat cooking techniques you can try.

Equipment: have at least one nonstick pan, and/or use vegetable cooking sprays. If using oils for flavor, measure rather than pour, and try some of the more flavorful varieties such as extra virgin olive oil, sesame oil or walnut oil. Have a fat separator to remove the fat from pan drippings or broth. Remember that most of these separators are made from a material that does not withstand high temperatures.

Seasoning: Make good use of all fresh and dried herbs, onions, shallots, fresh garlic, fresh ginger root, Dijon mustard, fresh lemons, limes, flavored vinegars, wines and sherry.

Minimize fats from meats: Plan each meat portion carefully so that it becomes secondary to the vegetable and grains that are being served. Remove as much visible fat as possible before cooking. It is only the fat in the marbling (not the outside) that adds to the flavor of cooked meat. Similarly, try to avoid the fat-intensive skin when preparing and eating poultry.

Choose low-fat dairy products: Always look for the "% M.F." or "% total fat" on the label of any dairy product. Use low-fat milk and yogurt (2% is specified for recipes in this book), reduced-fat cheeses (for example, 5% ricotta), evaporated skim milk and light sour cream.

ENJOY!

Always remember that the most important word in healthy eating is "enjoy." Food should not only nourish but should be an enjoyable part of family life. The recipes in this book are designed to help one achieve this balance.

Helen Chambers RD
Lorraine Fullum-Bouchard RD

Nutritionist's Notes

1. *All recipes have been analysed for the ingredients given in the main body of the recipe. Where substitute or optional ingredients are used (for example, in the Tips portion of the recipe), nutritional values may change.*

2. *Certain fat contents have been assumed for dairy products used in recipes. These include: ricotta cheese (5%); light sour cream (1%); and light cream cheese (17%).*

3. *Nutritional values have been rounded to the nearest whole number for all components except saturated fat, where values of less than 1 gram are rounded to the nearest tenth of a gram. For all other components, values less than 0.45 are not considered to be significant and are rounded down to zero.*

*A*PPETIZERS

APPETIZER TIPS

1. Dips can be prepared up to a day ahead. Be sure to mix well just before serving, since excess liquid can separate. Serve with crackers, bread, tortilla chips and vegetables.

2. Chill cold appetizers for at least 2 hours before serving.

3. Bake hot appetizers just before serving to ensure the best taste.

CHUNKY ARTICHOKE DIP

TIP

Serve with vegetables or crackers.

To make tortilla or pita crisps for this or any other dip, cut tortilla or pita into wedges and put on a sprayed baking sheet. Brush lightly with oil and bake at 350°F (180°C) for 5 to 10 minutes, or until lightly browned.

Serve either at room temperature or chilled.

MAKE AHEAD

Prepare up to a day in advance; stir before serving.

1	can (19 oz [398 mL]) artichoke hearts, drained	1
1/4 cup	5% ricotta cheese	50 mL
1/4 cup	light sour cream or 2% yogurt	50 mL
1/4 cup	chopped fresh parsley	50 mL
1/4 cup	chopped green onions, about 2 medium	50 mL
3 tbsp	light mayonnaise	45 mL
3 tbsp	grated Parmesan cheese	45 mL
1 tsp	minced garlic	5 mL

1. Put artichoke hearts, ricotta, sour cream, parsley, green onions, mayonnaise, Parmesan and garlic in food processor; process until slightly chunky.

PER SERVING

Calories	56
Protein	3 g
Fat, total	3 g
Fat, saturated	0.9 g
Carbohydrates	5 g
Sodium	198 mg
Cholesterol	6 mg
Fiber	0 g

AVOCADO TOMATO SALSA

TIP

Serve with crackers or tortilla crisps.

For an authentic, intense flavor, use 1/2 tsp (2 mL) finely diced chili pepper, or more chili powder.

MAKE AHEAD

Prepare up to 4 hours ahead; stir before serving.

2 cups	finely chopped plum tomatoes	500 mL
1/2 cup	finely chopped ripe but firm avocado (about 1/2 avocado)	125 mL
1/3 cup	chopped fresh coriander	75 mL
1/4 cup	chopped green onions (about 2 medium)	50 mL
1 tbsp	olive oil	15 mL
1 tbsp	lime or lemon juice	15 mL
1 tsp	minced garlic	5 mL
1/8 tsp	chili powder	1 mL

1. In serving bowl, combine tomatoes, avocado, coriander, green onions, olive oil, lime juice, garlic and chili powder; let marinate 1 hour before serving.

PER SERVING

Calories	53
Protein	1 g
Fat, total	4 g
Fat, saturated	0.6 g
Carbohydrates	4 g
Sodium	8 mg
Cholesterol	0 mg
Fiber	1 g

CREAMY PESTO DIP

TIP

To toast pine nuts, put in nonstick skillet over medium-high heat for 3 minutes, stirring occasionally. Or put them on a baking sheet and toast in a 400°F (200°C) oven for 5 minutes. Whichever method you choose, watch carefully – nuts burn quickly.

If basil is not available, use parsley or spinach leaves.

MAKE AHEAD

Prepare early in the day and keep covered and refrigerated.

1 cup	well-packed basil leaves	250 mL
2 tbsp	toasted pine nuts	25 mL
2 tbsp	grated Parmesan cheese	25 mL
2 tbsp	olive oil	25 mL
2 tsp	lemon juice	10 mL
1 tsp	minced garlic	5 mL
1/2 cup	5% ricotta cheese	125 mL
1/4 cup	light sour cream	50 mL

1. Put basil, pine nuts, Parmesan, olive oil, lemon juice and garlic in food processor; process until finely chopped, scraping sides of bowl down once. Add ricotta and sour cream and process until smooth. Serve with pita or tortilla crisps, or fresh vegetables.

PER SERVING (8)

Calories	67
Protein	4 g
Fat, total	5 g
Fat, saturated	2 g
Carbohydrates	2 g
Sodium	53 mg
Cholesterol	8 mg
Fiber	0 g

TUNA AND WHITE BEAN SPREAD

Serves 8

TIP

White navy pea beans can also be used. If you cook your own dry beans, 1/2 cup (125 mL) dry yields approximately 1 1/2 cups (375 mL) of cooked beans.

MAKE AHEAD

Prepare up to a day ahead; keep covered and refrigerated. Stir before using.

1 cup	canned, cooked white kidney beans, drained	250 mL
1	can (6.5 oz [184 g]) tuna in water, drained	1
1 1/2 tsp	minced garlic	7 mL
2 tbsp	lemon juice	25 mL
2 tbsp	light mayonnaise	25 mL
1/4 cup	5% ricotta cheese	50 mL
3 tbsp	minced red onions	45 mL
1/4 cup	minced fresh dill (or 1 tsp [5 mL] dried)	50 mL
1 tbsp	grated Parmesan cheese	15 mL
1/4 cup	diced red pepper	50 mL

1. Place beans, tuna, garlic, lemon juice, mayonnaise and ricotta in food processor; pulse on and off until combined but still chunky. Place in serving bowl.

2. Stir onions, dill, Parmesan and red pepper into bean mixture.

PER SERVING	
Calories	73
Protein	8 g
Fat, total	2 g
Fat, saturated	0.5 g
Carbohydrates	7 g
Sodium	188 mg
Cholesterol	6 mg
Fiber	2 g

ENGLISH MUFFIN TOMATO OLIVE BRUSCHETTA

Serves 8

TIP

Instead of using your toaster, toast the muffin halves on a baking sheet 3 inches (7.5 cm) under a preheated broiler for 2 minutes.

To avoid excess liquid, remove seeds from tomatoes. Plum tomatoes will give a firmer texture.

MAKE AHEAD

You can make the tomato mixture a few hours ahead, but don't top the muffins until you're ready to bake and serve.

Preheat oven to 450°C (230°C)

2 cups	diced tomatoes (2 medium), preferably plum	500 mL
2 tbsp	olive oil	25 mL
3 tbsp	chopped fresh basil (or 1 tsp [5 mL] dried)	45 mL
1 tsp	minced garlic	5 mL
1/4 cup	chopped black olives	50 mL
4	English muffins	4
1 oz	goat cheese	25 g

1. In bowl, combine tomatoes, olive oil, basil, garlic and olives; set aside.

2. Split and toast English muffins and place on baking sheet. Top each muffin half with 1/4 cup (50 mL) of the tomato mixture. Crumble the goat cheese and sprinkle over top of muffins.

3. Bake for 5 minutes or until cheese melts and topping is warmed through. Cut in quarters and serve.

PER SERVING

Calories	122
Protein	4 g
Fat, total	5 g
Fat, saturated	0.5 g
Carbohydrates	16 g
Sodium	140 mg
Cholesterol	0 mg
Fiber	1 g

CHICKEN SATAY WITH PEANUT SAUCE

TIP

These satays can be barbecued for approximately 10 minutes or until chicken is cooked.

Chicken can be replaced with fresh salmon, pork or beef.

This sauce can be used as a marinade for beef or fish.

These appetizers have a fair amount of protein. Have a main course with less protein.

MAKE AHEAD

Prepare sauce up to 2 days in advance. Keep refrigerated.

PER SERVING

Calories	167
Protein	23 g
Fat, total	6 g
Fat, saturated	1 g
Carbohydrates	5 g
Sodium	218 mg
Cholesterol	53 mg
Fiber	1 g

Preheat oven to 425°F (220°C)
Baking pan sprayed with vegetable spray

1 lb	skinless, boneless chicken breasts	500 g

Peanut Sauce

2 tbsp	peanut butter	25 mL
2 tbsp	chicken stock	25 mL
2 tbsp	chopped fresh coriander	25 mL
1 tbsp	rice wine vinegar	15 mL
1 tbsp	honey	15 mL
2 tsp	sesame oil	10 mL
2 tsp	soya sauce	10 mL
1 tsp	minced garlic	5 mL
1 tsp	minced ginger root	5 mL
1 tsp	sesame seeds, toasted	5 mL

1. In small bowl or food processor, combine peanut butter, chicken stock, coriander, vinegar, honey, sesame oil, soya sauce, garlic, ginger and sesame seeds. Set 3 tbsp (45 mL) aside.

2. Cut chicken into 1-inch (2.5 cm) cubes. Thread onto 10 small bamboo or barbecue skewers. Place skewers in prepared pan. Brush with half of the peanut sauce that has been set aside. Bake approximately 5 minutes. Turn over and brush the remaining 1 1/2 tbsp (20 mL) sauce and bake 5 more minutes or just until chicken is done. Serve with remaining peanut sauce.

HOISIN COCKTAIL MEATBALLS

Serves 8

TIP

Substitute ground beef with ground chicken, veal or pork.

★

Sauce can be warmed slightly before serving.

MAKE AHEAD

Prepare meatballs and sauce up to a day ahead. Broil just before serving.

Preheat broiler

12 oz	lean ground beef	375 g
4 tbsp	bread crumbs	60 mL
3 tbsp	chopped green onions (1 medium)	45 mL
3 tbsp	chopped coriander or parsley	45 mL
2 tbsp	hoisin sauce	25 mL
1 tbsp	soya sauce	15 mL
2 tsp	minced garlic	10 mL
1 tsp	minced ginger root	5 mL
1 tsp	sesame oil	5 mL

Sauce

2 tbsp	hoisin sauce	25 mL
2 tbsp	rice wine vinegar	25 mL
1 tbsp	sesame oil	15 mL
1 tbsp	soya sauce	15 mL
1 tbsp	water	15 mL
1 1/2 tsp	honey	7 mL
3/4 tsp	minced garlic	4 mL
1/2 tsp	minced ginger root	2 mL

1. In large bowl, combine beef, bread crumbs, green onions, coriander, hoisin sauce, soya sauce, garlic, ginger and sesame oil; mix thoroughly. Form into 32 meatballs, each approximately 1 inch (2.5 cm) in diameter. Cook under broiler for 6 minutes or until cooked through.

2. Meanwhile, in small bowl combine hoisin sauce, vinegar, sesame oil, soya sauce, water, honey, garlic and ginger. Serve meatballs with sauce.

PER SERVING	
Calories	160
Protein	9 g
Fat, total	9 g
Fat, saturated	3 g
Carbohydrates	10 g
Sodium	377 mg
Cholesterol	23 mg
Fiber	0 g

MINI PESTO SHRIMP TORTILLA PIZZAS

TIP

Using store-bought pesto adds more calories and fat. The sauce recipe on page 170 is delicious and the unused portion can be used over pasta. It can be frozen up to 3 weeks.

Two large tortillas can be used instead of the 4 small ones.

Any vegetables or other cheese, such as goat cheese, can be substituted.

MAKE AHEAD

Prepare the pizzas early in day. Keep covered and refrigerated until ready to bake.

Pizzas can also be prepared and frozen for up to 6 weeks.

PER SERVING

Calories	131
Protein	6 g
Fat, total	7 g
Fat, saturated	2 g
Carbohydrates	11 g
Sodium	159 mg
Cholesterol	23 mg
Fiber	1 g

Preheat oven to 400° F (200° C)
Baking sheet sprayed with vegetable spray

4	small flour tortillas	4
1/3 cup	pesto (store-bought or see sauce recipe on page 170)	75 mL
1/2 cup	finely chopped red peppers	125 mL
1/2 cup	finely chopped cooked shrimp	125 mL
2/3 cup	shredded part-skim mozzarella cheese	150 mL

1. Place tortillas on baking sheet. Divide pesto among tortillas; spread evenly.

2. Top tortillas with red peppers, shrimp and mozzarella.

3. Bake for 12 to 15 minutes or until cheese has melted and tortillas are crisp. Cut each into 4 pieces.

MUSHROOM PHYLLO PIZZA

Serves 8

TIP

Use wild mushrooms for an extra-special taste.

★

Feta cheese can replace goat cheese.

★

Bake just before serving so that the phyllo stays crisp.

MAKE AHEAD

Cook mushrooms early in the day and set aside.

Preheat oven to 425°F (220°C)

10- by 15-inch (25 cm by 37.5 cm) baking sheet sprayed with vegetable spray

3 tsp	margarine or butter	15 mL
6 cups	sliced mushrooms	1.5 L
2 tsp	minced garlic	10 mL
4	sheets phyllo pastry	4
1/3 cup	sliced black olives	75 mL
2 oz	goat cheese, crumbled	50 g

1. Heat 1 tsp (5 mL) of margarine in large nonstick skillet sprayed with vegetable spray over medium-high heat. Add mushrooms and garlic; cook 4 minutes or until tender and browned. Drain any excess liquid.

2. Melt remaining 2 tsp (10 mL) margarine. Layer 2 phyllo sheets on baking sheet; brush with melted margarine. Layer remaining 2 phyllo sheets on top; brush with remaining melted margarine. Fold ends of phyllo pastry under to create rim.

3. Spread mushroom mixture over phyllo; top with olives and goat cheese. Bake 8 to 10 minutes or until phyllo is browned.

PER SERVING	
Calories	87
Protein	3 g
Fat, total	4 g
Fat, saturated	0.5 g
Carbohydrates	10 g
Sodium	132 mg
Cholesterol	0 mg
Fiber	1 g

ORIENTAL EGG ROLLS WITH ALMOND SAUCE

TIP

Cooked shrimp, chicken or pork can replace crab.

Real crab can replace surimi.

MAKE AHEAD

Egg rolls can be prepared early in day, covered and refrigerated until ready to bake.

Prepare sauce up to 2 days in advance and keep refrigerated.

Preheat oven to 425° F (220°C)
Baking sheet sprayed with vegetable spray

Sauce

2 tbsp	finely chopped almonds	25 mL
4 tsp	soya sauce	20 mL
1 tbsp	sesame oil	15 mL
1 tbsp	honey	15 mL
2 tbsp	chicken stock or water	25 mL
1 tbsp	rice wine vinegar	15 mL
1 tsp	minced garlic	5 mL
1 tsp	minced ginger root	5 mL

Filling

3/4 cup	finely chopped red peppers	175 mL
3/4 cup	finely chopped snow peas	175 mL
1/2 cup	finely chopped green onions (4 medium)	125 mL
1 1/4 cups	bean sprouts	300 mL
3/4 cup	finely chopped crab legs or surimi (imitation crab)	175 mL
1/4 cup	chopped fresh coriander or parsley	50 mL
10	large egg roll wrappers	10

1. In food processor or in a bowl, combine almonds, soya sauce, sesame oil, honey, chicken stock, vinegar, garlic and ginger. Process or mix until well combined. Set aside.

2. In large nonstick skillet sprayed with vegetable spray, cook the red peppers, snow peas and green onions over medium-high heat for 4 minutes or until tender-crisp. Add bean sprouts, crab, and 2 tbsp (25 mL) of the sauce; cook, stirring, for 2 more minutes. Remove from heat and stir in coriander.

PER SERVING

Calories	84
Protein	4 g
Fat, total	3 g
Fat, saturated	0.4 g
Carbohydrates	11 g
Sodium	320 mg
Cholesterol	4 mg
Fiber	1 g

3. Keeping rest of wrappers covered with a cloth to prevent drying out, put 1 wrapper on work surface with a corner pointing towards you. Put 1/4 cup (50 mL) of the filling in the center. Fold the lower corner up over the filling, fold the two side corners in over the filling and roll the bundle away from you. Place on prepared pan and repeat until all wrappers are filled. Bake for 12 to 14 minutes until slightly browned, turning the egg rolls at the halfway point. Serve with dipping sauce.

GREEK EGG ROLLS WITH SPINACH AND FETA

Makes 10

TIP

If using fresh spinach, use half the package (5 oz [125 g]), wash and cook with water clinging to leaves until wilted and cooked (approximately 3 minutes). Drain, rinse with cold water, squeeze out excess mixture and chop.

Goat cheese can replace the feta cheese.

MAKE AHEAD

Prepare early in the day, cover and keep refrigerated until ready to bake.

Preheat oven to 425°F (220°C)
Baking sheet sprayed with vegetable spray

2 tsp	vegetable oil	10 mL
2 tsp	minced garlic	10 mL
3/4 cup	diced onions	175 mL
1 2/3 cup	diced mushrooms	400 mL
1 tsp	dried oregano	5 mL
half	package (10 oz [300 g]) frozen chopped spinach, thawed and drained	half
2 oz	feta cheese, crumbled	50 g
10	egg roll wrappers	10

1. In nonstick skillet, heat oil over medium-high heat. Add garlic, onions, mushrooms and oregano; cook for 5 minutes or until softened. Add spinach and feta; cook, stirring, for 2 minutes or until well mixed and cheese melts.

2. Keeping rest of egg roll wrappers covered with a cloth to prevent drying out, put one wrapper on work surface with a corner pointing towards you. Put 2 tbsp (25 mL) of the filling in the center. Fold the lower corner up over the filling, fold the two side corners in over the filling and roll the bundle away from you. Place on prepared pan and repeat until all wrappers are filled. Bake for 12 to 14 minutes until browned, turning the egg rolls at the halfway point.

PER SERVING

Calories	60
Protein	2 g
Fat, total	3 g
Fat, saturated	1 g
Carbohydrates	7 g
Sodium	96 mg
Cholesterol	5 mg
Fiber	1 g

GOAT CHEESE AND SPINACH PHYLLO TRIANGLES

Makes 12

PER SERVING

Calories	104
Protein	4 g
Fat, total	4 g
Fat, saturated	0.8 g
Carbohydrates	12 g
Sodium	107 mg
Cholesterol	4 mg
Fiber	1 g

Preheat oven to 400°F (200°C)
Baking sheet sprayed with vegetable spray

2 tsp	vegetable oil	10 mL
1 1/2 tsp	minced garlic	7 mL
1 cup	finely chopped red onions	250 mL
3/4 cup	finely chopped red peppers	175 mL
2/3 cup	cooked spinach, drained and chopped	150 mL
1/2 cup	5% ricotta cheese	125 mL
3 oz	goat cheese	75 g
3 tbsp	chopped fresh dill (or 1 tsp [5 mL] dried)	45 mL
1 tbsp	grated Parmesan cheese	15 mL
8	sheets phyllo pastry	8
2 tsp	melted margarine or butter	10 mL

1. Heat oil in nonstick skillet over medium heat; add garlic, red onions and red peppers and cook for 5 minutes, or until softened. Remove from heat; stir in spinach, ricotta, goat cheese, dill and Parmesan and mix well.

2. Lay two sheets of phyllo pastry, one on top of the other, on work surface in front of you. Cut lengthwise into three strips. Put 3 tbsp (45 mL) of filling near end of one strip; fold corner up to enclose filling and create a triangle-shaped bundle. Flip bundle repeatedly up and then over until all of phyllo strip has been used. Fill other two strips in same manner; place triangles on prepared baking sheet. Repeat with remaining phyllo sheets.

3. Brush triangles with melted margarine and bake for 10 minutes, or until browned.

SMOKED SALMON QUICHE BITES

Makes 25 squares

TIP

Instead of smoked salmon, use cooked shrimp, smoked trout or another tasty fish.

Use aged Cheddar for a more intense flavor.

MAKE AHEAD

Bake crust earlier in the day. Prepare filling as well, and bake entire dish just before serving.

Preheat oven to 375°F (190°C)

9-inch (2.5 L) square cake pan sprayed with vegetable spray

Crust

1 cup	all-purpose flour	250 mL
1/4 cup	cold butter	50 mL
2 tbsp	water	25 mL
2 tbsp	2% yogurt	25 mL

Custard

1 3/4 cup	5% ricotta cheese	425 mL
1	whole egg	1
1	egg white	1
3 tbsp	chopped fresh dill (or 1 tsp [5 mL] dried)	45 mL
1 tbsp	lemon juice	15 mL
4 oz	diced smoked salmon	125 g
1	green onion, chopped	1
1/2 cup	grated Cheddar cheese	125 mL
1/2 tsp	minced garlic	2 mL
2 tbsp	grated Parmesan cheese	25 mL
pinch	ground pepper	pinch

1. In bowl, combine flour, butter, water and yogurt just until crumbly and the mixture comes together; press into bottom of pan. Bake for 15 minutes, or until light brown.

2. Meanwhile, prepare custard. Place ricotta, whole egg, egg white, dill and lemon juice in bowl of food processor; process until puréed. Remove purée to a bowl, and stir in salmon, green onion, Cheddar cheese, garlic, Parmesan and pepper. Pour custard onto cooled crust; bake for 25 minutes or until filling is set. Let cool for 10 minutes before cutting into squares.

PER SQUARE

Calories	73
Protein	5 g
Fat, total	4 g
Fat, saturated	2 g
Carbohydrates	5 g
Sodium	105 mg
Cholesterol	18 mg
Fiber	0 g

CLOCKWISE FROM UPPER LEFT: MINI PESTO SHRIMP TORTILLA PIZZAS (PAGE 26); CHICKEN SATAY WITH PEANUT SAUCE (PAGE 24); PESTO AND RED PEPPER TORTILLA BITES (PAGE 35); ORIENTAL EGG ROLLS (PAGE 28)

DOUBLE SALMON AND DILL PÂTÉ

Serves 8

TIP

Leaving in the bones from the canned salmon increases the calcium content.

Also tastes great as a spread on french bread or served with vegetables.

Leftover cooked salmon can also be used instead of canned.

MAKE AHEAD

Prepare up to a day ahead and keep refrigerated.

1 cup	5% ricotta cheese	250 mL
1	can (7.5 oz [213 g]) salmon, drained and skin removed	1
1/4 cup	chopped green onions (about 2 medium)	50 mL
3 tbsp	chopped fresh dill (or 1 tsp [5 mL] dried dillweed)	45 mL
2 tbsp	lemon juice	25 mL
4 oz	smoked salmon, cut into thin shreds	125 g

1. Place ricotta, canned salmon, green onions, dill and lemon juice in bowl of food processor; process for 20 seconds or until smooth.

2. Transfer mixture to serving bowl and fold in shredded smoked salmon. Serve with crackers.

PER SERVING

Calories	91
Protein	10 g
Fat, total	4 g
Fat, saturated	2 g
Carbohydrates	1 g
Sodium	237 mg
Cholesterol	18 mg
Fiber	0 g

< RED AND YELLOW BELL PEPPER SOUP (PAGE 55)

EGGPLANT AND TUNA ANTIPASTO APPETIZER

Serves 8 to 10

TIP

Chill or serve warm with crackers or french bread.

This antipasto is also delicious as a sauce over 8 oz (250 g) of pasta.

MAKE AHEAD

Prepare up to 2 days before and stir before serving cold or before reheating.

1 tbsp	olive oil	15 mL
1 1/2 cups	peeled, chopped eggplant	375 mL
1 cup	sliced mushrooms	250 mL
3/4 cup	chopped red peppers	175 mL
1/2 cup	chopped onions	125 mL
2 tsp	minced garlic	10 mL
1 tsp	dried basil	5 mL
1/2 tsp	dried oregano	2 mL
1/2 cup	chicken stock or water	125 mL
1/2 cup	crushed tomatoes (canned or fresh)	125 mL
1/3 cup	sliced pimiento-stuffed green olives	75 mL
1/3 cup	bottled chili sauce	75 mL
2 tsp	drained capers	10 mL
1	can (6.5 oz [184 g]) tuna in water, drained	1

1. Spray a nonstick pan with vegetable spray. Heat oil in pan over medium-high heat; add eggplant, mushrooms, red peppers, onions, garlic, basil and oregano. Cook for 8 minutes, stirring occasionally, or until vegetables are softened.

2. Add stock, tomatoes, olives, chili sauce and capers; simmer uncovered for 6 minutes, stirring occasionally until most of the liquid is absorbed.

3. Transfer to bowl of food processor and add tuna; process for 20 seconds or until combined but still chunky.

PER SERVING (10)	
Calories	65
Protein	5 g
Fat, total	2 g
Fat, saturated	0.4 g
Carbohydrates	6 g
Sodium	411 mg
Cholesterol	3 mg
Fiber	2 g

PESTO AND RED PEPPER TORTILLA BITES

Serves 6 to 8

Preheat broiler

3 tbsp	pesto sauce (store-bought or sauce recipe on page 170)	45 mL
3 oz	goat cheese	75 g
1/4 cup	5% ricotta cheese	50 mL
1	large red pepper	1
3	10-inch (25-cm) flour tortillas	3
	or	
6	6-inch (15-cm) flour tortillas	6

1. In bowl or food processor, combine pesto, goat cheese and ricotta; mix until well combined.

2. Roast pepper under the broiler for 15 to 20 minutes, turning several times until charred on all sides; place in a bowl covered tightly with plastic wrap; let stand until cool enough to handle. Remove skin, stem and seeds; cut roasted pepper into thin strips.

3. If using larger tortillas, spread 1/4 cup (50 mL) filling on each tortilla; if using smaller tortillas, spread 2 tbsp (25 mL) on each tortilla. Spread filling to edges of tortillas, scatter red pepper strips on top, and roll tightly. Chill, wrapped in plastic wrap, for an hour. Cut into 1-inch (2.5 cm) pieces and serve.

TIP

If you're using a store-bought pesto sauce, the calories and fat will be higher. Prepare sauce recipe on page 170 and freeze unused sauce for another purpose.

If in a hurry, you don't need to chill the tortilla before cutting. Just use a sharp knife.

★

If tortillas are very small, increase the number to 8.

★

Try 4 oz (125 g) of roasted sweet peppers in a jar to replace fresh pepper. Use those which are packed in water.

MAKE AHEAD

Prepare up to a day ahead, keeping tightly wrapped in refrigerator.

PER SERVING (8)

Calories	142
Protein	5 g
Fat, total	7 g
Fat, saturated	1 g
Carbohydrates	16 g
Sodium	156 mg
Cholesterol	3 mg
Fiber	1 g

SEAFOOD TORTILLA PINWHEELS

Serves 6

Makes 24 pinwheels.

TIP

You may substitute crab legs (surimi, or imitation crab) for the shrimp.

The curly edges of green or red leaf lettuce are especially attractive in these pinwheels.

Two large tortillas can be used instead of 4 small ones.

MAKE AHEAD

Prepare tortillas early in the day and keep tightly covered in refrigerator.

3 oz	light cream cheese, softened	75 g
1/2 cup	5% ricotta cheese	125 mL
2 tbsp	chopped fresh dill (or 1 tsp [5mL] dried)	25 mL
2 tbsp	chopped green onions (1 medium)	25 mL
1 tbsp	light mayonnaise	15 mL
2 tsp	lemon juice	10 mL
4 oz	chopped cooked shrimp	125 g
1/4 cup	chopped red peppers	50 mL
4	small flour tortillas	4
	Lettuce leaves (optional)	

1. Place cream cheese, ricotta, dill, green onions, mayonnaise and lemon juice in a bowl; combine thoroughly. Stir in shrimp and red peppers.

2. Divide shrimp mixture among tortillas and spread to the edges; top with lettuce leaves (if using), overlapped to cover entire tortilla. Roll up tightly, cover and refrigerate for an hour to chill.

3. Cut each roll crosswise into 6 pieces and serve.

PER SERVING	
Calories	158
Protein	11 g
Fat, total	6 g
Fat, saturated	3 g
Carbohydrates	15 g
Sodium	304 mg
Cholesterol	51 mg
Fiber	1 g

SEAFOOD GARLIC ANTIPASTO

Serves 6

1 lb	scallops, squid or shrimp, or a combination, cut into pieces	500 g
3/4 cup	chopped snow peas	175 mL
3/4 cup	chopped red peppers	175 mL
1/2 cup	diced tomatoes	125 mL
1/3 cup	chopped red onions	75 mL
1/3 cup	minced coriander or dill	75 mL
1/4 cup	sliced black olives	50 mL
3 tbsp	lemon juice	45 mL
2 tbsp	olive oil	25 mL
1 1/2 tsp	minced garlic	7 mL
	Pepper to taste	

TIP

If suggested seafood is not used, try a firm white fish such as swordfish, haddock, or monkfish.

Replace fresh coriander or dill with 1 tsp (5 mL) of dried dill, but do not use dried coriander.

Green beans can replace snow peas.

MAKE AHEAD

Prepare early in the day and keep refrigerated. Mix before serving.

1. In a nonstick skillet sprayed with vegetable spray, cook the seafood over medium-high heat for 3 minutes, or until just done. Drain excess liquid, if any, and place seafood in serving bowl. Let cool slightly.

2. Add snow peas, red peppers, tomatoes, red onions, coriander and olives; mix well. Whisk together lemon juice, olive oil, garlic; pour over seafood mixture. Add pepper to taste. Chill for 1 hour before serving.

PER SERVING

Calories	127
Protein	14 g
Fat, total	5 g
Fat, saturated	0.7 g
Carbohydrates	6 g
Sodium	176 mg
Cholesterol	25 mg
Fiber	1 g

CHUNKY SUN-DRIED TOMATO AND GOAT CHEESE SPREAD

Serves 10

TIP

This spread may be made several days in advance and stored in the refrigerator.

Also great on bagels, toast and crackers.

MAKE AHEAD

Prepare entire dish earlier in the day, then bake just before serving.

Preheat oven to 425°F (220°C)

1/2 cup	sun-dried tomatoes (dry, not marinated in oil)	125 mL
1/3 cup	chopped black olives	75 mL
2 tbsp	grated Parmesan cheese	25 mL
1 tbsp	olive oil	15 mL
2 tbsp	water	25 mL
1 1/2 tsp	minced garlic	7 mL
5	English muffins	5
1 oz	goat cheese	25 g

1. Pour boiling water over sun-dried tomatoes. Let sit for 15 minutes, drain and chop.

2. Place sun dried tomatoes, olives, Parmesan, olive oil, water and garlic in bowl of food processor; pulse until combined, but still chunky.

3. Split muffins and toast them in toaster or oven; spread each muffin half with approximately 1 tbsp (15 mL) of tomato mixture. Crumble goat cheese and sprinkle over top of muffins.

4. Bake for 5 minutes or until cheese melts and muffins are heated through. Cut in quarters and serve.

PER SERVING	
Calories	215
Protein	7 g
Fat, total	7 g
Fat, saturated	1 g
Carbohydrates	31 g
Sodium	433 mg
Cholesterol	2 mg
Fiber	1 g

$\mathcal{S}$OUPS

SOUP TIPS

1. For soup stock, use 1 tsp (5 mL) powdered stock to 1 cup (250 mL) of boiling water for 1 cup (250 mL) of stock. Or use stock cubes, following package instructions. Nothing can beat homemade stock, though. Freeze stocks in small batches for easy use. Look for low-sodium stock if you are on a low-salt diet.

2. Using a large nonstick saucepan sprayed with vegetable spray allows you to sauté vegetables with minimal fat and ensures that the food will not stick to the pan.

3. Always simmer soup covered, on a medium-low heat, stirring occasionally.

4. When puréeing soup, process it in batches to achieve an even, smooth texture.

5. If soup appears too thick after reheating, add more stock. This often happens when pasta is used in a soup.

6. For more fiber, use unpeeled vegetables.

7. Leftover vegetables are ideal for making soups.

8. To ensure that vegetables such as broccoli, asparagus or zucchini retain good color, add them during the last 5 minutes of cooking.

9. Since carrots take longer to become tender, chop them more finely than other vegetables.

10. When a recipe calls for canned crushed tomatoes, you can use whole canned tomatoes, puréed in a food processor with the juice, or use fresh puréed tomatoes.

11. For a tasty and sophisticated garnish, add a dollop of light sour cream or yogurt to each bowl of soup.

12. Most soups can be frozen for up to 2 months. Reheat gently. However, the best taste is achieved when the soup is freshly cooked.

VEGETABLE BEAN CHICKEN SOUP

Serves 6

TIP

Bok choy, napa, or Chinese cabbage can be used. Otherwise, substitute romaine lettuce.

Leeks can have a lot of hidden dirt — to clean thoroughly, slice in half lengthwise and wash under cold running water, getting between the layers where dirt hides.

Any canned beans can replace red kidney beans.

If green beans are unavailable, substitute chopped broccoli or zucchini.

MAKE AHEAD

Prepare soup up to a day in advance, but leave Step 2 until just before serving.

PER SERVING	
Calories	160
Protein	12 g
Fat, total	3 g
Fat, saturated	0.3 g
Carbohydrates	24 g
Sodium	934 mg
Cholesterol	16 mg
Fiber	5 g

2 tsp	vegetable oil	10 mL
1 1/2 tsp	minced garlic	7 mL
3/4 cup	chopped onions	175 mL
1 cup	chopped leeks	250 mL
1 cup	chopped carrots	250 mL
5 cups	chicken stock	1.25 L
1 1/4 cups	peeled, chopped potatoes	300 mL
2	bay leaves	2
1/2 tsp	dried basil	2 mL
1/2 tsp	dried oregano	2 mL
2 cups	chopped bok choy	500 mL
1 cup	drained canned red kidney beans	250 mL
1 cup	trimmed green beans	250 mL
6 oz	skinless, boneless chicken breast, cut into 1/2-inch (1-cm) cubes	150 g
1/3 cup	chopped fresh parsley	75 mL
1/4 tsp	ground black pepper	1 mL

1. In nonstick saucepan sprayed with vegetable spray, heat oil over medium heat. Add garlic, onions, leeks and carrots; cook 4 minutes or until onions are softened, stirring occasionally. Add stock, potatoes, bay leaves, basil and oregano; bring to a boil. Cover, reduce heat to low and simmer for 20 minutes or until potatoes are tender.

2. Stir in bok choy, kidney beans, green beans and chicken. Cover and cook for 5 minutes or until chicken is just done. Stir in parsley and pepper and serve.

BEEF AND BEAN COUSCOUS MINESTRONE

TIP

Replace zucchini with broccoli or cauliflower for a change.

★

If bok choy or napa is unavailable, substitute romaine lettuce.

★

Couscous can be replaced with small shell pasta.

MAKE AHEAD

Prepare soup up to a day in advance, but wait until reheating to add couscous, zucchini, green beans and bok choy. Add extra stock if too thick.

2 tsp	vegetable oil	10 mL
2 tsp	minced garlic	10 mL
1 cup	chopped onions	250 mL
1 cup	chopped carrots	250 mL
8 oz	diced round beef	250 g
5 cups	beef or chicken stock	1.25 L
1 cup	canned white kidney beans, drained	250 mL
1	can (19 oz [540 mL]) whole tomatoes	1
2	bay leaves	2
1 1/2 tsp	dried basil	7 mL
1/2 tsp	dried oregano	2 mL
1 cup	chopped zucchini	250 mL
1 cup	green beans	250 mL
1/4 cup	couscous	50 mL
2 cups	sliced bok choy or napa cabbage	500 mL
	Grated Parmesan cheese (optional)	

1. In large saucepan sprayed with vegetable spray, heat oil over medium heat; add garlic, onions, and carrots and cook for 5 minutes or until onion and carrot are softened. Add beef and cook, stirring, for 3 to 5 minutes or until beef is no longer pink. Add stock, beans, tomatoes, bay leaves, basil, and oregano; bring to a boil. Cover, reduce heat to low and simmer for 40 minutes or until carrot and beef are tender, stirring occasionally while crushing the tomatoes with the back of the spoon.

2. Stir in zucchini, green beans and couscous; cover and cook for 10 minutes or until vegetables are tender. Stir in bok choy or cabbage; cover and cook for 2 minutes or until wilted. Serve sprinkled with Parmesan.

PER SERVING

Calories	136
Protein	11 g
Fat, total	2 g
Fat, saturated	0.4 g
Carbohydrates	19 g
Sodium	923 mg
Cholesterol	12 mg
Fiber	4 g

Cabbage Beef Barley Soup

TIP

A squeeze of lemon juice and 2 tsp (10 mL) brown sugar give a sweet-and-sour quality to this soup.

The addition of beef bones enhances the intensity of this soup's flavor.

MAKE AHEAD

Prepare and refrigerate up to a day ahead and reheat gently before serving, adding more stock if too thick.

2 tsp	vegetable oil	10 mL
1 tsp	minced garlic	5 mL
1 cup	chopped onions	250 mL
1 cup	chopped carrots	250 mL
1/2 cup	chopped celery	125 mL
8 oz	boneless inside round steak, cut into 1/2-inch (1-cm) cubes	250 g
4 cups	shredded cabbage	1 L
1	can (19 oz [540 mL]) tomatoes, puréed	1
4 cups	beef or chicken stock	1 L
1 cup	peeled diced potatoes	250 mL
1/4 cup	barley	50 mL
1 1/2 tsp	caraway seeds	7 mL

1. In large nonstick saucepan sprayed with vegetable spray, heat oil over medium heat. Add garlic, onions, carrots, celery and steak; cook for 5 minutes or until beef is no longer pink. Add cabbage. Cook, stirring, for 2 minutes, or until cabbage wilts.

2. Add tomatoes, stock, potatoes, barley and caraway; bring to a boil. Cover, reduce heat to low and simmer for 35 to 40 minutes, or until barley is tender.

PER SERVING

Calories	125
Protein	9 g
Fat, total	2 g
Fat, saturated	0.4 g
Carbohydrates	18 g
Sodium	712 mg
Cholesterol	12 mg
Fiber	4 g

CAULIFLOWER, LEEK AND SPICY SAUSAGE SOUP

TIP

Leeks can have a lot of hidden dirt — to clean thoroughly, slice in half lengthwise and wash under cold running water, getting between the layers where dirt hides.

For a milder taste, use sweet sausage.

MAKE AHEAD

Prepare and refrigerate up to a day ahead. Reheat gently before serving, adding more stock if too thick.

4 oz	spicy sausage, chopped and casing removed	125 g
2 tsp	vegetable oil	10 mL
2 tsp	minced garlic	10 mL
2 cups	chopped leeks	500 mL
4 cups	chicken stock	1 L
3 cups	cauliflower florets	750 mL
1 cup	peeled, diced potato	250 mL

1. In a small nonstick skillet, sauté sausage just until browned and cooked, approximately 5 minutes. Drain all excess fat, and set sausage aside.

2. In nonstick saucepan sprayed with vegetable spray, heat oil over medium heat. Add garlic and leeks; cook for 5 minutes or until softened. Add stock, cauliflower and potatoes; bring to a boil. Cover, reduce heat to low and simmer for 25 minutes or until potato is tender. Transfer to food processor and purée until smooth. Add sausage just before serving.

PER SERVING

Calories	152
Protein	6 g
Fat, total	6 g
Fat, saturated	3 g
Carbohydrates	14 g
Sodium	789 mg
Cholesterol	16 mg
Fiber	2 g

CLAM AND SCALLOP CHOWDER

TIP

Shrimp or squid or any firm white fish can be used instead of scallops.

★

If using frozen scallops, defrost and drain excess liquid.

MAKE AHEAD

Prepare up to a day ahead, but do not add scallops and clams until just ready to serve.

2	cans (5 oz [142 g]) baby clams	2
1 tsp	vegetable oil	5 mL
1 tsp	minced garlic	5 mL
1 cup	chopped onions	250 mL
3/4 cup	chopped celery	175 mL
3/4 cup	chopped carrots	175 mL
2 cups	chicken or fish stock	500 mL
1	can (19 oz [540 mL]) tomatoes, puréed	1
1 1/2 cups	peeled, diced potatoes	375 mL
1 tsp	dried basil	5 mL
1 tsp	dried oregano	5 mL
1	bay leaf	1
8 oz	scallops, sliced	250 g

1. Drain clams, reserving liquid; measure out 1 1/2 cups (375 mL) of clams for chowder and reserve the rest for another use.

2. In a nonstick saucepan sprayed with vegetable spray, heat oil over medium heat. Add garlic, onions, celery and carrots; cook for 4 minutes or until onion is softened. Add the reserved clam liquid, stock, tomatoes, potato, basil, oregano and bay leaf; bring to a boil. Cover, reduce heat to low and simmer for 35 minutes or until potatoes are tender. Stir in scallops and clams; cook for 5 minutes longer or until scallops are just done at center.

PER SERVING

Calories	188
Protein	20 g
Fat, total	2 g
Fat, saturated	0.3 g
Carbohydrates	20 g
Sodium	690 mg
Cholesterol	46 mg
Fiber	3 g

CLAM MINESTRONE

TIP

If fennel is unavailable, substitute celery and increase fennel seed to 2 tsp (10 mL).

Couscous is a good substitute for macaroni, but use only 1/4 cup (50 mL).

Dill will add a distinctive flavor if used instead of the parsley.

MAKE AHEAD

Prepare soup up to a day ahead, adding zucchini, clams and macaroni just before serving. Reheat until pasta is cooked.

2	cans (5 oz [142 g]) clams	2
2 tsp	vegetable oil	10 mL
2 tsp	minced garlic	10 mL
3/4 cup	chopped onions	175 mL
3/4 cup	chopped carrots	175 mL
3/4 cup	chopped fennel	175 mL
5 cups	chicken or fish stock	1.25 L
1 1/2 cups	peeled, diced potatoes	375 mL
1 1/2 tsp	fennel seed	7 mL
1/4 tsp	ground black pepper	1 mL
1/8 tsp	salt	0.5 mL
1 1/2 cups	chopped zucchini	375 mL
1/3 cup	elbow macaroni	75 mL
2 tbsp	grated Parmesan cheese	25 mL
1/2 cup	chopped fresh parsley	125 mL

1. Drain clams, reserving all liquid. Measure out 1 1/2 cups (375 mL) of clams for chowder and reserve the rest for another use.

2. In nonstick saucepan sprayed with vegetable spray, heat oil over medium heat. Add garlic, onions, carrots and fennel; cook for 5 minutes or until onions are softened. Add reserved clam juice, stock, potatoes, fennel seed, pepper and salt; bring to a boil. Cover, reduce heat to low and simmer for 20 minutes or until vegetables are tender.

3. Stir in zucchini, reserved clams and macaroni. Cover and cook for another 12 minutes or until pasta is tender but firm. Serve sprinkled with Parmesan and parsley.

PER SERVING (8)	
Calories	136
Protein	12 g
Fat, total	3 g
Fat, saturated	0.5 g
Carbohydrates	16 g
Sodium	789 mg
Cholesterol	26 mg
Fiber	2 g

CREAMY SALMON DILL BISQUE

6 oz	salmon fillet	150 g
2 tsp	margarine or butter	10 mL
1 tsp	minced garlic	5 mL
1 cup	chopped onions	250 mL
1 cup	chopped carrots	250 mL
1/2 cup	chopped celery	125 mL
1 tbsp	tomato paste	15 mL
2 1/4 cups	chicken stock	550 mL
1 1/2 cups	peeled, chopped potatoes	375 mL
1/2 cup	2% milk	125 mL
1/4 cup	chopped fresh dill	50 mL

1. In nonstick pan sprayed with vegetable spray, cook salmon over high heat for 3 minutes, then turn and cook 2 minutes longer, or until just barely done at center. Set aside.

2. Melt margarine in nonstick saucepan sprayed with vegetable spray over medium heat. Add garlic, onions, carrots, and celery; cook for 5 minutes or until onion is softened. Add tomato paste, stock and potatoes; bring to a boil. Cover, reduce heat to low and simmer for 20 minutes or until carrots and potatoes are tender.

3. Transfer soup to food processor or blender and purée. Return to saucepan and stir in milk and dill. Flake the cooked salmon. Add to soup and serve.

BLACK BEAN SOUP

Serves 4 or 5

2 tsp	vegetable oil	10 mL
2 tsp	minced garlic	10 mL
1 cup	chopped onions	250 mL
1 cup	chopped carrots	250 mL
1	can (19 oz [540mL]) black beans, drained (or 12 oz [375 g] cooked beans)	1
3 cups	chicken stock	750 mL
3/4 tsp	ground cumin	4 mL
1/4 cup	chopped coriander or parsley	50 mL

1. In a nonstick saucepan sprayed with vegetable spray, heat oil over medium heat; add garlic, onions and carrots and cook, stirring occasionally, for 4 minutes or until the onion is softened.

2. Add beans, stock and cumin; bring to a boil. Cover, reduce heat to medium low and simmer for 20 minutes or until carrots are softened. Transfer to food processor and purée until smooth.

3. Ladle into bowls; sprinkle with coriander.

PER SERVING (5)	
Calories	147
Protein	8 g
Fat, total	3 g
Fat, saturated	0.3 g
Carbohydrates	25 g
Sodium	741 mg
Cholesterol	0 mg
Fiber	8 g

CAULIFLOWER AND WHITE BEAN SOUP

1 tsp	vegetable oil	5 mL
1 tsp	minced garlic	5 mL
1 cup	chopped onions	250 mL
3 2/3 cups	chicken stock	900 mL
3 cups	cauliflower florets	750 mL
1 1/2 cups	canned white kidney beans, drained	375 mL
1 cup	peeled diced potatoes	250 mL
1/4 tsp	ground black pepper	1 mL
1/4 cup	chopped fresh dill (or 1 tsp [5 mL] dried dillweed)	50 mL
2 tbsp	chopped chives or green onions	25 mL

1. In nonstick saucepan sprayed with vegetable spray, heat oil over medium heat. Add garlic and onions; cook for 4 minutes or until softened. Add stock, cauliflower, kidney beans, potatoes, pepper and dried dillweed, if using; bring to a boil. Cover, reduce heat to low and simmer for 20 to 25 minutes or until vegetables are tender.

2. Transfer soup to food processor or blender; purée. Serve garnished with fresh dill, if using, and chives.

LEEK SPLIT-PEA SOUP

1 tbsp	vegetable oil	15 mL
2 tsp	minced garlic	10 mL
2 cups	chopped leeks	500 mL
1/2 cup	chopped carrots	125 mL
5 1/2 cups	chicken stock	1.375 L
1 cup	peeled diced potatoes	250 mL
3/4 cup	split peas	175 mL
1/4 tsp	ground black pepper	1 mL

1. In nonstick saucepan sprayed with vegetable spray, heat oil over medium heat. Add garlic, leeks and carrots; cook for 4 minutes or until onion is softened. Add stock, potatoes, split peas and pepper; bring to a boil. Cover, reduce heat to low and simmer for 40 minutes, or until peas are tender.

2. Transfer soup to food processor or blender; purée.

THREE-BEAN SOUP

Serves 6

TIP

Any combination of cooked beans will work well.

If cooking your own beans, use 1 cup (250 mL) of dry to make 3 cups (750 mL) cooked.

MAKE AHEAD

Prepare and refrigerate up to a day ahead and reheat gently before serving, adding more stock if too thick.

2 tsp	vegetable oil	10 mL
2 tsp	minced garlic	10 mL
3/4 cup	chopped onions	175 mL
3/4 cup	chopped carrots	175 mL
4 cups	chicken or vegetable stock	1 L
1 1/4 cups	canned chick peas, drained	300 mL
1 1/4 cups	canned red kidney beans, drained	300 mL
1 1/4 cups	canned white kidney beans, drained	300 mL
1 tsp	dried basil	5 mL
1/4 cup	chopped fresh parsley	50 mL

1. In saucepan sprayed with vegetable spray, heat oil over medium heat; add garlic, onions and carrots and cook for 5 minutes or until onion is softened. Add chicken stock and 1 cup (250 mL) each of the chick peas and red and white kidney beans; add basil. Bring to a boil. Cover, reduce heat to low and let simmer for 15 minutes or until carrots are tender.

2. Transfer soup to blender or food processor and purée. Return puréed soup to saucepan and stir in remaining 1/4 cup (50 mL) each chick peas, red and white kidney beans. Cook gently for 5 minutes or until heated through. Serve garnished with parsley.

PER SERVING

Calories	187
Protein	10 g
Fat, total	3 g
Fat, saturated	0.3 g
Carbohydrates	31 g
Sodium	974 mg
Cholesterol	0 mg
Fiber	9 g

POTATO CHEDDAR CHEESE SOUP

TIP

For maximum flavor, use aged Cheddar cheese.

If fresh herbs are unavailable, add 2 tsp (10 mL) dried herbs during the cooking.

MAKE AHEAD

Prepare and refrigerate up to a day ahead and reheat gently before serving, adding more stock if too thick.

1 tsp	vegetable oil	5 mL
1 tsp	minced garlic	5 mL
1 cup	chopped onion	250 mL
3 1/2 cups	peeled, diced potatoes	875 mL
3 cups	chicken stock	750 mL
3/4 cup	grated Cheddar cheese (about 3 oz [75 g])	175 mL
1/2 cup	2% milk	125 mL
1/4 cup	chopped fresh parsley or dill	50 mL

1. Heat oil in nonstick saucepan over medium heat. Add garlic and onions; cook for 4 minutes or until softened. Add potatoes and stock; bring to a boil. Cover, reduce heat to low and simmer for 20 minutes or until potatoes are tender.

2. Remove 1/2 cup (125 mL) potato-onion mixture without liquid and set aside. Transfer remainder of soup to food processor or blender and purée. Return puréed soup to saucepan; stir in Cheddar cheese, milk, parsley and reserved potato-onion mixture. Cook for 1 minute or until cheese melts.

PER SERVING

Calories	253
Protein	10 g
Fat, total	9 g
Fat, saturated	5 g
Carbohydrates	33 g
Sodium	857 mg
Cholesterol	25 mg
Fiber	3 g

CURRIED BROCCOLI SWEET POTATO SOUP

Serves 6

TIP

Increase curry to 1 1/2 tsp (7 mL) for more intense flavor.

MAKE AHEAD

Prepare and refrigerate up to a day ahead and reheat gently before serving, adding more stock if too thick.

2 tsp	vegetable oil	10 mL
1 1/2 tsp	minced garlic	7 mL
1 1/2 cups	chopped onions	375 mL
1 tsp	curry powder	5 mL
4 cups	chicken stock	1 L
4 cups	broccoli florets	1 L
3 cups	peeled, diced sweet potato	750 mL
2 tbsp	honey	25 mL

1. Heat oil in nonstick saucepan over medium heat. Add garlic, onions and curry; cook for 4 minutes or until softened. Add stock, broccoli and sweet potatoes; bring to a boil. Cover, reduce heat to low and simmer for 30 minutes or until vegetables are tender.

2. Transfer soup to food processor or blender; add honey and purée.

PER SERVING

Calories	150
Protein	4 g
Fat, total	2 g
Fat, saturated	0.3 g
Carbohydrates	31 g
Sodium	648 mg
Cholesterol	0 mg
Fiber	4 g

GREEN ONION, POTATO AND DILL SOUP

TIP

The blue cheese really adds flavor to this soup. If you don't want it, substitute another strong-flavored cheese, such as Swiss or goat cheese.

Substitute 2 tsp (10 mL) dried dill if fresh is unavailable. Add it during cooking.

MAKE AHEAD

Prepare and refrigerate up to a day ahead and reheat gently before serving, adding more stock if too thick.

2 tsp	vegetable oil	10 mL
2 tsp	minced garlic	10 mL
2 2/3 cups	chopped green onions	650 mL
3 cups	chicken stock	750 mL
2 1/3 cups	diced potatoes	575 mL
3 tbsp	chopped fresh dill	45 mL
1 1/2 oz	blue cheese or other strong cheese, crumbled	45 g

1. In saucepan, heat oil over medium heat; add garlic and green onions. Cook for 4 minutes, stirring occasionally. Add stock and potatoes; bring to a boil. Cover, reduce heat to low and cook for 20 to 25 minutes or until potatoes are tender.

2. Transfer soup to a blender or food processor and purée. Return purée to saucepan and stir in chopped dill and blue cheese; cook for 2 minutes or until blue cheese melts.

PER SERVING	
Calories	166
Protein	6 g
Fat, total	6 g
Fat, saturated	2 g
Carbohydrates	25 g
Sodium	854 mg
Cholesterol	8 mg
Fiber	3 g

RED AND YELLOW BELL PEPPER SOUP

TIP

Orange peppers can be used instead of red or yellow.

If desired, coriander can be added before puréeing for a more intense flavor.

Roasted peppers in a jar (packed in water) can replace fresh peppers. Use about 4 oz (125 g) peppers in a jar for each fresh pepper required.

MAKE AHEAD

Roast peppers earlier in the day and set aside.

Prepare both soups earlier in day, and keep them separate until serving.

PER SERVING	
Calories	99
Protein	3 g
Fat, total	2 g
Fat, saturated	0.2 g
Carbohydrates	19 g
Sodium	644 mg
Cholesterol	0 mg
Fiber	3 g

Preheat oven to broil

2	red peppers	2
2	yellow peppers	2
2 tsp	vegetable oil	10 mL
2 tsp	minced garlic	10 mL
1 1/2 cups	chopped onions	375 mL
1 1/4 cups	chopped carrots	300 mL
1/2 cup	chopped celery	125 mL
4 cups	chicken or vegetable stock	1 L
1 1/2 cups	diced, peeled potatoes	375 mL
	Pepper to taste	
1/4 cup	chopped fresh coriander, dill or basil	50 mL

1. Roast the peppers under the broiler for 15 to 20 minutes, turning several times until charred on all sides. Place in a bowl covered tightly with plastic wrap; let stand until cool enough to handle. Remove skin, stem and seeds.

2. In a nonstick saucepan sprayed with vegetable spray, heat oil over medium heat. Add garlic, onion, carrots and celery; cook for 8 minutes or until vegetables are softened, stirring occasionally. Add stock and potatoes; bring to a boil. Reduce heat to low; cover, and let cook for 20 to 25 minutes or until carrots and potatoes are tender.

3. Put the red peppers in food processor and process until smooth. Add half of the soup mixture to the red pepper purée and process until smooth. Season with pepper and pour into serving bowl. Rinse out food processor. Put yellow peppers in food processor and process until smooth; add remaining soup to yellow pepper purée and process until smooth. Season with pepper and pour into another serving bowl. To serve, ladle some of the red pepper soup into one side of individual bowl, at the same time ladling some of the yellow pepper soup into the other side of the bowl. Add coriander to soup and serve.

CHUNKY RED PEPPER AND TOMATO SOUP

Serves 4

TIP

If using dried basil, add 1 tsp (5 mL) during the cooking.

For a spicier taste, use 1/2 tsp (2 mL) fresh chopped chili pepper.

MAKE AHEAD

Prepare and refrigerate up to a day ahead and reheat gently before serving, adding more stock if too thick.

2 tsp	vegetable oil	10 mL
1 1/2 tsp	minced garlic	7 mL
1 cup	chopped onions	250 mL
4 1/2 cups	chopped tomatoes	1.125 L
1 1/4 cups	chopped red peppers	300 mL
2 cups	chicken stock	500 mL
pinch	chili flakes	pinch
1/4 cup	chopped fresh basil or dill	50 mL

1. Heat oil in nonstick saucepan over medium heat. Add garlic and onions; cook for 4 minutes or until softened.

2. Reserve 1/2 cup (125 mL) each of tomatoes and red peppers; set aside. Add remaining tomatoes and red peppers to saucepan; cook for 10 minutes, stirring often. Add stock and chili flakes; bring to a boil. Cover, reduce heat to low and simmer 20 minutes.

3. Transfer soup to food processor and purée. Return to saucepan and stir in reserved tomatoes, red peppers, and basil.

PER SERVING	
Calories	108
Protein	3 g
Fat, total	3 g
Fat, saturated	0.3 g
Carbohydrates	19 g
Sodium	492 mg
Cholesterol	0 mg
Fiber	4 g

CREAMY PUMPKIN SOUP

TIP

Serve with a small dollop of low-fat sour cream or yogurt.

In season, fresh cooked pumpkin is great in this soup.

MAKE AHEAD

Prepare and refrigerate up to a day ahead and reheat gently before serving, adding more stock if too thick.

2 tsp	vegetable oil	10 mL
1 tsp	minced garlic	5 mL
1 1/2 cups	chopped onions	375 mL
1 1/2 cups	chopped carrots	375 mL
3 1/2 cups	chicken stock	875 mL
1 tsp	cinnamon	5 mL
1/2 tsp	ground ginger	2 mL
1/8 tsp	nutmeg	0.5 mL
1 1/2 cups	canned pumpkin purée	375 mL
1 cup	2% milk	250 mL
2 tbsp	honey	25 mL

1. In nonstick saucepan sprayed with vegetable spray, heat oil over medium-high heat. Add garlic, onions and carrots; cook for 10 minutes, stirring frequently, or until onions are browned and softened. Add stock, cinnamon, ginger, nutmeg and pumpkin; bring to a boil. Cover, reduce heat to low and simmer for 20 minutes or until carrot is tender.

2. Transfer soup to food processor or blender; purée until smooth. Return soup to saucepan. Stir in milk and honey and heat gently.

PER SERVING	
Calories	174
Protein	5 g
Fat, total	4 g
Fat, saturated	1 g
Carbohydrates	32 g
Sodium	871 mg
Cholesterol	5 mg
Fiber	4 g

CURRIED CARROT ORANGE SOUP

Serves 6

TIP

Leeks can have a lot of hidden dirt — to clean thoroughly, slice in half lengthwise and wash under cold running water, getting between the layers where dirt hides.

For an elegant presentation, serve with a small dollop of low-fat sour cream or yogurt.

When grating zest of an orange, be careful not to scrape the white underneath the zest. It is bitter.

MAKE AHEAD

Prepare and refrigerate up to a day ahead and reheat gently before serving, adding more stock if too thick.

1 tsp	vegetable oil	5 mL
1 1/2 tsp	minced garlic	7 mL
1 tsp	curry powder	5 mL
1 cup	chopped onions or sliced leeks	250 mL
1 lb	carrots, peeled and sliced	500 g
3 3/4 cups	chicken stock	925 mL
1 cup	peeled, diced sweet potatoes	250 mL
1/2 cup	orange juice	125 mL
2 tbsp	honey	25 mL
1 tbsp	grated orange zest (1 large orange)	15 mL

1. In nonstick saucepan sprayed with vegetable spray, heat oil over medium heat. Add garlic, curry, onions and carrots; cook for 5 minutes or until onions are softened. Add stock and sweet potatoes; bring to a boil. Cover, reduce heat to low and simmer for 25 minutes or until carrots and sweet potatoes are tender.

2. Transfer soup to food processor or blender; purée. Return to saucepan and stir in orange juice, honey and zest.

PER SERVING

Calories	119
Protein	2 g
Fat, total	1 g
Fat, saturated	0.1 g
Carbohydrates	26 g
Sodium	624 mg
Cholesterol	0 mg
Fiber	3 g

SALADS

SALAD TIPS

1. Use fresh crisp vegetables for salads. If cooking vegetables such as snow peas, asparagus or broccoli, be certain to cook only until tender-crisp by steaming, boiling or microwaving. Drain and rinse with cold water until no longer warm. This prevents discoloration.

2. Fresh herbs are preferable to dried, since the flavors are more intense. When substituting, the ratio of fresh to dried is 3:1. Therefore, 1 tbsp (15 mL) fresh equals 1 tsp (5 mL) dried.

3. Try a variety of greens for salad, such as Boston lettuce, Bibb lettuce, radicchio, red leaf lettuce and endive. Avoid iceberg lettuce, which has few nutrients and little flavor.

4. If excess liquid is a problem when you use tomatoes, either deseed them or use plum tomatoes.

5. Prepare a salad up to 4 hours before serving, then cover and refrigerate. If prepared earlier, the vegetables will give off excess liquid and lose their crispness.

6. Prepare dressing early in the day, or up to 2 days ahead. Keep covered and refrigerate. Do not pour over salad until just ready to serve.

FOUR-TOMATO SALAD

TIP

Any combination of tomatoes can be used if those specified here are not available.

Yellow, larger tomatoes, if available, are great to add.

Removing seeds from field tomatoes will eliminate excess liquid.

Do not toss this salad until just ready to serve.

MAKE AHEAD

Prepare dressing early in the day only if using dried basil. Salad portion can be prepared early in the day.

1/2 cup	sun-dried tomatoes	125 mL
2 cups	sliced field tomatoes	500 mL
2 cups	halved red or yellow cherry tomatoes	500 mL
2 cups	quartered plum tomatoes	500 mL
1 cup	sliced red onions	250 mL
Dressing		
3 tbsp	olive oil	45 mL
1/4 cup	balsamic vinegar	50 mL
1 1/2 tsp	minced garlic	7 mL
1/2 cup	chopped fresh basil (or 2 tsp [10 mL] dried)	125 mL
1/8 tsp	ground black pepper	0.5 mL

1. Pour boiling water over sun-dried tomatoes. Let rest for 15 minutes until softened. Drain and slice.

2. Place sun-dried tomatoes, field tomatoes, cherry tomatoes, plum tomatoes, red onions and fresh basil in serving bowl or on platter.

3. Whisk together olive oil, balsamic vinegar, garlic and pepper; pour over tomatoes.

PER SERVING	
Calories	134
Protein	3 g
Fat, total	8 g
Fat, saturated	1 g
Carbohydrates	17 g
Sodium	116 mg
Cholesterol	0 mg
Fiber	3 g

GREEK BARLEY SALAD

TIP

Great variation on traditional Greek salad.

Remove seeds of tomatoes to eliminate excess liquid.

MAKE AHEAD

Prepare early in the day and refrigerate until ready to use.

3 cups	chicken stock or water	750 mL
3/4 cup	barley	175 mL
1 1/2 cups	diced cucumbers	375 mL
1 1/2 cups	diced tomatoes	375 mL
3/4 cup	chopped red onions	175 mL
3/4 cup	chopped green peppers	175 mL
1/3 cup	sliced black olives	75 mL
2 oz	feta cheese, crumbled	50 g

Dressing

2 tbsp	olive oil	25 mL
2 tbsp	lemon juice	25 mL
1 1/2 tsp	minced garlic	7 mL
1/3 cup	chopped fresh oregano (or 2 tsp [10 mL] dried)	75 mL

1. In medium saucepan, bring stock or water to the boil; add barley. Cover, reduce heat and simmer for 40 to 45 minutes, or just until tender. Drain well, rinse with cold water and place in large serving bowl, along with cucumbers, tomatoes, red onions, green peppers, black olives and feta cheese; toss well.

2. In small bowl whisk together oil, lemon juice, garlic and oregano; pour over salad and toss well. Refrigerate until chilled.

PER SERVING	
Calories	197
Protein	5 g
Fat, total	8 g
Fat, saturated	2 g
Carbohydrates	29 g
Sodium	658 mg
Cholesterol	9 mg
Fiber	6 g

POLYNESIAN WILD RICE SALAD

Serves 4 to 6

TIP

This recipe can be prepared using all wild rice or all white rice.

Great salad for brunch or picnic. Sits well for hours.

MAKE AHEAD

Prepare up to a day ahead. Keep refrigerated and stir well before serving.

2 cups	chicken stock	500 mL
1/2 cup	white rice	125 mL
1/2 cup	wild rice	125 mL
1 cup	halved snow peas	250 mL
1 cup	chopped red peppers	250 mL
3/4 cup	chopped celery	175 mL
2/3 cup	sliced water chestnuts	150 mL
1/2 cup	canned mandarin oranges, drained	125 mL
2	medium green onions, chopped	2

Dressing

2 tsp	orange juice concentrate, thawed	10 mL
2 tsp	honey	10 mL
1 tsp	soya sauce	5 mL
1 tsp	vegetable oil	5 mL
1/2 tsp	sesame oil	2 mL
1/2 tsp	lemon juice	2 mL
1/2 tsp	minced garlic	2 mL
1/4 tsp	minced ginger root	1 mL

1. Bring stock to boil in medium saucepan; add wild rice and white rice. Cover, reduce heat to medium low and simmer for 15 to 20 minutes, or until rice is tender and liquid is absorbed. Rinse with cold water. Put rice in serving bowl.

2. In a saucepan of boiling water or microwave, blanch snow peas for 1 or 2 minutes or until tender-crisp; refresh in cold water and drain. Add to serving bowl along with red peppers, celery, water chestnuts, mandarin oranges and green onions; toss well.

3. In small bowl, whisk together orange juice concentrate, honey, soya sauce, vegetable oil, sesame oil, lemon juice, garlic and ginger; pour over salad and toss well.

PER SERVING (6)	
Calories	169
Protein	5 g
Fat, total	2 g
Fat, saturated	0.2 g
Carbohydrates	36 g
Sodium	388 mg
Cholesterol	0 mg
Fiber	2 g

RICE, BLACK BEAN AND RED PEPPER SALAD

TIP

This recipe can be prepared using all wild rice or all white rice.

Canned black beans can be difficult to find. Cook your own dry beans — 1/2 cup (125 mL) of dry beans yields approximately 1 1/2 cups (375 mL) cooked. Cook in simmering water for 1 hour or until beans are tender. Otherwise, any other canned beans can be used.

For best taste, allow to chill before serving.

MAKE AHEAD

Prepare entire salad early in the day, keeping refrigerated. Stir well before serving.

PER SERVING

Calories	251
Protein	8 g
Fat, total	8 g
Fat, saturated	1 g
Carbohydrates	40 g
Sodium	437 mg
Cholesterol	0 mg
Fiber	5 g

2 cups	chicken stock or water	500 mL
1/2 cup	wild rice	125 mL
1/2 cup	white rice	125 mL
1 cup	chopped red peppers	250 mL
1 cup	chopped snow peas	250 mL
1 cup	canned black beans, drained	250 mL
1/2 cup	corn kernels	125 mL
1/3 cup	chopped red onions	75 mL
1/3 cup	chopped fresh coriander or parsley	75 mL
1	medium green onion, chopped	1

Dressing

3 tbsp	olive oil	45 mL
2 tbsp	lemon juice	25 mL
1 tbsp	red wine vinegar	15 mL
1 tsp	minced garlic	5 mL

1. Bring stock or water to boil in a saucepan; add wild rice and white rice. Cover, reduce heat to medium-low and simmer for 20 minutes or until rice is tender. Remove from heat and let stand for 5 minutes, or until all liquid is absorbed. Rinse with cold water and put in large serving bowl.

2. Add red peppers, snow peas, black beans, corn, red onions, coriander and green onion to rice and toss to combine.

3. In small bowl whisk together olive oil, lemon juice, red wine vinegar and garlic; pour over salad and toss well.

FOUR-TOMATO SALAD (PAGE 61) ➤

GREEK ORZO SEAFOOD SALAD

Serves 8

TIP

Orzo is a rice-shaped pasta. If unavailable, substitute a small shell pasta.

Substitute squid or any firm white fish for part or all of the shrimp or scallops.

Definitely use fresh lemon juice — bottled will give too tart a taste. If a less intense lemon flavor is desired, use 3 tbsp (45 mL) instead of 1/4 cup (50 mL).

MAKE AHEAD

Prepare early in the day and keep refrigerated. This tastes fine the next day.

PER SERVING	
Calories	314
Protein	15 g
Fat, total	10 g
Fat, saturated	3 g
Carbohydrates	42 g
Sodium	174 mg
Cholesterol	53 mg
Fiber	2 g

1 3/4 cups	orzo	425 mL
8 oz	shrimp or scallops or a combination, chopped	250 g
1 cup	halved snow peas	250 mL
12 oz	tomatoes, chopped	375 g
3 oz	feta cheese, crumbled	75 g

Dressing

1/4 cup	olive oil	50 mL
1/4 cup	freshly squeezed lemon juice	50 mL
1 tbsp	dried oregano (or 1/3 cup [75 mL] chopped fresh)	15 mL
2 tsp	minced garlic	10 mL
2 tsp	grated lemon zest	10 mL
1/4 tsp	ground black pepper	1 mL

1. In large pot of boiling water cook the orzo for 8 to 10 minutes or until tender but firm; rinse under cold water and drain. Put in large serving bowl.

2. In nonstick skillet sprayed with vegetable spray, cook shrimp or scallops over high heat for 2 minutes or until just done at center. Drain any excess liquid. Add to orzo in serving bowl.

3. In a saucepan of boiling water, blanch snow peas for 1 minute, or until tender-crisp; refresh in cold water and drain. Place in serving bowl, along with tomatoes and feta cheese.

4. In small bowl whisk together olive oil, lemon juice, oregano, garlic, lemon zest and pepper; pour over salad and toss well. Chill before serving.

◄ POTATO PESTO SALAD (PAGE 67)

ORIENTAL CHICKEN SALAD WITH MANDARIN ORANGES, SNOW PEAS AND ASPARAGUS

Serves 6

TIP

Replace chicken with shrimp, pork or steak.

★

Broccoli or green beans can replace asparagus.

★

Thinly sliced carrots (julienned) can replace bean sprouts.

MAKE AHEAD

Prepare salad and dressing early in the day, keeping separate until ready to serve. Dressing can keep for days.

PER SERVING	
Calories	155
Protein	17 g
Fat, total	3 g
Fat, saturated	0.5 g
Carbohydrates	17 g
Sodium	434 mg
Cholesterol	33 mg
Fiber	2 g

12 oz	skinless, boneless chicken breasts	375 g
1 cup	asparagus cut into 1-inch (2.5 cm) pieces	250 mL
1 1/4 cups	halved snow peas	300 mL
1 cup	sliced baby corn cobs	250 mL
1 cup	bean sprouts	250 mL
1 cup	canned mandarin oranges, drained	250 mL
1 1/2 cups	sliced red or green peppers	375 mL
3/4 cup	sliced water chestnuts	175 mL
2	medium green onions, chopped	2

Dressing

2 tbsp	orange juice concentrate, thawed	25 mL
1 tbsp	rice wine vinegar	15 mL
1 tbsp	soya sauce	15 mL
2 tsp	honey	10 mL
2 tsp	vegetable oil	10 mL
1 tsp	sesame oil	5 mL
1 tsp	minced ginger root	5 mL
1 tsp	minced garlic	5 mL

1. In nonstick skillet sprayed with vegetable spray, sauté chicken breasts and cook approximately 7 minutes, or until browned on both sides and just done at center. Let chicken cool, then cut into 1/2 inch (1 cm) cubes and place in large serving bowl.

2. In boiling water or microwave, blanch asparagus for 2 minutes or until tender-crisp; refresh in cold water and drain. As well, cook snow peas for 45 seconds or until tender-crisp; refresh in cold water and drain. Place in serving bowl with chicken. Add baby corn, bean sprouts, mandarin oranges, red peppers, water chestnuts and green onions to bowl and toss.

3. In small bowl, whisk together orange juice concentrate, vinegar, soya sauce, honey, vegetable oil, sesame oil, ginger and garlic; pour over salad and toss.

PESTO POTATO SALAD

TIP

Use 3/4 cup (175 mL) store-bought pesto instead of making your own. Keep in mind that calories and fat will be higher.

If basil is unavailable, try spinach or parsley leaves.

Roasted corn kernels (1 cob) make a delicious replacement for canned kernels. Broil or barbecue corn for 15 minutes or until charred.

MAKE AHEAD

Prepare potatoes, pesto and vegetables up to a day ahead. Toss before serving.

Tastes great the next day.

PER SERVING (10)	
Calories	154
Protein	4 g
Fat, total	6 g
Fat, saturated	1 g
Carbohydrates	22 g
Sodium	124 mg
Cholesterol	1 mg
Fiber	3 g

2 lb	scrubbed whole red potatoes with skins on	1 kg

Pesto

1 1/4 cups	packed fresh basil leaves	300 mL
3 tbsp	olive oil	45 mL
2 tbsp	toasted pine nuts	25 mL
2 tbsp	grated Parmesan cheese	25 mL
1 tsp	minced garlic	5 mL
1/4 tsp	salt	1 mL
1/4 cup	chicken stock or water	50 mL
1 cup	halved snow peas	250 mL
3/4 cup	chopped red onions	175 mL
3/4 cup	chopped red peppers	175 mL
3/4 cup	chopped green peppers	175 mL
1/2 cup	corn kernels	125 mL
2	medium green onions, chopped	2
2 tbsp	toasted pine nuts	25 mL
2 tbsp	lemon juice	25 mL

1. Put potatoes in saucepan with cold water to cover; bring to a boil and cook for 20 to 25 minutes, or until easily pierced with a sharp knife. Drain and set aside.

2. Meanwhile, put basil, olive oil, pine nuts, Parmesan, garlic and salt in food processor; process until finely chopped. With the processor running, gradually add stock through the feed tube; process until smooth.

3. In saucepan of boiling water or microwave, blanch snow peas for 1 or 2 minutes, or until tender-crisp; refresh in cold water and drain. Place in large serving bowl, along with pesto, red onions, red and green peppers, corn, green onions, pine nuts and lemon juice. When potatoes are cool enough to handle, cut into wedges and add to serving bowl; toss well to combine.

ORIENTAL COLESLAW

Serves 8 to 10

TIP

Other vegetables such as green beans or broccoli can replace snow peas.

Great variation on usual coleslaw.

MAKE AHEAD

Prepare salad and dressing early in the day. Best if tossed just before serving.

3/4 cup	chopped snow peas	175 mL
3 cups	shredded green cabbage	750 mL
3 cups	shredded red cabbage	750 mL
1 cup	sliced water chestnuts	250 mL
1 cup	sliced red peppers	250 mL
3/4 cup	canned mandarin oranges, drained	175 mL
2	medium green onions, chopped	2

Dressing

3 tbsp	brown sugar	45 mL
2 tbsp	rice wine vinegar	25 mL
2 tbsp	vegetable oil	25 mL
1 tbsp	soya sauce	15 mL
1 tbsp	sesame oil	15 mL
1 tsp	minced garlic	5 mL
1 tsp	minced ginger root	5 mL

1. In saucepan of boiling water or microwave, blanch snow peas just until tender-crisp, approximately 1 to 2 minutes; refresh in cold water and drain. Place in serving bowl with shredded cabbage, water chestnuts, red peppers, mandarin oranges and green onions; toss well to combine.

2. In small bowl whisk together brown sugar, vinegar, vegetable oil, soya sauce, sesame oil, garlic and ginger; pour over salad and toss well.

PER SERVING (10)	
Calories	81
Protein	1 g
Fat, total	4 g
Fat, saturated	0.4 g
Carbohydrates	12 g
Sodium	116 mg
Cholesterol	0 mg
Fiber	2 g

SPINACH SALAD WITH ORANGES AND MUSHROOMS

Serves 6

TIP

Use 1 1/2 cups (375 mL) canned, drained mandarins to replace the orange.

Oyster mushrooms or other wild mushrooms are exceptionally tasty.

Orange juice concentrate provides the intense flavor — if you substitute orange juice, flavor will be less pronounced. Refreeze the remainder of thawed concentrate for making juice later.

MAKE AHEAD

Prepare salad early in the day, keeping refrigerated. Prepare dressing up to 2 days ahead. Pour over salad just before serving.

	PER SERVING	
Calories		177
Protein		5 g
Fat, total		10 g
Fat, saturated		1 g
Carbohydrates		21 g
Sodium		88 mg
Cholesterol		0 mg
Fiber		5 g

8 cups	packed fresh spinach leaves, washed, dried and torn into bite-sized pieces	2 L
1 1/2 cups	sliced mushrooms	375 mL
3/4 cup	sliced water chestnuts	175 mL
1/2 cup	sliced red onions	125 mL
1/4 cup	raisins	50 mL
2 tbsp	sliced or chopped almonds, toasted	25 mL
1	orange, peeled and sections cut into pieces	1

Dressing

3 tbsp	olive oil	45 mL
3 tbsp	balsamic vinegar	45 mL
2 tbsp	orange juice concentrate, thawed	25 mL
1 tbsp	honey	15 mL
1 tsp	grated orange zest	5 mL
1 tsp	minced garlic	5 mL

1. In large serving bowl, combine spinach, mushrooms, water chestnuts, red onions, raisins, almonds and orange pieces; toss well.

2. In small bowl whisk together olive oil, balsamic vinegar, orange juice concentrate, honey, orange zest and garlic; pour over salad and toss.

THAI BEEF SALAD

8 oz	boneless steak, sliced thinly	250 g
1 3/4 cups	halved snow peas	425 mL
5 cups	well-packed romaine lettuce, washed, dried and torn into bite-size pieces	1.25 L
1 cup	chopped cucumber	250 mL
3/4 cup	sliced red onions	175 mL
3/4 cup	sliced water chestnuts	175 mL
3/4 cup	canned mandarin oranges, drained	175 mL
1	medium red pepper, sliced	1

Dressing

1 1/2 tbsp	orange juice concentrate, thawed	20 mL
4 tsp	honey	20 mL
1 tbsp	rice wine vinegar	15 mL
1 tbsp	soya sauce	15 mL
2 tsp	vegetable oil	10 mL
2 tsp	sesame oil	10 mL
1 tsp	minced garlic	5 mL
3/4 tsp	minced ginger root	4 mL
1/2 tsp	grated orange zest	2 mL

1. In nonstick skillet sprayed with vegetable spray, cook beef over high heat for 90 seconds or until just done at center. Drain any excess liquid. Put in large serving bowl.

2. In a saucepan of boiling water or microwave, blanch snow peas for 1 or 2 minutes, or until tender-crisp; refresh in cold water and drain. Place in serving bowl, along with lettuce, cucumber, red onions, water chestnuts, mandarin oranges and red pepper.

3. In small bowl whisk together orange juice concentrate, honey, vinegar, soya sauce, vegetable oil, sesame oil, garlic, ginger and orange zest; pour over salad and toss well.

SALMON SALAD WITH PEANUT LIME DRESSING

Serves 8

TIP

Dressing is great as a marinade or for stir-fry. Keeps well for days in refrigerator.

Great with tuna, swordfish or other tasty fish.

If you wish, use canned salmon or tuna.

MAKE AHEAD

Prepare salad and dressing early in the day. Keep separate until ready to serve.

8 oz	skinless salmon, cut into 1/2-inch (1-cm) cubes	250 g
2 cups	halved snow peas	500 mL
6 cups	well-packed romaine lettuce, washed, dried and torn into bite-size pieces	1.5 L
2 cups	sliced red peppers	500 mL
1 cup	sliced baby corn cobs	250 mL
1/2 cup	chopped fresh coriander or parsley	125 mL

Dressing

3 tbsp	lime juice	45 mL
2 tbsp	peanut butter	25 mL
2 tbsp	water	25 mL
2 tbsp	honey	25 mL
1 tbsp	soya sauce	15 mL
1 tbsp	vegetable oil	15 mL
2 tsp	sesame oil	10 mL
1 1/2 tsp	minced garlic	7 mL
1 tsp	minced ginger	5 mL

1. Heat nonstick skillet sprayed with vegetable spray over high heat; add salmon cubes and cook for 2 1/2 minutes, turning frequently, or until just done at center. Set aside.

2. Blanch snow peas in boiling water or microwave for 1 minute or until tender-crisp; refresh in cold water and drain. Place in serving bowl with salmon, romaine, red peppers, baby corn and coriander; toss gently.

3. In small bowl whisk together lime juice, peanut butter, water, honey, soya sauce, vegetable oil, sesame oil, garlic and ginger; pour over salad and toss gently.

PER SERVING

Calories	141
Protein	9 g
Fat, total	7 g
Fat, saturated	0.9 g
Carbohydrates	13 g
Sodium	324 mg
Cholesterol	16 mg
Fiber	3 g

MUSSEL AND SWEET PEPPER SALAD

Serves 6

TIP

Clams are an ideal substitute for mussels; or you can use a combination of both, but steam separately.

Coriander can replace dill.

To clean mussels, cut off any beards that are visible and discard any that are opened and will not close when you tap them.

MAKE AHEAD

Prepare early in the day. Stir again before serving.

1/3 cup	white wine or water	75 mL
2 lb	mussels	1 kg
3/4 cup	chopped asparagus	175 mL
1 cup	chopped red peppers	250 mL
3/4 cup	chopped green peppers	175 mL
1/2 cup	chopped red onions	125 mL
1/3 cup	chopped fresh dill (or 2 tsp [10 mL] dried)	75 mL
2 tbsp	olive oil	25 mL
1 1/2 tbsp	balsamic vinegar	20 mL
1 tsp	minced garlic	5 mL
2 tbsp	lemon juice	25 mL
1/8 tsp	ground black pepper	0.5 mL

1. Bring the wine to a boil in large heavy saucepan; add mussels and cover. Let cook for approximately 5 minutes, or until shells open. Discard any mussels that do not open. Remove mussels from shells and place in serving bowl.

2. In saucepan of boiling water or microwave, steam asparagus for 4 minutes or until tender-crisp; add to serving bowl along with red peppers, green peppers, onions, dill, olive oil, vinegar, garlic, lemon juice and pepper. Toss well to mix. Refrigerate until chilled.

PER SERVING	
Calories	109
Protein	7 g
Fat, total	5 g
Fat, saturated	0.8 g
Carbohydrates	7 g
Sodium	147 mg
Cholesterol	14 mg
Fiber	1 g

TURKEY PESTO SALAD

2 cups	diced, cooked turkey	500 mL
4 cups	well-packed washed, dried and torn romaine lettuce	1 L
3/4 cup	chopped red peppers	175 mL
3/4 cup	chopped green peppers	175 mL
1/2 cup	sliced red onions	125 mL
1	medium green onion, chopped	1
2 oz	feta cheese, crumbled	50 g

Pesto Dressing

1 cup	well-packed basil leaves	250 mL
2 tbsp	grated Parmesan cheese	25 mL
2 tbsp	olive oil	25 mL
1 tbsp	toasted pine nuts	15 mL
1 tsp	minced garlic	5 mL
2 tbsp	light sour cream	25 mL
1 tbsp	lemon juice	15 mL

1. In large serving bowl combine turkey, lettuce, red peppers, green peppers, red onions, green onion and feta cheese.

2. Put basil, Parmesan, olive oil, pine nuts and garlic in food processor; process until finely chopped, scraping sides of bowl once. Add sour cream and lemon juice and process until smooth. Pour over salad and toss well to combine. Garnish with a few toasted pine nuts (toast in skillet until browned, approximately 2 minutes).

SWEET CINNAMON WALDORF SALAD

TIP

For a nice change, use a combination of peas and apples to total 2 1/2 cups (625 mL).

Children like this salad as a dessert.

MAKE AHEAD

Prepare salad early in the day. Refrigerate and toss well just before serving. Keeps well for 2 days in refrigerator.

2 1/2 cups	diced apples	625 mL
3/4 cup	diced celery	175 mL
1 cup	red or green seedless grapes, quartered	250 mL
1 cup	chopped red or green peppers	250 mL
1/3 cup	raisins	75 mL
1/2 cup	canned mandarin oranges, drained	125 mL
2 tbsp	finely chopped pecans	25 mL

Dressing

1/4 cup	light mayonnaise	50 mL
1/4 cup	light (1%) sour cream	50 mL
2 tbsp	honey	25 mL
1 tbsp	lemon juice	15 mL
1/2 tsp	cinnamon	2 mL

1. In serving bowl, combine apples, celery, grapes, sweet peppers, raisins, mandarin oranges and pecans.

2. In small bowl, combine mayonnaise, sour cream, honey, lemon juice and cinnamon; mix thoroughly. Pour over salad and toss.

PER SERVING (8)	
Calories	116
Protein	1 g
Fat, total	3 g
Fat, saturated	0.4 g
Carbohydrates	24 g
Sodium	116 mg
Cholesterol	2 mg
Fiber	2 g

FISH AND SEAFOOD

FISH AND SEAFOOD TIPS

1. Fish must be fresh. It should have a bright color, a firm texture and a sweet smell. Whole fish should look plump and have shiny, clear, protruding eyes.

2. Store fish in the coldest part of the refrigerator. Ideally, place whole fish in a dish surrounded with ice. Replace ice when necessary. Do not allow fish to sit in water. Wash fillets, pat dry, then wrap in plastic wrap and keep very cold. Fish will last up to 3 days like this.

3. Wrap frozen fish very tightly so no air can penetrate. Avoid fish with ice crystals or discoloration. These are signs of freezer burn and result in dry fish. Darker, oily fish can be frozen up to 10 weeks, and lean whiter fish up to 4 months.

4. Defrost fish in refrigerator on a plate, pouring off excess liquid as necessary, or in microwave following manufacturer's instructions.

5. Sauté fish in a nonstick skillet sprayed with vegetable spray, without any oil or butter. This reduces calories and fat. Sauté just until fish is opaque and just cooked. Do not overcook, or fish will be dry. The liquid from the fish prevents sticking.

6. If baking, measure fish at the thickest point and bake for 10 minutes per inch (2.5 cm) at 425°F to 450°F (220°C to 230°C). If the fish is frozen, double the time. This guideline can be applied to any cooking method. If not sautéing, fish can be broiled, baked, steamed, microwaved, grilled or poached. If a sauce or filling is placed over fish, the baking time will be increased. Check at 5-minute intervals.

7. Fish and seafood can replace one another in any of the recipes that follow.

8. Firm white fish include halibut, haddock, orange roughy, sea bass, snapper and grouper. Be sure not to substitute a flaky white fillet, or it will fall apart in the cooking.

9. Shellfish can include any combination of shrimp, scallop, lobster, squid or crab meat. Imitation crab meat — surimi — is a combination of white fishes and is less expensive than real crab. Use it as you would crab meat.

FISH WITH TOMATO, BASIL AND CHEESE TOPPING

TIP

This dish suits any type of fish.

If goat cheese is too intense for you, try ricotta or feta.

Baking time is increased according to fish guidelines, due to the added sauce.

MAKE AHEAD

Tomato mixture can be prepared earlier in the day and refrigerated.

Preheat oven to 425° F (220° C)

Baking dish sprayed with vegetable spray

1 cup	chopped tomatoes	250 mL
1/2 cup	grated mozzarella cheese	125 mL
1/4 cup	sliced black olives	50 mL
1/4 cup	chopped green onions (about 2 medium)	50 mL
2 oz	goat cheese	50 g
1 tsp	minced garlic	5 mL
1 1/2 tsp	dried basil	7 mL
1 lb	fish fillets	500 g

1. In bowl, combine tomatoes, mozzarella, black olives, green onions, goat cheese, garlic and basil; mix well.

2. Place fish in prepared pan; top with tomato mixture. Bake uncovered approximately 15 minutes for each 1-inch (2.5 cm) thickness of fish fillet, or until fish flakes easily with a fork.

PER SERVING	
Calories	195
Protein	27 g
Fat, total	7 g
Fat, saturated	2 g
Carbohydrates	5 g
Sodium	287 mg
Cholesterol	63 mg
Fiber	1 g

CRUNCHY FISH WITH CUCUMBER DILL RELISH

Serves 4

Relish

2 cups	finely chopped cucumbers	500 mL
1/3 cup	chopped fresh dill	75 mL
1/3 cup	2% yogurt	75 mL
1/4 cup	finely diced green onions (about 2 medium)	50 mL
1/4 cup	finely diced green peppers	50 mL
3 tbsp	light mayonnaise	45 mL
1 tsp	minced garlic	5 mL

Crunchy Fish

2 cups	corn flakes	500 mL
1 tbsp	grated Parmesan cheese	15 mL
1 tsp	minced garlic	5 mL
1/2 tsp	dried basil	2 mL
1	egg	1
3 tbsp	2% milk	45 mL
3 tbsp	all-purpose flour	45 mL
1 lb	firm white fish fillets	500 g
1 tbsp	margarine or butter	15 mL

1. Relish: In bowl, combine cucumbers, dill, yogurt, green onions, green peppers, mayonnaise and garlic; mix to combine and set aside.

2. Put corn flakes, Parmesan, garlic and basil in food processor; process until fine and put on a plate. In shallow bowl whisk together egg and milk. Dust fish with flour.

3. Dip fish fillets in egg wash, then coat with crumb mixture. In large nonstick skillet sprayed with vegetable spray, melt margarine over medium heat. Add fillets and cook for 5 minutes or until browned, turn and cook for 2 minutes longer, or until fish is browned and flakes easily when pierced with a fork. Serve topped with cucumber dill relish.

PER SERVING

Calories	274
Protein	27 g
Fat, total	9 g
Fat, saturated	2 g
Carbohydrates	20 g
Sodium	429 mg
Cholesterol	112 mg
Fiber	1 g

FISH FILLETS WITH CORN AND RED PEPPER SALSA

TIP

After broiling pepper, put in small bowl and cover tightly with plastic wrap; this allows the skin to be removed easily.

The fresh pepper can be replaced with 4 oz (125 g) sweet pepper packed in water in a jar.

Roasted corn gives an exceptional flavor in this recipe. Either barbecue or broil until just cooked and charred, along with pepper. Remove kernels with a sharp knife.

MAKE AHEAD

Prepare salsa earlier in the day and refrigerate.

Preheat broiler

Baking dish sprayed with vegetable spray

1 lb	fish fillets	500 g

Salsa

1	large red pepper	1
1 1/2 cups	corn kernels	375 mL
1/3 cup	chopped red onions	75 mL
1/4 cup	chopped fresh coriander	50 mL
2 tbsp	fresh lime or lemon juice	25 mL
3 tsp	olive oil	15 mL
2 tsp	minced garlic	7 mL

1. Salsa: Broil red pepper for 15 to 20 minutes, turning occasionally, until charred on all sides. Remove pepper and set oven at 425° F (220° C). When pepper is cool, remove skin, seeds and stem. Chop and put in small bowl along with corn, onions, coriander, lime juice, 2 tsp (10 mL) of olive oil and 1 tsp (5 mL) of the garlic; mix well.

2. Put fish in single layer in prepared baking dish and brush with remaining 1 tsp (5 mL) garlic and 1 tsp (5 mL) oil. Bake uncovered for 10 minutes per inch (2.5 cm) thickness of fish or until fish flakes easily when pierced with a fork. Serve with salsa.

PER SERVING	
Calories	211
Protein	24 g
Fat, total	5 g
Fat, saturated	1 g
Carbohydrates	19 g
Sodium	320 mg
Cholesterol	54 mg
Fiber	2 g

FISH WITH SUN-DRIED TOMATO PESTO, FETA AND BLACK OLIVES

Preheat oven to 425° F (220° C)

Baking dish sprayed with vegetable spray

1 1/2 lbs	fish fillets	750 g
1 oz	feta cheese, crumbled	25 g
2 tbsp	chopped black olives	25 mL

Sauce

1/4 cup	well-packed, chopped sun-dried tomatoes	50 mL
2 tbsp	chopped fresh basil or parsley	25 mL
1 1/2 tbsp	olive oil	20 mL
1 1/2 tbsp	grated Parmesan cheese	20 mL
1 tbsp	toasted pine nuts	15 mL
1 tsp	minced garlic	5 mL
1/3 cup	chicken stock	75 mL

1. Sauce: Put sun-dried tomatoes, basil, olive oil, Parmesan, pine nuts and garlic in food processor; process until finely chopped. With machine running, gradually add stock through feed tube; process until smooth.

2. Put fish in single layer in prepared baking dish; spread sun-dried pesto on top. Sprinkle with feta and olives. Bake uncovered for 15 minutes per inch (2.5 cm) thickness of fish or until fish flakes easily when pierced with a fork.

PER SERVING	
Calories	172
Protein	24 g
Fat, total	7 g
Fat, saturated	2 g
Carbohydrates	2 g
Sodium	295 mg
Cholesterol	60 mg
Fiber	0 g

FISH WITH SMOKED SALMON AND GREEN PEAS

MAKE AHEAD

Prepare sauce up to 24 hours ahead. Add more stock or milk if too thick.

Preheat oven to 425° F (220° C)

Baking dish sprayed with vegetable spray

1 lb	fish fillets or steaks	500 g
1/4 cup	chopped green onions (about 2 medium)	50 mL
2 oz	smoked salmon, diced	50 g

Sauce

2 tsp	margarine or butter	10 mL
4 tsp	all-purpose flour	20 mL
1/2 cup	fish or chicken stock	125 mL
1/2 cup	2% milk	125 mL
1/3 cup	frozen peas	75 mL
3 tbsp	chopped fresh dill (or 2 tsp [10 mL] dried)	50 mL

1. Sauce: Melt the margarine in small saucepan over medium-low heat; add the flour and cook, stirring, for 1 minute. Add stock and milk, stirring or whisking constantly, until mixture starts to simmer and thicken slightly, 5 to 7 minutes. Stir peas and dill into sauce, and pour over fish.

2. Bake until fish is just done at center, and flakes easily with a fork, 10 minutes for every inch (2.5 cm) thickness. Remove fish from oven.

3. Sprinkle with green onions and smoked salmon pieces and serve.

PER SERVING

Calories	175
Protein	26 g
Fat, total	5 g
Fat, saturated	1 g
Carbohydrates	6 g
Sodium	376 mg
Cholesterol	60 mg
Fiber	1 g

SWORDFISH WITH MANGO CORIANDER SALSA

TIP

Any firm fish can be substituted. Try tuna or shark.

Parsley or dill can be substituted for coriander.

This salsa can be used over chicken or pork.

MAKE AHEAD

Make salsa early in the day and refrigerate.

Start barbecue or preheat oven to 425° F (220° C)

1 1/2 lbs	swordfish steaks	750 g
1 tsp	vegetable oil	5 mL

Salsa

1 1/2 cups	finely diced mango or peach	375 mL
3/4 cup	finely diced red peppers	175 mL
1/2 cup	finely diced green peppers	125 mL
1/2 cup	finely diced red onions	125 mL
1/4 cup	chopped fresh coriander	50 mL
2 tbsp	lemon juice	25 mL
2 tsp	olive oil	10 mL
1 tsp	minced garlic	5 mL

1. Brush fish with 1 tsp (5 mL) of oil on both sides. Barbecue or bake fish for 10 minutes per inch (2.5 cm) thickness, or until it flakes easily when pierced with a fork.

2. Meanwhile, in bowl combine mango, red peppers, green peppers, red onions, coriander, lemon juice, olive oil and garlic; mix thoroughly. Serve over fish.

PER SERVING	
Calories	197
Protein	22 g
Fat, total	7 g
Fat, saturated	2 g
Carbohydrates	11 g
Sodium	101 mg
Cholesterol	43 mg
Fiber	2 g

ORANGE SOYA-GLAZED SWORDFISH WITH MUSHROOMS

Serves 4

TIP

Wild mushrooms, especially oyster, are a special taste treat in this dish.

★

Any firm fish, such as tuna, orange roughy or halibut, can be substituted for swordfish.

MAKE AHEAD

Sauce can be prepared up to 24 hours ahead. Reheat and add more water if too thick.

Preheat oven to 425° F (220° C)

Baking dish sprayed with vegetable spray

1 lb	swordfish	500 g
1 tsp	margarine or butter	5 mL
1/2 lb	mushrooms, sliced	250 g
1/4 cup	chopped green onions (about 2 medium)	50 mL

Glaze

2 tbsp	soya sauce	25 mL
2 tbsp	orange juice concentrate	25 mL
2 tbsp	honey	25 mL
2 tbsp	water	25 mL
1 tsp	minced garlic	5 mL
1 tsp	minced ginger	5 mL
3/4 tsp	cornstarch	4 mL

1. Glaze: In small saucepan whisk together soya sauce, orange juice concentrate, honey, water, garlic, ginger and cornstarch; cook over medium heat for 3 minutes or until sauce thickens.

2. Put swordfish in single layer in baking dish; pour sauce over and bake uncovered for 10 minutes per inch (2.5 cm) thickness of fish, or until fish flakes easily when pierced with a fork.

3. Meanwhile, melt margarine over high heat in non-stick skillet; add mushrooms and cook for 4 minutes or until mushrooms are browned. Add green onions and cook for 1 minute. Pour onion-mushroom mixture over fish and serve.

PER SERVING

Calories	201
Protein	24 g
Fat, total	6 g
Fat, saturated	1 g
Carbohydrates	13 g
Sodium	553 mg
Cholesterol	44 mg
Fiber	1 g

PECAN-COATED SWORDFISH WITH LEMON SAUCE

Serves 4

TIP

Try almonds or cashews instead of pecans.

Tuna, shark or any firm white fish would be a good substitute for swordfish.

MAKE AHEAD

Prepare fish earlier in the day and refrigerate before baking.

Prepare sauce earlier in the day. Add more stock before serving if sauce is too thick.

Preheat oven to 425° F (220° C)

Baking dish sprayed with vegetable spray

1	egg	1
3 tbsp	2% milk	45 mL
1/2 cup	finely chopped pecans	125 mL
2 tbsp	seasoned bread crumbs	25 mL
1 lb	swordfish	500 g
3 tbsp	all-purpose flour	45 mL
2 tsp	vegetable oil	10 mL

Sauce

2/3 cup	chicken stock	150 mL
2 tbsp	lemon juice	25 mL
2 tbsp	sugar	25 mL
2 tsp	cornstarch	10 mL
1/2 tsp	grated lemon zest	2 mL
2 tbsp	chopped fresh parsley	25 mL

1. In shallow bowl whisk together egg and milk. Combine pecans and bread crumbs and put on a plate. Dust fish with flour, dip in egg wash and coat with pecan mixture.

2. Heat oil in large nonstick skillet sprayed with vegetable spray over medium heat; add fish and cook for 2 minutes per side or until both sides are golden. Place in prepared baking dish. Bake uncovered for 10 minutes per inch (2.5 cm) thickness of fish or until fish flakes easily when pierced with a fork.

3. While fish bakes, in saucepan whisk together stock, lemon juice, sugar, cornstarch and lemon zest; cook over medium heat for 3 or 4 minutes or until sauce thickens slightly. Pour sauce over fish and sprinkle with parsley.

PER SERVING

Calories	341
Protein	27 g
Fat, total	19 g
Fat, saturated	3 g
Carbohydrates	17 g
Sodium	528 mg
Cholesterol	99 mg
Fiber	1 g

FISH WITH CORNBREAD AND DILL STUFFING

Serves 4

TIP

Salmon, trout or whitefish is ideal. Ask to have fish butter-flied, scaled and deboned.

This cornbread stuffing is also ideal for chicken or turkey.

MAKE AHEAD

Prepare entire stuffing with vegetables up to one day in advance.

PER SERVING

Calories	465
Protein	33 g
Fat, total	14 g
Fat, saturated	3 g
Carbohydrates	52 g
Sodium	324 mg
Cholesterol	123 mg
Fiber	4 g

Preheat oven to 400° F (200° C)

8-inch (2 L) square baking dish sprayed with vegetable spray

Cornbread

1/2 cup	cornmeal	125 mL
1/2 cup	all-purpose flour	125 mL
1 1/2 tbsp	granulated sugar	20 mL
1 1/2 tsp	baking powder	7 mL
3/4 cup	2% yogurt	175 mL
3/4 cup	corn kernels	175 mL
1	egg	1
1 1/2 tbsp	melted margarine or butter	20 mL
2 tsp	vegetable oil	10 mL
1 1/2 tsp	minced garlic	7 mL
1 cup	chopped onions	250 mL
1 cup	sliced mushrooms	250 mL
1 cup	chopped green or red peppers	250 mL
1/4 cup	chopped fresh dill (or 2 tsp [10 mL] dried)	50 mL
1	whole 2-lb (1 kg) fish, rinsed under cold water	1
1 tsp	vegetable oil	5 mL
1 tsp	minced garlic	5 mL
1/3 cup	chicken stock or water	75 mL
1/3 cup	white wine	75 mL

1. In large bowl stir together cornmeal, flour, sugar and baking powder. In another bowl combine yogurt, corn, egg and margarine. Add the wet ingredients to the dry ingredients and stir just until combined. Pour batter into prepared pan and bake for 15 to 18 minutes or until cake tester inserted in center comes out clean.

2. In nonstick skillet sprayed with vegetable spray, heat oil over medium heat. Add garlic and onions and cook for 4 minutes or until softened. Add mushrooms and peppers and cook for 5 minutes or until vegetables are tender. Stir in dill and remove from heat.

3. Crumble the cooled cornbread into a large bowl. Add vegetable mixture and combine thoroughly. Stuff half of the mixture into fish. Place remaining mixture in dish and serve warmed with fish. Place fish in baking pan sprayed with vegetable spray and brush fish with oil and garlic. Pour stock and wine into pan. Cover and bake for 35 to 45 minutes or until fish flakes easily when pierced with a fork.

SALMON FILLETS WITH BLACK BEAN SAUCE

Serves 4

TIP

Whole black bean sauce is less salty tasting than the puréed version. If whole black bean sauce is unavailable, increase the sugar to taste.

Other fish fillets, such as sole, trout, or orange roughy, are good alternatives to salmon.

MAKE AHEAD

Prepare sauce up to 48 hours ahead and keep refrigerated. Stir again before using.

Preheat oven to 425° F (220° C)

Baking dish sprayed with vegetable spray

1 lb	salmon fillets	500 g
1/4 cup	chopped green onions (about 2 medium)	50 mL

Sauce

1/2 cup	chicken stock	125 mL
5 tsp	brown sugar	25 mL
1 tbsp	black bean sauce	15 mL
2 tsp	rice wine vinegar	10 mL
2 tsp	soya sauce	10 mL
2 tsp	sesame oil	10 mL
1 1/4 tsp	cornstarch	6 mL
3/4 tsp	minced ginger root	4 mL
1/2 tsp	minced garlic	2 mL

1. Put salmon fillets in single layer in prepared baking dish.

2. Sauce: In saucepan whisk together stock, brown sugar, black bean sauce, vinegar, soya sauce, sesame oil, cornstarch, ginger and garlic; cook over medium heat, stirring, for 4 minutes or until sauce thickens slightly. Pour over fish and bake uncovered 10 minutes per inch (2.5 cm) thickness of fish, or until fish flakes easily when pierced with a fork. Serve sprinkled with green onions.

PER SERVING

Calories	196
Protein	23 g
Fat, total	8 g
Fat, saturated	2 g
Carbohydrates	7 g
Sodium	417 mg
Cholesterol	56 mg
Fiber	0 g

SALMON OVER WHITE-AND-BLACK-BEAN SALSA

Start barbecue or preheat oven to 425° F (220° C)

1 lb	salmon fillets	500 g

Salsa:

1 cup	canned black beans, drained	250 mL
1 cup	canned white navy beans, drained	250 mL
3/4 cup	chopped tomatoes	175 mL
1/2 cup	chopped green peppers	125 mL
1/4 cup	chopped red onions	50 mL
1/4 cup	chopped fresh coriander	50 mL
2 tbsp	balsamic vinegar	25 mL
2 tbsp	lemon juice	25 mL
1 tbsp	olive oil	15 mL
1 tsp	minced garlic	5 mL

1. Salsa: In bowl combine black beans, white beans, tomatoes, green peppers, red onions and coriander. In small bowl whisk together vinegar, lemon juice, olive oil and garlic; pour over bean mixture and toss to combine.

2. Barbecue fish or bake uncovered for approximately 10 minutes for each 1-inch (2.5 cm) thickness of fish, or until fish flakes with a fork. Serve fish over bean salsa.

TIP

Swordfish or tuna can be substituted for salmon.

Other varieties of beans can be substituted if black or white navy beans are unavailable.

★

If you're not using canned beans, 1 cup (250 mL) dry yields 3 cups (750 mL) cooked.

MAKE AHEAD

Prepare bean mixture earlier in the day and keep refrigerated. Stir before serving.

PER SERVING

Calories	319
Protein	32 g
Fat, total	9 g
Fat, saturated	2 g
Carbohydrates	29 g
Sodium	313 mg
Cholesterol	56 mg
Fiber	9 g

CREAMY SEAFOOD STRUDEL

Serves 6

TIP

Substitute any firm white fish for the scallops and shrimp.

Substitute wild mushrooms for the regular type.

MAKE AHEAD

Prepare entire filling and sauce earlier in the day, adding more milk if sauce is too thick. For best taste, roll in phyllo just before baking and serving.

Preheat oven to 375° F (190° C)
Baking sheet sprayed with vegetable spray

4 oz	diced scallops	125 g
4 oz	diced shrimp	125 g
1 tsp	vegetable oil	5 mL
2 tsp	minced garlic	10 mL
1 1/2 cups	chopped mushrooms	375 mL
1 cup	chopped green or red peppers	250 mL
1/3 cup	chopped fresh dill (or 1 tbsp [15 mL] dried)	75 mL
1/4 cup	chopped green onions (about 2 medium)	50 mL

Sauce

2 tsp	margarine or butter	10 mL
1 1/2 tbsp	all-purpose flour	20 mL
1/2 cup	2% milk	125 mL
1/2 cup	chicken stock	125 mL
2 tbsp	grated Parmesan cheese	25 mL
2 tsp	margarine or butter	10 mL
5	sheets phyllo pastry	5

1. In nonstick skillet sprayed with vegetable spray, cook scallops and shrimp over high heat for 1 minute, or until just done at center; drain any excess liquid and set aside.

2. Heat oil in nonstick skillet over medium heat; add garlic, mushrooms and peppers and cook for 4 minutes or until softened. Drain any excess liquid. Stir in dill and green onions and remove from heat.

3. Sauce: Melt margarine in saucepan over medium heat; add flour and cook, stirring, for 1 minute. Gradually add milk and stock, stirring constantly until sauce begins to thicken, and simmer approximately 2 minutes. Stir in Parmesan and remove from heat. Toss together seafood, vegetables and cheese sauce. Let cool for 5 minutes.

PER SERVING	
Calories	169
Protein	11 g
Fat, total	6 g
Fat, saturated	1 g
Carbohydrates	18 g
Sodium	269 mg
Cholesterol	38 mg
Fiber	1 g

4. Melt margarine. Layer two phyllo sheets one on top of the other. Brush with margarine. Layer two more phyllo sheets on top, and brush with margarine. Layer last phyllo sheet on top and spread filling over top to within 1 inch (2.5 cm) of edges. Starting at long edge, roll up tightly. Place on prepared baking sheet and brush with remaining melted margarine. Bake for 20 to 25 minutes or until browned.

SALMON FAJITAS IN HOISIN SAUCE

Serves 3	

TIP

Seafood or any firm white fish can substitute for the salmon.

Substitute chopped broccoli for snow peas.

Handle cooked salmon gently, since it flakes easily.

MAKE AHEAD

Prepare sauce up to one day in advance. Keep refrigerated.

Preheat oven to 425° F (220° C)

Baking sheet sprayed with vegetable spray

8 oz	salmon, thinly sliced	250 g
1 tsp	vegetable oil	5 mL
1 1/4 cups	halved snow peas	300 mL
1 1/4 cups	thinly sliced red or green peppers	300 mL
1/3 cup	chopped green onions (about 3 medium)	75 mL
3 tbsp	chopped fresh coriander or parsley	45 mL
6	small tortillas	6

Sauce
2 tbsp	hoisin sauce	25 mL
1 tbsp	honey	15 mL
2 tsp	soya sauce	10 mL
2 tsp	lemon juice	10 mL
2 tsp	sesame oil	10 mL
1 1/2 tsp	minced garlic	7 mL
1 tsp	minced ginger root	5 mL
1/2 tsp	cornstarch	2 mL

1. Sauce: In small bowl whisk together hoisin sauce, honey, soya sauce, lemon juice, sesame oil, garlic, ginger and cornstarch; set aside.

2. In nonstick skillet sprayed with vegetable spray, cook salmon over high heat for 2 minutes, or until just barely done at center; set aside.

3. Heat oil in nonstick skillet over medium heat. Add snow peas and red peppers; cook for 4 minutes or until tender. Stir sauce again and add to vegetables, along with green onions and coriander. Cook for 1 minute, or until slightly thickened. Remove from heat and gently stir in salmon.

4. Divide salmon filling among tortillas; roll up and put on prepared baking sheet. Bake for 5 minutes or until heated through.

PER SERVING	
Calories	448
Protein	24 g
Fat, total	14 g
Fat, saturated	3 g
Carbohydrates	58 g
Sodium	650 mg
Cholesterol	37 mg
Fiber	4 g

PESTO SEAFOOD PAELLA

TIP

If basil is unavailable, substitute parsley, or use a combination.

Substitute any firm fish for scallops and squid. Shrimps also go well.

MAKE AHEAD

Prepare pesto up to 24 hours in advance and refrigerate. Pesto can be frozen for up to 2 weeks.

Prepare rice mixture earlier in the day and reheat before mixing rest of the dish together.

1 tsp	vegetable oil	5 mL
2 tsp	minced garlic	10 mL
1 cup	chopped onions	250 mL
1 cup	chopped green or red peppers	250 mL
3/4 cup	wild rice	175 mL
3/4 cup	white rice	175 mL
2 1/2 cups	chicken stock	625 mL
8 oz	scallops	250 g
8 oz	squid	250 g

Pesto

1 1/2 cups	packed fresh basil leaves	375 mL
2 1/2 tbsp	grated Parmesan cheese	35 mL
2 1/2 tbsp	olive oil	35 mL
2 1/2 tbsp	toasted pine nuts	35 mL
1 1/2 tsp	minced garlic	7 mL
5 tbsp	chicken stock or water	75 mL

1. In saucepan sprayed with vegetable spray, heat oil over medium heat; add garlic, onions and green peppers and cook for 4 minutes or until softened. Add wild rice, white rice and stock; bring to a boil. Cover, reduce heat to medium-low and simmer for 30 minutes, or until rice is tender and liquid absorbed.

2. Meanwhile, put basil, Parmesan, olive oil, pine nuts and garlic in food processor; process until finely chopped, scraping down sides of bowl once. With machine running, gradually add stock through the feed tube; process until smooth.

3. In nonstick skillet sprayed with vegetable spray, cook scallops and squid over high heat until just done at center (approximately 1 or 2 minutes); remove from skillet. Drain any excess liquid. Toss together rice mixture, pesto and seafood. Place in serving dish.

PER SERVING (6)	
Calories	346
Protein	20 g
Fat, total	11 g
Fat, saturated	2 g
Carbohydrates	43 g
Sodium	564 mg
Cholesterol	103 mg
Fiber	3 g

SAUTÉED CRAB CAKES WITH CHUNKY DILL TARTAR SAUCE

1/2 tsp	vegetable oil	2 tsp
1 tsp	minced garlic	5 mL
1/2 cup	chopped onions	125 mL
12 oz	imitation crab (sea legs, Krab legs or Krab flakes)	375 g
2/3 cup	seasoned bread crumbs	150 mL
1/4 cup	chopped fresh dill (or 2 tsp [10 mL] dried)	50 mL
1	whole egg	1
1	egg white	1
2 tbsp	light mayonnaise	25 mL
2 tsp	lemon juice	10 mL
1 tbsp	margarine or butter	15 mL

Chunky Dill Tartar Sauce

3 tbsp	light mayonnaise	45 mL
3 tbsp	light sour cream	45 mL
2 tbsp	finely chopped green peppers	25 mL
2 tbsp	finely chopped red onions	25 mL
2 tbsp	chopped fresh dill (or 1/2 tsp [2 mL] dried)	25 mL
2 tsp	lemon juice	10 mL

1. Heat oil in small nonstick skillet over medium heat; add garlic and onions and cook for 5 minutes or until softened. Put in food processor along with crab, bread crumbs, dill, whole egg, egg white, mayonnaise and lemon juice. Pulse on and off until finely chopped. Form each 1/3 cup (75 mL) into a patty.

2. Sauce: In small bowl combine mayonnaise, sour cream, green peppers, onions, dill and lemon juice; set aside.

3. Melt margarine in large nonstick skillet sprayed with vegetable spray over medium heat. Add crab cakes and cook for 6 minutes, or until golden; turn and cook for 6 minutes longer, or until golden and hot. Serve with chunky dill tartar sauce.

ZUCCHINI STUFFED WITH CRABMEAT, TOMATOES AND DILL

Serves 4

TIP

Try yellow zucchini if available.

★

Diced, cooked shrimp can substitute for crabmeat.

★

Imitation crab (surimi) can also be used.

MAKE AHEAD

Shells can be filled up to a day ahead, covered and kept in refrigerator. Bake for 20 minutes to heat thoroughly.

PER SERVING

Calories	113
Protein	10 g
Fat, total	3 g
Fat, saturated	0.9 g
Carbohydrates	12 g
Sodium	756 mg
Cholesterol	4 mg
Fiber	3 g

Preheat oven to 400° F (200° C)

Baking sheet

4	zucchini	4
2 tsp	margarine or butter	10 mL
1 tsp	minced garlic	5 mL
1/3 cup	chopped onions	75 mL
6 oz	chopped crabmeat	150 g
1/3 cup	chopped tomatoes	75 mL
3 tbsp	seasoned bread crumbs	45 mL
3 tbsp	chopped fresh dill (or 2 tsp [10 mL] dried)	45 mL
2 tbsp	light sour cream	25 mL
2 tbsp	chopped green onions (about 1 medium)	25 mL
1 tbsp	grated Parmesan cheese	15 mL

1. Trim ends of zucchini. Cook in boiling water, covered, for 5 minutes or until tender. Rinse with cold water and drain. Cut in half lengthwise; scoop out pulp, leaving shell intact. Chop pulp and squeeze out moisture. Set aside. Place shells on baking sheet.

2. In nonstick saucepan, heat margarine over medium heat; cook garlic and onions for 4 minutes or until softened. Add zucchini pulp and cook for 4 minutes more.

3. Place vegetable mixture in food processor along with crabmeat, tomatoes, bread crumbs, dill, sour cream and green onions. Pulse on and off just until finely chopped. Divide among shells. Sprinkle with Parmesan.

4. Bake for 10 minutes or until heated through.

SCALLOPS IN BLACK BEAN SAUCE WITH ASPARAGUS AND OYSTER MUSHROOMS

Serves 4

TIP

Whole black bean sauce is less salty than the puréed version. If puréed sauce is too salty, increase honey to taste.

Regular mushrooms are acceptable as a substitute. They give off more liquid, so drain off excess.

Any firm seafood can be used.

Broccoli can be substituted for asparagus.

MAKE AHEAD

Prepare sauce up to 48 hours ahead. Keep refrigerated and stir again before using.

PER SERVING

Calories	222
Protein	23 g
Fat, total	6 g
Fat, saturated	0.7 g
Carbohydrates	20 g
Sodium	604 mg
Cholesterol	37 mg
Fiber	2 g

1 lb	scallops	500 g
1 tsp	vegetable oil	5 mL
2 1/2 cups	asparagus cut into 1-inch (2.5 cm) pieces	625 mL
2 cups	sliced oyster mushrooms	500 mL
2	medium green onions, chopped	2

Sauce

3/4 cup	chicken stock	175 mL
2 tbsp	black bean sauce	25 mL
2 tbsp	honey	25 mL
2 tsp	rice wine vinegar	10 mL
2 tsp	soya sauce	10 mL
2 tsp	sesame oil	10 mL
1 tbsp	cornstarch	15 mL
1 tsp	minced garlic	5 mL
1 tsp	minced ginger root	5 mL

1. Heat a nonstick skillet sprayed with vegetable spray over high heat; add scallops and cook for 2 to 3 minutes, turning frequently, or until just cooked at center. Remove from heat and drain any excess liquid.

2. In small bowl, whisk together stock, black bean sauce, honey, vinegar, soya sauce, sesame oil, cornstarch, garlic and ginger; set aside.

3. Heat oil in nonstick pan over medium-high heat. Cook asparagus and mushrooms for 5 minutes or until tender-crisp. Drain any excess liquid. Stir sauce again and add to pan. Cook for 1 minute or until bubbly and thickened slightly. Return scallops to pan and cook for 30 seconds or until heated through. Serve over rice or pasta. Garnish with green onions.

SWORDFISH WITH MANGO CORIANDER SALSA (PAGE 83) ➤

SEAFOOD KEBABS WITH PINEAPPLE AND GREEN PEPPER IN APRICOT GLAZE

Serves 4

TIP

Swordfish, shrimps, or scallops are a good choice for fish.

★

Peach jam can substitute for the apricot jam.

★

If fresh pineapple is unavailable, use canned.

MAKE AHEAD

Prepare kebabs and the glaze up to 24 hours ahead, keeping separate until just ready to cook.

Start barbecue or preheat oven to 425° F (220° C)

1 lb	firm white fish, cut into 2-inch (5-cm) cubes	500 g
16	dried apricots	16
1	green pepper, cut into 16 chunks	1
16	pineapple chunks	16

Glaze

1/3 cup	apricot jam	75 mL
2 tbsp	lemon juice	25 mL
1 tbsp	vegetable oil	15 mL
1 tbsp	water	15 mL
1 tbsp	chopped fresh coriander or parsley	15 mL
1 tsp	Dijon mustard	5 mL
1 tsp	minced garlic	5 mL
3/4 tsp	curry powder	4 mL

1. Alternately thread fish cubes, apricots, green pepper and pineapple chunks onto 4 long or 8 short barbecue skewers.

2. Glaze: In small bowl whisk together apricot jam, lemon juice, oil, water, coriander, mustard, garlic and curry. Brush kebabs with some of sauce; reserve remainder of sauce to serve with cooked kebabs.

3. Barbecue or bake kebabs for 5 to 8 minutes, turning once, or just until seafood is opaque.

PER SERVING

Calories	317
Protein	23 g
Fat, total	5 g
Fat, saturated	0.6 g
Carbohydrates	47 g
Sodium	118 mg
Cholesterol	54 mg
Fiber	3 g

< ROASTED CHICKEN WITH APRICOT ORANGE GLAZE AND COUSCOUS STUFFING (PAGE 116)

SEAFOOD AND VEGETABLE ORANGE STIR-FRY

Serves 4

TIP

Use any firm seafood or fish. Chicken or pork can also be used.

Broccoli can be replaced with asparagus or snow peas.

MAKE AHEAD

Prepare sauce up to one day in advance.

Sauce

1/2 cup	chicken or fish stock	125 mL
1/3 cup	orange marmalade	75 mL
5 tsp	soya sauce	25 mL
5 tsp	rice wine vinegar	25 mL
1 tbsp	cornstarch	15 mL
1 tsp	minced ginger	5 mL
1 tsp	minced garlic	5 mL
1 lb	squid cut in rings or scallops	500 g
1 tsp	vegetable oil	5 mL
3 cups	chopped broccoli	750 mL
1	medium red pepper, sliced	1

1. Sauce: In small bowl combine stock, marmalade, soya sauce, vinegar, cornstarch, ginger and garlic; mix thoroughly and set aside.

2. In large nonstick wok (or skillet) sprayed with vegetable spray, cook seafood over high heat, stirring constantly, for 3 to 5 minutes or until just done; remove from pan and set aside. Drain any excess liquid.

3. Respray wok with vegetable spray, and add oil to wok. Add broccoli and cook, stirring constantly, for 3 minutes or until beginning to soften; add red pepper and cook for 3 minutes more, or until vegetables are tender-crisp. Stir the sauce again and add to wok along with cooked seafood; cook for 1 minute or until slightly thickened. Serve alongside rice.

PER SERVING

Calories	220
Protein	21 g
Fat, total	3 g
Fat, saturated	0.5 g
Carbohydrates	29 g
Sodium	624 mg
Cholesterol	264 mg
Fiber	3 g

SQUID RINGS WITH CREAMY TOMATO DIP

	Serves 4	

TIP

Instead of bread crumbs, try crushed cornflake crumbs for a crunchier texture.

MAKE AHEAD

Prepare breaded squid earlier in the day. Cover and refrigerate before baking.

Sauce can be made up to 48 hours in advance.

Preheat oven to 400° F (200° C)

Baking sheet sprayed with vegetable spray

12 oz	squid	375 g
3 tbsp	all-purpose flour	45 mL
1	egg	1
2 tbsp	2% milk	25 mL
3/4 cup	bread crumbs	175 mL
1/4 cup	grated Parmesan cheese	50 mL
1 tbsp	chopped fresh parsley	15 mL
1 tsp	minced garlic	5 mL
1/2 tsp	chili powder	2 mL

Sauce

3 tbsp	light mayonnaise	45 mL
1 1/2 tbsp	tomato paste	20 mL
1 1/2 tbsp	2% yogurt	20 mL
1 1/2 tbsp	water	20 mL
1 tsp	minced garlic	5 mL
3/4 tsp	dried basil	4 mL

1. Clean squid and cut crosswise into 1/2-inch (1-cm) wide rings. Dust with flour. Whisk egg and milk together in shallow bowl. Combine bread crumbs, Parmesan, parsley, garlic and chili powder and place on plate. Dip squid rings in egg wash, then coat with bread crumb mixture. Place on prepared baking sheet and bake for 5 to 8 minutes, or until just done at center.

2. Meanwhile, in small bowl stir together mayonnaise, tomato paste, yogurt, water, garlic and basil. Serve squid rings with tomato sauce dip.

PER SERVING	
Calories	248
Protein	20 g
Fat, total	8 g
Fat, saturated	2 g
Carbohydrates	22 g
Sodium	399 mg
Cholesterol	257 mg
Fiber	1 g

MUSSELS WITH PESTO

1/4 cup	white wine or chicken stock	50 mL
2 lbs	cleaned mussels	1 kg

Pesto

1 1/4 cups	packed fresh basil	300 mL
3 tbsp	olive oil	45 mL
2 tbsp	toasted pine nuts	25 mL
2 tbsp	grated Parmesan cheese	25 mL
1 tsp	minced garlic	5 mL
1/4 cup	chicken stock	50 mL

1. Pesto: Put basil, olive oil, pine nuts, Parmesan and garlic in food processor; process until finely chopped, scraping down sides of bowl once. With machine running, gradually add stock through feed tube; process until smooth.

2. Put pesto and wine in large heavy-bottomed saucepan. Bring to a boil; add mussels and cover. Cook, shaking the saucepan for 2 minutes, or just until mussels open. Discard any that do not open.

CHICKEN

CHICKEN TIPS

1. When you buy skinless, boneless chicken breasts, each piece is actually one half breast. The recipes will usually call for a 4 oz (125 g) breast per person. Do not be concerned about the weight of each breast as long as 4 servings do not exceed 1 lb (500 g), or 6 servings 1 1/2 lb (750 g).

2. Pounding boneless chicken breasts makes stuffing easier, and the breasts cook more quickly. If you don't pound them, allow a longer cooking time.

3. At home, remove the wrapping and wash the chicken with cold water. Wrap chicken loosely in foil and place in the coldest part of the refrigerator for up to 48 hours. If freezing, wrap chicken in a plastic freezer bag and freeze for up to 4 months.

4. Thaw poultry in the refrigerator (5 hours per pound [10 hours per kilogram]), in a bowl of cold water (1 hour per pound [2 hours per kilogram]), or in a microwave. Do not defrost at room temperature; harmful bacteria may develop. Never refreeze raw chicken after thawing. Cooked chicken may be frozen.

    Note: Raw chicken contains bacteria that can cause illness. Thorough cooking destroys bacteria. After working with raw chicken, wash hands, cutting board and utensils with hot water and soap. Never place cooked chicken on a plate where raw chicken has been.

5. Always cook chicken until it is no longer pink and juices run clear. It must never be served rare, since harmful bacteria may remain.

6. Boneless chicken breasts can be replaced with turkey, veal or pork scallopini.

7. The nutritional analysis for some chicken recipes reflects cooking with the skin on but the skin being removed before eating. When you do this, the chicken retains the flavor through the cooking, but your fat consumption is greatly reduced.

8. Most of the fat in chicken is in the skin. A 3-oz (75-g) breast with skin has 8 g of fat; without skin, only 3 g. Cooking chicken with the skin on protects the delicate meat underneath and holds in precious juices. Fortunately, the fat from the skin isn't absorbed into the meat. A chicken breast cooked with the skin on, then removed, has approximately the same amount of fat as a breast cooked without the skin.

9. Buy chicken with moist skin, tender flesh and a fresh smell.

10. Stuff bird just before roasting; harmful bacteria could contaminate the stuffing if done earlier.

11. Try not to overcook chicken, as it will become dry.

12. If you have a sauce that was used as a marinade for the raw chicken, remember to boil the remaining marinade if serving with cooked chicken; this will eliminate harmful bacteria that may remain from the raw chicken.

CHICKEN WITH RICE, GREEN OLIVES AND TOMATO SAUCE

Serves 4

TIP

Bone-in chicken breasts can be used, or a combination of both can be used. Bone-in breast will cook in less time than legs.

A combination of wild and white rice can be used.

MAKE AHEAD

Brown chicken earlier in the day and refrigerate until ready to complete cooking.

Preheat oven to 400° F (200° C)

9- by 13-inch baking dish (3.5 L) sprayed with vegetable spray

4	chicken legs	4
1/3 cup	all-purpose flour	75 mL
2 tsp	vegetable oil	10 mL
2 tsp	minced garlic	10 mL
1 1/2 cups	chopped onions	375 mL
1 1/2 cups	chopped green peppers	375 mL
1 cup	white rice	250 mL
1	can (19 oz [540 mL]) tomatoes, puréed	1
1 1/2 cups	chicken stock	375 mL
1/2 cup	sliced stuffed green olives	125 mL
2 tsp	drained capers	10 mL
2 tsp	dried basil	10 mL
1 1/2 tsp	dried oregano	7 mL
1	bay leaf	1

1. In large nonstick skillet sprayed with vegetable spray, heat 1 tsp (5 mL) of the oil over high heat. Dust chicken with flour. Cook for 8 minutes, turning often, or until browned on all sides. Put in prepared baking dish.

2. In nonstick skillet, heat remaining 1 tsp (5 mL) oil over medium heat. Add garlic, onions and green peppers; cook for 4 minutes or until softened. Stir in rice, tomatoes, stock, olives, capers, basil, oregano and bay leaf; bring to a boil and pour over chicken. Cover tightly with aluminum foil and bake for 30 minutes, or until juices run clear when leg is pierced at thickest point and rice is tender. Remove skin before eating.

PER SERVING

Calories	522
Protein	34 g
Fat, total	10 g
Fat, saturated	2 g
Carbohydrates	76 g
Sodium	964 mg
Cholesterol	92 mg
Fiber	8 g

CHICKEN FAGIOLI
(BEAN TOMATO SAUCE)

TIP

Use bone-in chicken breasts instead of legs; reduce browning time to 4 minutes and reduce cooking time to 20 minutes.

White kidney beans or a combination can be used.

A great dish to reheat.

MAKE AHEAD

Brown chicken earlier in the day and refrigerate until ready to cook with sauce.

4	chicken legs	4
1/4 cup	all-purpose flour	50 mL
2 tsp	vegetable oil	10 mL
2 tsp	minced garlic	10 mL
1/2 cup	chopped onions	125 mL
1/3 cup	chopped carrots	75 mL
1/3 cup	chopped celery	75 mL
1 1/2 cups	red kidney beans, drained	375 mL
1 cup	pureed canned tomatoes	250 mL
3/4 cup	chicken stock	175 mL
1 1/2 tsp	dried basil	7 mL
1 tsp	dried oregano	5 mL

1. In large nonstick skillet sprayed with vegetable spray, heat 1 tsp (5 mL) of the oil over high heat. Dust chicken with flour and cook for 8 minutes, turning often, or until browned on all sides. Set aside and wipe skillet clean.

2. Reduce heat to medium. Add remaining 1 tsp (5 mL) oil to skillet. Add garlic, onions, carrots and celery; cook for 5 minutes or until softened. Mash 1/2 cup (125 mL) of the kidney beans; add mashed and whole beans, tomatoes, stock, basil and oregano to skillet. Bring to a boil, reduce heat to medium-low, add browned chicken pieces, cover and cook for 30 minutes or until juices run clear when legs are pierced at thickest point. Stir occasionally. Remove skin before eating.

PER SERVING	
Calories	316
Protein	33 g
Fat, total	7 g
Fat, saturated	1 g
Carbohydrates	31 g
Sodium	538 mg
Cholesterol	92 mg
Fiber	8 g

CHICKEN WITH BLACK BEAN SAUCE AND SAUTÉED MUSHROOMS

Serves 4

TIP

Try using oyster mushrooms instead of regular button mushrooms.

Of the two kinds of bottled black bean sauce available — whole black bean sauce and puréed black bean garlic sauce — the whole bean sauce is lower in sodium.

MAKE AHEAD

Prepare sauce and mushrooms earlier in the day. Add more stock if sauce is too thick.

Preheat oven to 400° F (200° C)

Baking dish

2 tsp	vegetable oil	10 mL
4	chicken legs	4
1/3 cup	all-purpose flour	75 mL
2 1/2 cups	sliced mushrooms	625 mL

<u>Sauce</u>

1 cup	chicken stock	250 mL
3 tbsp	honey	45 mL
3 tbsp	black bean sauce	45 mL
1 tbsp	soya sauce	15 mL
1 tbsp	rice wine vinegar	15 mL
1 tbsp	sesame oil	15 mL
1 tbsp	cornstarch	15 mL
2 tsp	minced garlic	10 mL
1 tsp	minced ginger root	5 mL
1/2 cup	chopped green onions (about 4 medium)	125 mL

1. In large nonstick skillet sprayed with vegetable spray, heat oil over high heat. Dust chicken pieces with flour; cook for 8 minutes, turning often, or until well-browned on all sides. Transfer to baking dish. Bake for 30 to 40 minutes or until juices run clear when pierced at thickest point. Pour off fat and place on serving platter and keep covered.

2. In a nonstick skillet sprayed with vegetable spray, sauté mushrooms until just cooked (approximately 4 minutes). Drain any excess liquid and set aside.

3. Meanwhile, in saucepan whisk together stock, honey, black bean sauce, soya sauce, vinegar, sesame oil, cornstarch, garlic and ginger until smooth; cook over medium heat for 5 minutes, or until slightly thickened. Add mushrooms and pour over baked chicken. Garnish with green onions. Remove skin before eating.

PER SERVING

Calories	344
Protein	28 g
Fat, total	12 g
Fat, saturated	2 g
Carbohydrates	30 g
Sodium	708 mg
Cholesterol	92 mg
Fiber	2 g

CHICKEN BREASTS STUFFED WITH BRIE CHEESE, RED PEPPER AND GREEN ONIONS

Serves 4

TIP

Instead of serving each breast whole, slice each crosswise into medallions and fan out on plates.

Replace chicken with turkey, veal or pork scallopini.

Brie is a high-fat cheese, but 2 oz (50 g) divided among 4 servings makes it acceptable.

MAKE AHEAD

Prepare chicken breasts early in the day, sauté, then refrigerate. Bake for an extra 5 minutes just prior to serving.

PER SERVING

Calories	284
Protein	33 g
Fat, total	11 g
Fat, saturated	4 g
Carbohydrates	12 g
Sodium	637 mg
Cholesterol	134 mg
Fiber	0 g

Preheat oven to 425° F (220° C)

Baking sheet sprayed with vegetable spray

2 oz	Brie cheese, at room temperature	50 g
3 tbsp	finely chopped red peppers	45 mL
3 tbsp	finely chopped green onions (about 2 medium)	45 mL
1 tsp	minced garlic	5 mL
1	egg	1
2 tbsp	2% milk	25 mL
1/2 cup	seasoned bread crumbs	125 mL
1 lb	skinless, boneless chicken breasts (about 4)	500 g
1 tbsp	vegetable oil	15 mL

1. In small bowl, mix Brie, red peppers, green onions and garlic. In small bowl whisk together egg and milk. Put bread crumbs on a plate.

2. Between sheets of waxed paper, pound breasts to 1/4-inch (5 mm) thickness. Put 1 tbsp (15 mL) Brie mixture at a short end of each breast. Roll up tightly; secure edge with a toothpick.

3. Dip each chicken roll in egg wash, then in bread crumbs. Heat oil in large nonstick skillet sprayed with vegetable spray, cook over high heat for 3 minutes, turning often, or until browned on all sides. Put on prepared baking sheet and bake for 10 minutes or until just done at centre. Remove toothpicks before serving.

SWEET AND SOUR BAKED CHICKEN WITH RED PEPPER, SNOW PEAS AND CARROTS

Serves 4

TIP

Bone-in chicken breasts can be used instead of legs, or a combination of both can be used. Cook less time for breasts (approximately 20 minutes).

Other vegetables, such as green beans, broccoli or zucchini can be used.

MAKE AHEAD

Cook vegetables and prepare sauce earlier in the day. If sauce thickens, add a little water. Bake chicken just before serving.

Preheat oven to 400° F (200° C)

Baking dish sprayed with vegetable spray

3 tsp	vegetable oil	15 mL
4	chicken legs	4
1/4 cup	all-purpose flour	50 mL
1 cup	chopped red peppers	250 mL
3/4 cup	chopped red onions	175 mL
1/2 cup	chopped green peppers	125 mL
1/2 cup	chopped carrots	125 mL
3/4 cup	chopped snow peas	175 mL
1/2 cup	sliced water chestnuts	125 mL

Sauce

1/2 cup	orange juice	125 mL
3 tbsp	brown sugar	45 mL
2 tbsp	soya sauce	25 mL
2 tbsp	lemon juice	25 mL
2 tbsp	ketchup	25 mL
1 tbsp	cornstarch	15 mL
1 1/2 tsp	minced garlic	7 mL
1 1/2 tsp	minced ginger root	7 mL

1. In large nonstick skillet sprayed with vegetable spray, heat 2 tsp (10 mL) of the oil over medium-high heat. Dust chicken legs with flour and cook for 8 minutes, turning often, or until browned on all sides. Put in prepared baking dish with 1/4 cup (50 mL) water. Wipe out skillet and spray again with vegetable spray.

2. Heat remaining 1 tsp (5 mL) oil in nonstick skillet. Add red peppers, onions, green peppers and carrots; cook for 8 minutes or until softened. Add a little water if vegetables begin to burn. Stir in snow peas and water chestnuts; cook for 2 minutes longer. Scatter vegetables on top of chicken.

PER SERVING

Calories	320
Protein	28 g
Fat, total	8 g
Fat, saturated	1 g
Carbohydrates	34 g
Sodium	641 mg
Cholesterol	93 mg
Fiber	3 g

3. In saucepan, whisk together orange juice, brown sugar, soya sauce, lemon juice, ketchup, cornstarch, garlic and ginger until smooth; cook over medium heat for 5 minutes or until thickened slightly. Pour over chicken and vegetables and bake covered for 20 minutes, and 20 minutes uncovered, or until juices run clear when legs are pierced at thickest point. Occasionally baste with sauce. Remove skin before eating.

CHICKEN WITH ROASTED PEPPER AND PROSCIUTTO

Serves 4

TIP

Use 4 oz (125 g) of bottled roasted red peppers rather than roasting your own.

Serve chicken breasts whole or slice crosswise into medallions and fan out on the plate for a pretty presentation.

If prosciutto is unavailable, use thin slices of smoked ham.

If a more intense flavor is desired, use a stronger tasting cheese.

MAKE AHEAD

Assemble chicken breasts early in the day, and refrigerate before baking. Bake 5 minutes longer due to refrigeration.

PER SERVING

Calories	269
Protein	34 g
Fat, total	7 g
Fat, saturated	2 g
Carbohydrates	14 g
Sodium	717 mg
Cholesterol	78 mg
Fiber	0 g

Preheat oven to broil

Baking sheet sprayed with vegetable spray

1	small red pepper	1
1 lb	skinless, boneless chicken breasts (about 4)	500 g
1 oz	sliced prosciutto (4 thin slices)	25 g
2 oz	mozzarella cheese, cut into 4 equal-sized pieces	50 g
1	egg white	1
2 tbsp	water	25 mL
2/3 cup	seasoned bread crumbs	150 mL
2 tsp	vegetable oil	10 mL

1. Broil red pepper for 15 to 20 minutes, turning often until charred on all sides. Preheat oven to 425° F (220° C). Put pepper in bowl and cover tightly with plastic wrap. When cool enough to handle, remove stem, skin and seeds, and cut into thin strips.

2. Pound chicken breasts between sheets of waxed paper to 1/4-inch (5-mm) thickness. Divide prosciutto slices among flattened chicken breasts. Place a piece of cheese at the short end of each breast, and place roasted pepper strips on top of the cheese. Starting at the filling end, carefully roll the breasts up tightly. Use a toothpick to hold chicken breast together.

3. In small bowl, whisk together egg white and water. Put bread crumbs on a plate. Dip each chicken roll in egg white mixture, then in bread crumbs. Heat oil in nonstick skillet sprayed with vegetable spray. Cook over high heat for 3 minutes, turning often, or until browned on all sides. Transfer to prepared baking sheet and bake for 10 to 15 minutes. Remove toothpicks before serving.

CHICKEN AND EGGPLANT PARMESAN

Serves 4

TIP

Turkey, veal or pork scallopini can replace chicken.

★

A stronger cheese, such as Swiss, can replace mozzarella.

★

A great dish to reheat the next day.

MAKE AHEAD

Prepare earlier in the day, refrigerate and bake at 350° F (180° C) until warm (approximately 10 minutes).

Preheat oven to 425° F (220° C)

Baking sheet sprayed with vegetable spray

4	crosswise slices of eggplant, skin on, approximately 1/2 inch (1 cm) thick	4
1	whole egg	1
1	egg white	1
1 tbsp	water or milk	15 mL
2/3 cup	seasoned bread crumbs	150 mL
3 tbsp	chopped fresh parsley (or 2 tsp [10 mL] dried)	45 mL
1 tbsp	grated Parmesan cheese	15 mL
1 lb	skinless, boneless chicken breasts (about 4)	500 g
2 tsp	vegetable oil	10 mL
1 tsp	minced garlic	5 mL
1/2 cup	tomato pasta sauce	125 mL
1/2 cup	grated mozzarella cheese	125 mL

1. In small bowl, whisk together whole egg, egg white and water. On plate stir together bread crumbs, parsley and Parmesan. Dip eggplant slices in egg wash, then coat with bread-crumb mixture. Place on prepared pan and bake for 20 minutes, or until tender, turning once.

2. Meanwhile, pound chicken breasts between sheets of waxed paper to 1/4-inch (5-mm) thickness. Dip chicken in remaining egg wash, then coat with remaining bread-crumb mixture. Heat oil and garlic in nonstick skillet sprayed with vegetable spray and cook for 4 minutes, or until golden brown, turning once.

3. Spread 1 tbsp (15 mL) of tomato sauce on each eggplant slice. Place one chicken breast on top of each eggplant slice. Spread another 1 tbsp (15 mL) of tomato sauce on top of each chicken piece. Sprinkle with cheese and bake for 5 minutes or until cheese melts.

PER SERVING	
Calories	317
Protein	36 g
Fat, total	10 g
Fat, saturated	3 g
Carbohydrates	20 g
Sodium	612 mg
Cholesterol	130 mg
Fiber	2 g

CHINESE LEMON CHICKEN ON A BED OF RED PEPPERS AND SNOW PEAS

TIP

This is a beautiful looking dish. If you substitute any vegetables, try to keep contrasting colors.

Replace chicken with turkey, veal or pork scallopini.

MAKE AHEAD

Prepare sauce earlier in the day. Add a little water if too thick before serving.

1 tsp	vegetable oil	5 mL
1 1/2 cups	thinly sliced red peppers	375 mL
1 1/2 cups	sugar snap peas or halved snow peas	375 mL
1 lb	skinless, boneless chicken breasts (about 4)	500 g
1/4 cup	all-purpose flour	50 mL
2 tsp	vegetable oil	10 mL

Sauce

1 cup	chicken stock	250 mL
3 tbsp	lemon juice	45 mL
2 tbsp	granulated sugar	25 mL
1 tbsp	vegetable oil	15 mL
4 tsp	cornstarch	20 mL
1 tsp	sesame oil	5 mL
1 tsp	grated lemon zest	5 mL
1/2 tsp	minced garlic	2 mL
2 tbsp	chopped fresh parsley	25 mL

1. In a large nonstick skillet sprayed with vegetable spray, heat 1 tsp (5 mL) oil over medium heat and sauté red peppers and peas just until tender-crisp (approximately 3 minutes). Place in serving dish.

2. Between sheets of waxed paper, pound chicken breasts to 1/4-inch (5-mm) thickness. Dust with flour. In large nonstick skillet sprayed with vegetable spray, heat oil; sauté chicken until browned on both sides and just cooked (approximately 6 to 8 minutes).

3. In saucepan combine stock, lemon juice, sugar, oil, cornstarch, sesame oil, lemon zest and garlic; cook over medium heat for 2 to 3 minutes or until thickened. Pour some sauce over chicken. Sprinkle with parsley. Serve individual servings with remaining sauce.

PER SERVING	
Calories	290
Protein	29 g
Fat, total	10 g
Fat, saturated	1 g
Carbohydrates	20 g
Sodium	313 mg
Cholesterol	66 mg
Fiber	2 g

SAUTÉED CHICKEN WITH TROPICAL FRUIT SAUCE

TIP

Dates can replace the apricots.

If fresh pineapple is available, add to sauce when you've finished cooking.

Veal or turkey scallopini can replace chicken.

MAKE AHEAD

Sauce can be made up to a day ahead. Reheat gently, adding more stock if too thick.

PER SERVING	
Calories	253
Protein	29 g
Fat, total	3 g
Fat, saturated	0.6 g
Carbohydrates	27 g
Sodium	668 mg
Cholesterol	66 mg
Fiber	1 g

Sauce

3/4 cup	canned pineapple bits, drained	175 mL
1/2 cup	orange or pineapple juice	125 mL
1/2 cup	chicken stock	125 mL
1/4 cup	chopped dried apricots	50 mL
2 tbsp	brown sugar	25 mL
1 tbsp	soya sauce	15 mL
1 tbsp	cornstarch	15 mL
1 tsp	minced garlic	5 mL
1 tsp	grated orange zest	5 mL
1	egg white	1
2 tbsp	water	25 mL
3/4 cup	seasoned bread crumbs	175 mL
1 1/2 lb	skinless, boneless chicken breasts (approximately 6)	750 g
1 tsp	vegetable oil	5 mL

1. In small saucepan, combine pineapple, juice, stock, apricots, brown sugar, soya sauce, cornstarch, garlic and zest until smooth and well blended; cook over medium heat for 5 minutes, or until slightly thickened. Reduce heat to low and keep warm.

2. In shallow bowl, whisk together egg white and water. Put bread crumbs on a plate. Between sheets of waxed paper pound breasts to 1/4-inch (5-mm) thickness.

3. Dip chicken in egg wash, then in bread crumbs. In large nonstick skillet sprayed with vegetable spray, heat oil over medium-high heat. Cook for 2 minutes per side, or until just done at center. Serve with sauce.

ALMOND CHICKEN BREASTS WITH CREAMY TARRAGON MUSTARD SAUCE

TIP

Try other nuts, such as cashews or pecans.

Try veal or turkey scallopini instead of chicken.

MAKE AHEAD

Bread chicken breasts and prepare sauce earlier in the day. Cook just before serving.

1 lb	skinless, boneless chicken breasts	500 g
3 tbsp	all-purpose flour	45 mL
1	egg white	1
3 tbsp	water	45 mL
1/3 cup	finely chopped almonds	75 mL
1/2 cup	seasoned bread crumbs	125 mL
2 tsp	vegetable oil	10 mL

Sauce

1/4 cup	light mayonnaise	50 mL
1/4 cup	light sour cream	50 mL
1 tsp	Dijon mustard	5 mL
1 tsp	dried tarragon	5 mL

1. Between sheets of waxed paper, pound breasts to 1/4-inch (5-mm) thickness. Dust with flour. In shallow bowl, whisk together egg white and water. Combine almonds and bread crumbs and place on a plate.

2. In nonstick skillet sprayed with vegetable spray, heat oil over medium-high heat. Dip breasts in egg wash, then in crumb mixture. Cook for 3 minutes on one side; turn and cook for 2 minutes longer or until just done at center.

3. Meanwhile, in small saucepan whisk together mayonnaise, sour cream, mustard and tarragon; heat over low heat just until warm. Serve over chicken.

PER SERVING

Calories	304
Protein	32 g
Fat, total	12 g
Fat, saturated	2 g
Carbohydrates	16 g
Sodium	672 mg
Cholesterol	70 mg
Fiber	1 g

CHINESE CHICKEN WITH GARLIC GINGER SAUCE

3 lb	whole chicken	1.5 kg

Sauce

1/3 cup	chicken stock	75 mL
1/4 cup	chopped green onions (about 2 medium)	50 mL
3 tbsp	vegetable oil	45 mL
4 tsp	soya sauce	20 mL
1 tsp	minced garlic	5 mL
1 tsp	minced ginger root	5 mL

1. Remove neck and giblets from chicken and discard. Place chicken in large saucepan and add water to cover. Cover saucepan and bring to a boil over high heat. Reduce heat to low and simmer, covered, for 45 minutes, or until juices run clear from chicken leg when pierced.

2. Meanwhile, whisk together stock, green onions, oil, soya sauce, garlic and ginger in a small bowl.

3. Remove chicken from pot and let cool slightly. Remove skin; cut into serving pieces. Serve with dipping sauce.

Serves 6

TIP

This is delicious served cold.

This is a simple-looking chicken dish, but unbelievably tasty. Great for leftovers.

Increase garlic and ginger to taste

MAKE AHEAD

Prepare up to a day ahead and serve at room temperature.

PER SERVING	
Calories	156
Protein	17 g
Fat, total	9 g
Fat, saturated	1 g
Carbohydrates	1 g
Sodium	337 mg
Cholesterol	53 mg
Fiber	0 g

ROASTED CHICKEN WITH APRICOT ORANGE GLAZE AND COUSCOUS STUFFING

Serves 4 to 6

PER SERVING (6)	
Calories	429
Protein	23 g
Fat, total	5 g
Fat, saturated	0.9 g
Carbohydrates	74 g
Sodium	769 mg
Cholesterol	53 mg
Fiber	3 g

Preheat oven to 400° F (200° C)

Roasting pan with rack

3 lb	roasting chicken	1.5 kg

Couscous stuffing

1 tbsp	orange juice concentrate, thawed	15 mL
1 tbsp	chopped fresh coriander or parsley	15 mL
2 tsp	hoisin sauce	10 mL
1 1/2 tsp	honey	7 mL
1 tsp	minced garlic	5 mL
1/2 tsp	minced ginger root	2 mL
1 tsp	sesame oil	5 mL
1 tsp	vegetable oil	5 mL
1 3/4 cups	chicken stock	425 mL
1 cup	couscous	250 mL
1 cup	chopped snow peas	250 mL
2/3 cup	chopped red onions	150 mL
1/2 cup	chopped carrots	125 mL
1/2 cup	chopped dried apricots	125 mL

Apricot glaze

3/4 cup	apricot or peach jam	175 mL
1/2 cup	chicken stock	125 mL
3 tbsp	orange juice concentrate, thawed	45 mL
1 tbsp	soya sauce	15 mL
1 tsp	minced garlic	5 mL
1 tsp	minced ginger root	5 mL
1 tbsp	cornstarch	15 mL
1 cup	chicken stock	250 mL

1. Stuffing: In small bowl whisk together orange juice concentrate, coriander, hoisin, honey, garlic, ginger, sesame oil and vegetable oil; set aside. Bring stock to

a boil in saucepan; stir in couscous, cover and remove from heat. Let stand for 5 minutes; fluff with a fork. In bowl combine couscous, snow peas, red onions, carrots, dried apricots and orange juice sauce.

2. Loosely stuff chicken with some of the couscous stuffing. Place on rack in roasting pan sprayed with vegetable spray. Put remaining couscous stuffing in a casserole dish and cover. Set aside.

3. Glaze: In bowl, whisk together apricot jam, stock, orange juice concentrate, soya sauce, garlic and ginger. Measure out 1/2 cup (125 mL) of the glaze; combine with cornstarch and 1/2 cup (125 mL) of the chicken stock and set aside. Pour remaining 1/2 cup (125 mL) chicken stock into roasting pan under chicken. Spread some of the remaining apricot glaze (without cornstarch) over chicken; bake for 1 hour, or until juices run clear when leg is pierced at thickest point. Baste chicken with apricot glaze every 15 minutes as it roasts. Put casserole with stuffing in oven for last 30 minutes of roasting time. Let chicken rest for 10 minutes before carving.

4. Meanwhile, remove juices, if any, from roasting pan and place in saucepan. Add reserved apricot glaze-cornstarch mixture; heat over medium heat for 2 minutes or until slightly thickened. Serve chicken with sauce and stuffing. Remove skin before eating.

CHICKEN STIR-FRY WITH ASPARAGUS, BOK CHOY AND OYSTER SAUCE

Serves 4

12 oz	skinless, boneless chicken breast, cut into thin strips	375 g
2 tsp	vegetable oil	10 mL
2 cups	asparagus cut into 1-inch (2.5 cm) pieces	500 mL
1 cup	sliced red peppers	250 mL
4 cups	sliced bok choy or napa cabbage	1 L
1 cup	water chestnuts	250 mL

Sauce

3/4 cup	chicken stock	175 mL
3 tbsp	oyster sauce	45 mL
1 1/2 tbsp	rice wine vinegar	22 mL
2 tbsp	honey	25 mL
1 tbsp	soya sauce	15 mL
1 tbsp	cornstarch	15 mL
1 1/2 tsp	minced garlic	7 mL
1 1/2 tsp	minced ginger root	7 mL
1/2 cup	chopped green onions (about 4 medium)	125 mL

1. Sauce: In bowl, whisk together stock, oyster sauce, vinegar, honey, soya sauce, cornstarch, garlic and ginger; set aside.

2. In a nonstick skillet or wok sprayed with vegetable spray, stir-fry chicken strips for 3 to 4 minutes, stirring constantly, or until just cooked at center. Remove chicken from skillet.

3. Heat oil in skillet over high heat. Add asparagus and red pepper strips and stir-fry for 3 minutes, stirring constantly, or until tender-crisp. Add bok choy and water chestnuts and stir-fry for 1 minute or until bok choy wilts. Stir sauce again and add to wok along with chicken strips. Cook for 2 minutes or until thickened slightly. Garnish with green onions.

PER SERVING	
Calories	228
Protein	24 g
Fat, total	4 g
Fat, saturated	0.5 g
Carbohydrates	26 g
Sodium	1280 mg
Cholesterol	49 mg
Fiber	3 g

TURKEY SCALLOPINI WITH PESTO CREAM SAUCE

Serves 4

TIP

If you can't find turkey scallopini, get your butcher to cut thin crosswise slices from a turkey breast for you. Otherwise, substitute chicken or veal scallopini.

If you use store-bought pesto, calories and fat will be higher.

MAKE AHEAD

Prepare pesto sauce up to a day ahead, or freeze for up to 3 weeks. Cook just before serving.

Sauce

1/3 cup	pesto (store-bought, or see sauce recipe on page 170)	75 mL
1 1/2 tbsp	light sour cream	22 mL
1 1/2 tbsp	grated Parmesan cheese	22 mL
1 lb	turkey scallopini	500 g
1/4 cup	all-purpose flour	50 mL
1 tbsp	vegetable oil	15 mL

1. In small bowl combine pesto, sour cream and Parmesan; set aside.

2. Between sheets of waxed paper, pound turkey to 1/4-inch (5-mm) thickness. Dust with flour.

3. In nonstick skillet sprayed with vegetable spray, heat oil over medium-high heat. Cook 2 minutes per side, or until just done at center. Serve with a dollop of pesto sauce on top.

PER SERVING

Calories	283
Protein	31 g
Fat, total	15 g
Fat, saturated	3 g
Carbohydrates	7 g
Sodium	200 mg
Cholesterol	74 mg
Fiber	1 g

PHYLLO CHICKEN AND SPINACH BAKE

TIP

Be sure to squeeze out excess moisture from spinach. Half a cup (125 mL) of cooked spinach is equivalent to 3 cups (750 mL) fresh spinach (or 1/2 package of frozen) after it's cooked, drained and squeezed dry.

Ground beef or veal can replace chicken.

MAKE AHEAD

Prepare entire filling up to a day ahead, then layer in phyllo. Bake 5 minutes longer.

Preheat oven to 400° F (200° C)

9- by 13-inch baking dish (3.5 L)

Sauce

1 tbsp	margarine or butter	15 mL
2 tbsp	all-purpose flour	25 mL
1 cup	2% milk	250 mL
3/4 cup	chicken stock	175 mL
1 1/2 tsp	Dijon mustard	7 mL
2/3 cup	grated Cheddar cheese	150 mL
1 tsp	minced garlic	5 mL
3/4 cup	finely chopped onions	175 mL
3/4 cup	finely chopped mushrooms	175 mL
12 oz	lean ground chicken	375 g
1/2 cup	frozen spinach, cooked, drained and finely chopped	125 mL
1/3 cup	seasoned bread crumbs	75 mL
1	egg	1
10	sheets phyllo pastry	10
2 1/2 tsp	melted margarine or butter	12 mL

1. In saucepan, melt margarine over medium heat; add flour and cook, stirring, for 1 minute. Gradually add milk and stock, stirring constantly, until sauce begins to simmer and thicken slightly (approximately 5 minutes). Stir in mustard and cheese and remove from heat.

2. In nonstick skillet sprayed with vegetable spray over medium heat, cook garlic, onions and mushrooms for 5 minutes, or until softened. Remove vegetables and set aside. Add chicken to skillet and cook for 5 minutes, stirring to break up chicken, or until no longer pink. Remove from heat and drain fat from skillet. Add cooked vegetables and stir in spinach, bread crumbs and egg. Add above sauce and mix well.

PER SERVING

Calories	387
Protein	23 g
Fat, total	17 g
Fat, saturated	6 g
Carbohydrates	35 g
Sodium	709 mg
Cholesterol	88 mg
Fiber	2 g

3. Melt margarine and lay out 2 sheets of phyllo pastry in baking dish. Brush phyllo with margarine. Lay out 2 more sheets and brush again. Then, lay out one sheet and spread out entire filling over top. Repeat with remaining phyllo, brushing every 2 sheets. Brush top sheet with remaining margarine and tuck in edges. Bake for 20 to 25 minutes or until phyllo turns brown.

TURKEY RATATOUILLE CHILI

TIP

Great combination of ratatouille and chili in one dish.

Great as a family meal. Serve with french bread.

★

Ground pork, veal or chicken can replace turkey.

MAKE AHEAD

Prepare up to a day ahead and reheat gently, adding extra chicken stock if too thick.

2 tsp	vegetable oil	10 mL
2 tsp	minced garlic	10 mL
1 cup	chopped onions	250 mL
1 2/3 cups	chopped zucchini	400 mL
1 2/3 cups	chopped peeled eggplant	400 mL
1 1/2 cups	chopped mushrooms	375 mL
12 oz	ground turkey	375 g
2 tbsp	tomato paste	25 mL
1	can (19 oz [540 mL]) tomatoes, puréed	1
2 cups	chicken stock	500 mL
1 1/3 cups	peeled chopped potatoes	325 mL
1 cup	canned red kidney beans, drained	250 mL
1 tbsp	chili powder	15 mL
1 1/2 tsp	dried basil	7 mL
1	bay leaf	1

1. In large nonstick saucepan sprayed with vegetable spray, heat oil over medium heat. Add garlic, onions, zucchini and eggplant; cook for 5 minutes or until softened. Add mushrooms and cook 2 minutes longer. Remove vegetables from skillet and set aside. Add turkey to skillet and cook for 3 minutes, stirring to break it up, or until no longer pink. Drain fat and add cooked vegetables to skillet.

2. Add tomato paste, tomatoes, stock, potatoes, beans, chili powder, basil and bay leaf; bring to a boil. Cover, reduce heat to low and simmer for 40 minutes, stirring occasionally.

PER SERVING (6)	
Calories	248
Protein	18 g
Fat, total	7 g
Fat, saturated	2 g
Carbohydrates	31 g
Sodium	496 mg
Cholesterol	39 mg
Fiber	8 g

MEAT

MEAT TIPS

1. Tightly wrapped fresh meat can be kept refrigerated for 2 days in a cold section of the refrigerator. Meat can be frozen for up to 6 months. Do not use meat that has freezer burn or discoloration.

2. Defrost meat in the refrigerator, or wrap in plastic and place in a bowl of cold water to quicken defrosting. An even faster method is to defrost in the microwave. Rotate meat every few minutes to ensure even defrosting.

3. Tender cuts of beef from the rib and sirloin areas contain a lot of fat and calories. Choose those from the flank, chuck or round. Buy lean cuts of meat and trim all excess fat.

4. To make lean cuts of meat tender, marinate them for at least 4 hours, or preferably overnight.

5. It's not necessary to marinate cuts such as rib eye, sirloin, porterhouse or filet. These are the most tender. Remove visible fat before cooking.

6. Beef, veal, lamb or pork can be substituted for one another in recipes. Pork should be thoroughly cooked until no longer pink. Do not overcook, or the meat will become dry.

7. If basting grilled or roasted meat with a sauce, remember to boil the remaining basting sauce if serving with cooked meat to destroy harmful bacteria.

FLANK STEAK IN HOISIN MARINADE WITH SAUTÉED MUSHROOMS

Serves 6

Preheat broiler or start barbecue

TIP

Wild mushrooms such as oyster or portbello are a highlight to this dish.

The longer a flank steak marinates, the tenderer the meat will be.

MAKE AHEAD

Prepare sauce up to 3 days ahead and keep refrigerated.

Marinade

1/4 cup	soya sauce	50 mL
1/4 cup	hoisin sauce	50 mL
1/4 cup	rice wine vinegar	50 mL
2 tbsp	brown sugar	25 mL
2 tbsp	vegetable oil	25 mL
1 tsp	minced ginger root	5 mL
1 tsp	minced garlic	5 mL
1 1/2 lb	flank steak	750 g
1 tsp	vegetable oil	5 mL
1 tsp	minced garlic	5 mL
3 cups	sliced mushrooms	750 mL
3/4 cup	chopped green onions	175 mL

1. In small bowl whisk together soya sauce, hoisin sauce, vinegar, brown sugar, oil, ginger and garlic. Pour over steak and let marinate in refrigerator at least 2 hours or overnight. Bring to room temperature before cooking.

2. In large nonstick skillet, heat oil over medium-high heat. Add garlic and mushrooms and cook for 3 minutes or until softened. Add green onions and cook for 1 minute longer.

3. Barbecue or broil steak, basting with some of the marinade, until cooked to desired "doneness" (approximately 15 minutes). Bring remaining marinade to a boil and simmer for 3 minutes. Serve steak with mushrooms and sauce. Cut the steak across the grain thinly to ensure tenderness.

PER SERVING

Calories	266
Protein	26 g
Fat, total	13 g
Fat, saturated	4 g
Carbohydrates	11 g
Sodium	768 mg
Cholesterol	44 mg
Fiber	1 g

BEEF TORTILLAS WITH CRISP VEGETABLES AND ORANGE ASIAN SAUCE

Serves 4

TIP

Rib eye, sirloin or tenderloin steak is great for this recipe.

Chicken or pork can replace steak. Leftover cooked meat can also be used.

Sauce can be used as a marinade over fish or chicken.

MAKE AHEAD

Prepare sauce up to 2 days ahead.

Prepare vegetables a few hours before serving. Sauté steak just before serving and add to reheated sauce, adding a little water if sauce thickens.

PER SERVING

Calories	429
Protein	21 g
Fat, total	12 g
Fat, saturated	2 g
Carbohydrates	61 g
Sodium	641 mg
Cholesterol	25 mg
Fiber	4 g

Preheat oven to 400° F (200° C)

Baking sheet sprayed with vegetable spray

Sauce

2 tbsp	orange juice concentrate, thawed	25 mL
2 tbsp	hoisin sauce	25 mL
1 tbsp	rice wine vinegar	15 mL
1 tbsp	soya sauce	15 mL
1 tbsp	water	15 mL
1 tbsp	honey	15 mL
1 1/2 tsp	cornstarch	7 mL
1 tsp	sesame oil	5 mL
2 tsp	vegetable oil	10 mL
8 oz	beef steak, cut into 1/8-inch (2-mm) thick slices	250 g
1 tsp	minced garlic	5 mL
3/4 cup	chopped onions	175 mL
1 1/3 cup	chopped mushrooms	325 mL
1 1/4 cup	chopped red peppers	300 mL
1/2 cup	chopped celery	125 mL
2/3 cup	sliced water chestnuts	150 mL
1/2 cup	chopped green onions (about 4 medium)	125 mL
8	small flour tortillas	8

1. In small bowl, whisk together orange juice concentrate, hoisin sauce, rice vinegar, soya sauce, water, honey, cornstarch and sesame oil; set aside.

2. In nonstick skillet sprayed with vegetable spray, sauté steak until just cooked, about 1 to 2 minutes. Drain any excess liquid. Remove steak from pan. Respray skillet with vegetable spray and add oil; sauté garlic and onions until browned, about 4 minutes. Add mushrooms, red peppers and celery, and sauté for 4 minutes just until vegetables are softened.

3. Stir sauce again and add to skillet along with water chestnuts and green onions; cook for 3 minutes or until sauce thickens. Remove from heat and stir in steak. Divide among tortillas. Roll up, place on baking sheet and bake for 5 minutes or until heated through.

ORIENTAL BEEF BUNDLES IN LETTUCE

Serves 4

12 oz	lean ground beef	375 g

Sauce

2 tbsp	hoisin sauce	25 mL
1 tbsp	rice wine vinegar	15 mL
2 tsp	minced garlic	10 mL
1 1/2 tsp	minced ginger root	7 mL
1 tsp	sesame oil	5 mL
1 tsp	vegetable oil	5 mL
1/3 cup	finely chopped carrots	75 mL
3/4 cup	finely chopped red or green peppers	175 mL
3/4 cup	finely chopped mushrooms	175 mL
1/2 cup	chopped water chestnuts	125 mL
2	green onions, chopped	2
2 tbsp	hoisin sauce	25 mL
1 tbsp	water	15 mL
8	large iceberg lettuce leaves	8

TIP

Use small flour tortillas instead of lettuce if you prefer.

Look for a large iceberg lettuce to get the best quality leaves.

Use other vegetables such as celery and oyster mushrooms as substitutes.

MAKE AHEAD

Prepare entire beef mixture earlier in the day. Reheat gently before placing in lettuce leaves.

1. Sauce: In small bowl, whisk together hoisin, vinegar, garlic, ginger and sesame oil; set aside.

2. In nonstick skillet sprayed with vegetable spray, cook beef over medium heat for 5 minutes, or until browned; remove from skillet. Drain any excess liquid.

3. In same nonstick skillet, heat oil over medium heat. Add carrots and cook for 3 minutes. Add red peppers and mushrooms and cook for 3 minutes or until softened. Return beef to pan along with water chestnuts and green onions. Add sauce and cook for 2 minutes.

4. Combine hoisin sauce and water in small bowl. Place a little over leaves. Divide beef mixture among lettuce leaves. Serve open or rolled up.

PER SERVING

Calories	252
Protein	17 g
Fat, total	15 g
Fat, saturated	5 g
Carbohydrates	12 g
Sodium	236 mg
Cholesterol	45 mg
Fiber	1 g

ORIENTAL BEEF BUNDLES IN LETTUCE (THIS PAGE) ➤

OVERLEAF - LARGE DISHES (L TO R): GREEK BAKED POTATOES STUFFED WITH TOMATOES, ➤
OLIVES AND CHEESE (PAGE 151); GREEK CHILI WITH BLACK OLIVES AND FETA
CHEESE (PAGE 132); SALMON OVER WHITE-AND-BLACK-BEAN SALSA (PAGE 89)

HOISIN GARLIC BURGERS

TIP

Ground chicken or veal can replace beef.

Serve these burgers in a pita bun, or over half a kaiser roll.

MAKE AHEAD

Prepare beef mixture up to a day ahead and form into burgers. Freeze up to 6 weeks.

Start barbecue or preheat oven to 450° F (230° C)

1 lb	lean ground beef	500 g
1/4 cup	bread crumbs	50 mL
1/4 cup	chopped green onions (about 2 medium)	50 mL
3 tbsp	chopped coriander or parsley	45 mL
2 tbsp	hoisin sauce	25 mL
2 tsp	minced garlic	10 mL
1 tsp	minced ginger root	5 mL
1	egg	1
2 tbsp	water	25 mL
2 tbsp	hoisin sauce	25 mL
1 tsp	sesame oil	5 mL

1. In bowl combine beef, bread crumbs, green onions, coriander, hoisin sauce, garlic, ginger and egg; mix well. Makes 4 to 5 burgers.

2. In small bowl whisk together water, hoisin sauce and sesame oil. Brush half of the sauce over top of burgers.

3. Place on greased grill and barbecue, or place on rack on baking sheet and bake for 10 to 15 minutes (or until no longer pink inside). Turn patties once and brush with remaining sauce.

PER SERVING (5)	
Calories	253
Protein	19 g
Fat, total	16 g
Fat, saturated	6 g
Carbohydrates	9 g
Sodium	245 mg
Cholesterol	92 mg
Fiber	0 g

◄ CHICKEN STIR-FRY WITH ASPARAGUS, BOK CHOY AND OYSTER SAUCE (PAGE 118)

RATATOUILLE MEAT LOAF CASSEROLE WITH CHEESE TOPPING

Serves 6	

Preheat oven to 350° F (180° C)

8-inch (2 L) square baking dish sprayed with vegetable spray

12 oz	lean ground beef	375 g
1/4 cup	bread crumbs	50 mL
3 tbsp	bottled barbecue sauce	45 mL
1 1/2 tsp	minced garlic	7 mL
1	egg	1

TIP

Use ground chicken or veal to replace beef.

Another cheese can replace goat cheese, such as feta, Cheddar or mozzarella.

Vegetable Mixture

2 tsp	vegetable oil	10 mL
1 1/2 tsp	minced garlic	7 mL
1 1/2 cups	chopped unpeeled eggplant	375 mL
1 cup	chopped zucchini	250 mL
1/2 cup	chopped onions	125 mL
1 cup	sliced mushrooms	250 mL
1 1/2 cups	tomato pasta sauce	375 mL
1/4 cup	sliced black olives	50 mL
1 1/2 tsp	dried basil	7 mL
1 tsp	dried oregano	5 mL
2 oz	goat cheese	50 g

MAKE AHEAD

Prepare beef mixture and cook vegetable mixture up to a day ahead. Bake just before serving. Great to reheat the next day.

1. In large bowl, combine beef, bread crumbs, barbecue sauce, garlic and egg; mix well and press into prepared pan.

2. In large nonstick skillet sprayed with vegetable spray, heat oil over medium heat. Add garlic, eggplant, zucchini and onions; cook for 5 minutes or until softened, stirring often. Add mushrooms and cook 2 minutes longer. Stir in tomato sauce, olives, basil and oregano. Pour vegetable mixture over meat and bake, uncovered, for 25 minutes or until beef is cooked. Dot with goat cheese and bake for another 5 minutes.

PER SERVING	
Calories	276
Protein	15 g
Fat, total	16 g
Fat, saturated	4 g
Carbohydrates	19 g
Sodium	536 mg
Cholesterol	66 mg
Fiber	2 g

PEPPERED BEEF STEAKS WITH TUNA CAPER SAUCE

Serves 8

Preheat broiler or start barbecue

1	can (6.5 oz [184 g]) water-packed tuna, drained	1
1/2 cup	chicken stock	125 mL
2 tbsp	light mayonnaise	25 mL
2 tbsp	olive oil	25 mL
1 tbsp	drained capers	15 mL
1 1/2 tsp	minced garlic	7 mL
3 lb	beef tenderloin steaks, about 8, each approximately 6 oz (150 g)	1.5 kg
3 tbsp	coarsely ground black pepper	45 mL

1. Put tuna, stock, mayonnaise, olive oil, capers and garlic in food processor; purée until smooth.

2. Rub approximately 1 tsp (5 mL) pepper onto each steak, covering all sides. Barbecue or cook under broiler for 5 minutes; turn and cook for 3 minutes longer for medium-rare. Warm sauce slightly and serve over top.

TIP

Use any other good quality steaks, such as sirloin, rib eye or porterhouse, totalling 3 lbs (1.5 kg).

Vary the amount of pepper according to taste. Veal tenderloin can also be used.

This sauce is great over other meats, fish or even pasta.

MAKE AHEAD

Prepare sauce up to a day ahead.

PER SERVING

Calories	320
Protein	40 g
Fat, total	16 g
Fat, saturated	5 g
Carbohydrates	1 g
Sodium	268 mg
Cholesterol	89 mg
Fiber	0 g

GREEK CHILI WITH BLACK OLIVES AND FETA CHEESE

Serves 4

TIP

Leave the skin on zucchini and eggplant for extra fiber.

Other canned beans can be used, such as chick peas, navy white beans or black beans.

Another cheese can replace feta, such as goat, Cheddar or mozzarella.

MAKE AHEAD

Prepare up to a day ahead and gently reheat, adding more stock if too thick.

Great as leftovers.

PER SERVING	
Calories	407
Protein	25 g
Fat, total	15 g
Fat, saturated	6 g
Carbohydrates	47 g
Sodium	1380 mg
Cholesterol	44 mg
Fiber	12 g

1 tsp	vegetable oil	5 mL
2 tsp	minced garlic	10 mL
1 cup	chopped onions	250 mL
1 cup	chopped zucchini	250 mL
1 cup	sliced mushrooms	250 mL
1 cup	chopped green peppers	250 mL
1 1/2 cups	chopped eggplant	375 mL
8 oz	lean ground beef or lamb	250 g
1	can (19 oz [540 mL]) tomatoes, puréed	1
1 1/2 cups	beef or chicken stock	375 mL
1 cup	canned red kidney beans, drained	250 mL
1 cup	canned white kidney beans, drained	250 mL
1/3 cup	sliced black olives	75 mL
1 tbsp	chili powder	15 mL
1 1/2 tsp	dried basil	7 mL
1 1/2 tsp	dried oregano	7 mL
2 oz	feta cheese, crumbled	50 g

1. In large nonstick saucepan sprayed with vegetable spray, heat oil over medium heat. Add garlic, onions, zucchini, mushrooms, green peppers and eggplant; cook for 8 minutes or until softened. Add beef and cook for 2 minutes, stirring to break it up, or until it is no longer pink. Drain any excess fat.

2. Mash 1/2 cup (125 mL) of the red kidney beans and 1/2 cup (125 mL) of the white kidney beans. Add tomatoes, stock, mashed and whole beans, olives, chili, basil and oregano to saucepan; bring to a boil. Reduce heat to low and simmer, covered, for 30 minutes. Sprinkle with cheese before serving.

LEG OF LAMB WITH PESTO AND WILD RICE

Serves 8

Preheat oven to 375° F (190° C)

Stuffing

1 tsp	vegetable oil	5 mL
2 tsp	minced garlic	10 mL
1 cup	chopped onions	250 mL
1 cup	chopped red or green peppers	250 mL
3/4 cup	wild rice	175 mL
3/4 cup	white rice	175 mL
3 cups	beef or chicken stock	750 mL
1/3 cup	store-bought pesto (or see sauce recipe on page 170)	75 mL
3 lb	boneless leg of lamb with a pocket	1 5 kg
1 tsp	vegetable oil	5 mL
1 tsp	minced garlic	5 mL
2/3 cup	beef stock	150 mL
1/2 cup	red or white wine	125 mL

1. In saucepan, heat oil over medium heat. Add garlic and onions and cook for 3 minutes or until softened. Add red peppers and cook for 2 minutes longer. Add rices and cook, stirring, for 3 minutes. Add stock; bring to a boil, cover, reduce heat to medium-low and simmer covered for 20 to 25 minutes or until rice is tender and liquid absorbed. Stir in pesto. Set aside to cool.

2. Stuff leg of lamb with some of the cooled rice mixture; put leftover stuffing in a casserole dish and cover. Rub lamb with oil and garlic and place on rack in roasting pan. Truss lamb with string. Pour stock and wine under lamb. Bake covered for 20 minutes, basting with pan juices every 10 minutes. Uncover lamb and bake another 20 to 25 minutes, basting every 10 minutes. Add extra stock if liquids evaporate. Put casserole dish with leftover stuffing in the oven for the last 20 minutes. Serve meat with juices.

LAMB VEGETABLE STEW OVER GARLIC MASHED POTATOES

Serves 4 to 6

TIP

Substitute stewing beef or veal for leg of lamb.

★

Vegetables of your own choice can replace those in recipe.

★

Do not use a food processor to purée potatoes as they will become sticky.

★

Great as leftovers.

MAKE AHEAD

Prepare mashed potatoes recipe up to a day ahead. Reheat gently before serving.

★

Prepare stew early in the day and gently reheat before serving.

PER SERVING (6)	
Calories	343
Protein	19 g
Fat, total	8 g
Fat, saturated	3 g
Carbohydrates	51 g
Sodium	504 mg
Cholesterol	40 mg
Fiber	7 g

3 tsp	vegetable oil	15 mL
12 oz	leg of lamb, visible fat removed, cut into 1-inch (2.5 cm) cubes	375 g
3 tbsp	flour	45 mL
1 cup	pearl onions	250 mL
2 tsp	minced garlic	10 mL
1 1/2 cups	sliced mushrooms	375 mL
1 1/2 cups	chopped leeks	375 mL
1 cup	sliced carrots	250 mL
1 cup	chopped green or yellow peppers	250 mL
3/4 cup	sliced zucchini	175 mL
1/4 cup	tomato paste	50 mL
1/3 cup	red or white wine	75 mL
2 cups	chopped tomatoes	500 mL
2 cups	beef or chicken stock	500 mL
2 tsp	dried rosemary	10 mL
1	bay leaf	1

Mashed Potatoes

1 1/2 lb	potatoes, peeled and quartered	750 g
1 tbsp	margarine or butter	15 mL
1 tbsp	minced garlic	15 mL
1 cup	chopped onions	250 mL
1/2 cup	chicken stock	125 mL
1/3 cup	light sour cream	75 mL
1/4 tsp	ground black pepper	1 mL

1. In large nonstick saucepan, heat 2 tsp (10 mL) of the oil over medium-high heat. Dust the lamb cubes in the flour and add to the saucepan. Cook for 5 minutes or until well-browned on all sides. Remove lamb from saucepan.

2. Blanch the pearl onions in a pot of boiling water for 1 minute; refresh in cold water and drain. Peel and set aside.

3. In same saucepan, heat remaining 1 tsp (5 mL) oil over medium heat; add garlic, mushrooms, leeks, carrots, green peppers, zucchini and pearl onions. Cook for 8 to 10 minutes or until softened and browned, stirring occasionally. Stir in tomato paste and wine. Return lamb to saucepan along with tomatoes, beef stock, rosemary and bay leaf. Bring to a boil, cover, reduce heat to medium-low, and simmer for 25 minutes or until carrots and meat are tender.

4. Meanwhile, put potatoes in a saucepan with water to cover; bring to a boil and cook for 15 minutes or until tender when pierced with the tip of a knife. In nonstick skillet, melt margarine over medium heat; add garlic and onions and cook for 4 minutes or until softened. Drain cooked potatoes and mash with chicken stock and sour cream. Stir in onion mixture and pepper. Place potato mixture on large serving platter and pour stew over top.

LAMB KEBABS WITH PECAN ORIENTAL SAUCE

Serves 4

Start barbecue or preheat broiler

TIP

Sauce can be used for other marinades or stir frys.

Beef steak cubes, boneless chicken or tender pork can replace lamb.

Other vegetables of your choice can be used. Mushrooms are a good option.

MAKE AHEAD

Prepare kebabs up to a day before to marinate. Sauce can be made up to 2 days before.

Sauce

1/4 cup	chopped pecans	50 mL
2 tbsp	water	25 mL
2 tbsp	brown sugar	25 mL
2 tbsp	lemon juice	25 mL
1 tbsp	soya sauce	15 mL
1 tbsp	vegetable oil	15 mL
2 tsp	sesame oil	10 mL
1 tsp	minced ginger root	5 mL
1 tsp	minced garlic	5 mL
12 oz	boneless lamb leg, cut into 3/4-inch (2-cm) cubes	375 g
1	red or green pepper, cut into 16 chunks	1
1	red onion, cut into 16 chunks	1
1 1/2 cups	snow peas	375 mL

1. Put pecans, water, brown sugar, lemon juice, soya sauce, vegetable and sesame oils, ginger and garlic in food processor; process until smooth. Pour half of sauce over lamb cubes and let marinate for 20 minutes or longer. Set aside the other half of the sauce.

2. Alternately thread lamb, sweet pepper chunks, onion chunks, and snow peas equally on 4 large or 8 small skewers. Barbecue for approximately 15 minutes, turning once or until lamb is medium rare (or desired level of doneness), basting with marinade sauce. Serve with remaining sauce.

PER SERVING

Calories	263
Protein	20 g
Fat, total	14 g
Fat, saturated	2 g
Carbohydrates	16 g
Sodium	318 mg
Cholesterol	52 mg
Fiber	3 g

PORK STIR-FRY WITH SWEET AND SOUR SAUCE, SNOW PEAS AND RED PEPPERS

Serves 4

TIP

Use beef steak or boneless chicken breast instead of pork.

★

Serve over pasta or rice.

MAKE AHEAD

Prepare sauce up to a day before.

Sauce

1 cup	chicken stock	250 mL
1/3 cup	brown sugar	75 mL
1/3 cup	ketchup	75 mL
2 tbsp	rice wine vinegar	25 mL
1 tbsp	soya sauce	15 mL
2 tsp	sesame oil	10 mL
4 tsp	cornstarch	20 mL
2 tsp	minced garlic	10 mL
1 1/2 tsp	minced ginger root	7 mL
12 oz	pork loin, cut into thin strips	375 g
1 tsp	vegetable oil	5 mL
1 1/2 cups	snow peas or sugar snap peas	375 mL
1 1/4 cups	red pepper strips	300 mL
3/4 cup	green pepper strips	175 mL
1/2 cup	chopped green onions (about 4 medium)	125 mL

1. In small bowl combine stock, brown sugar, ketchup, vinegar, soya sauce, sesame oil, cornstarch, garlic and ginger; set aside.

2. In nonstick wok or skillet sprayed with vegetable spray, cook the pork strips over high heat for 2 minutes, stirring constantly, or until just done at center; remove from wok.

3. Add oil to wok. Cook snow peas, red and green peppers for 3 minutes, stirring constantly, or until tender-crisp. Stir sauce again and add to wok along with pork. Cook for 45 seconds or until thickened. Garnish with green onions.

PER SERVING

Calories	266
Protein	21 g
Fat, total	6 g
Fat, saturated	1 g
Carbohydrates	34 g
Sodium	802 mg
Cholesterol	46 mg
Fiber	3 g

PORK FAJITAS WITH SWEET PEPPERS, CORIANDER AND CHEESE

Serves 3 or 4

TIP

Use pork chops or pork cutlets or substitute boneless chicken or beef steak.

Mozzarella cheese can replace Cheddar.

MAKE AHEAD

Prepare pork mixture earlier in the day. Reheat gently and fill tortillas.

Preheat oven to 425° F (220° C)

Baking sheet sprayed with vegetable spray

8 oz	pork tenderloin, cut into thin strips	250 g
2 tsp	vegetable oil	10 mL
1 1/2 tsp	minced garlic	7 mL
1 1/2 cups	thinly sliced onions	375 mL
1 1/2 cups	red pepper strips	375 mL
1/4 cup	fresh chopped coriander or parsley	50 mL
3 tbsp	chopped green onions (about 2 medium)	45 mL
6	small flour tortillas	6
1/2 cup	grated Cheddar cheese	125 mL
1/3 cup	bottled salsa	75 mL
1/4 cup	light sour cream	50 mL

1. In nonstick skillet sprayed with vegetable spray, cook the pork strips over high heat for 2 minutes, or until just done at center. Remove from skillet. Add oil. Cook garlic and onions for 4 minutes until browned. Add red pepper strips and cook over medium heat for 5 minutes, or until softened.

2. Remove from heat and stir in coriander, green onions and pork. Divide among tortillas. Top with Cheddar, salsa and sour cream. Roll up, place on baking sheet and bake for 5 minutes or until heated through.

PER SERVING (4)	
Calories	365
Protein	22 g
Fat, total	13 g
Fat, saturated	6 g
Carbohydrates	41 g
Sodium	528 mg
Cholesterol	50 mg
Fiber	3 g

VEAL WITH SPINACH, MUSHROOMS, OLIVES AND CHEESE SAUCE

Serves 4

Preheat oven to 450° F (230° C)

1 lb	veal scallopini	500 g
3 tbsp	flour	45 mL
2 tsp	vegetable oil	10 mL
2 tsp	minced garlic	10 mL
1 cup	chopped onions	250 mL
2 cups	sliced mushrooms	500 mL
1	package (10 oz [300g]) frozen chopped spinach, cooked, drained and squeezed dry	1
1 1/2 tsp	dried oregano	7 mL
1/4 tsp	ground black pepper	1 mL
1 tbsp	lemon juice	15 mL
1/4 cup	sliced black olives	50 mL
1/4 cup	chicken stock	50 mL
3 oz	feta cheese, crumbled	75 g
2/3 cup	tomato pasta sauce	150 mL

1. Between sheets of waxed paper, pound veal to 1/4-inch (5-mm) thickness. Heat 1 tsp (5 mL) of the oil in nonstick skillet sprayed with vegetable spray over medium-high heat. Dredge veal in flour and cook for 2 minutes per side or until just done at center. Place on baking dish.

2. Heat remaining 1 tsp (5 mL) oil in nonstick saucepan over medium heat. Add garlic and onions; cook for 4 minutes or until softened. Add mushrooms and cook for 3 minutes longer. Stir in spinach, oregano, black pepper, lemon juice, olives, stock and 2 oz (50 g) of the feta until well combined. Place over top of veal, pour over tomato sauce and sprinkle with remaining cheese.

3. Bake for 5 minutes, or just until hot.

TIP

Use boneless chicken breast, turkey or pork scallopini instead of veal.

A 10-oz (300-g) bag of fresh spinach can replace frozen spinach. Wash the spinach and cook with water clinging to leaves. Drain and squeeze dry.

Goat cheese, Cheddar or mozzarella can replace feta.

MAKE AHEAD

Prepare mushroom-spinach mixture up to a day before. Reheat gently before placing on veal.

PER SERVING

Calories	311
Protein	31 g
Fat, total	12 g
Fat, saturated	4 g
Carbohydrates	21 g
Sodium	666 mg
Cholesterol	104 mg
Fiber	3 g

ROLLED VEAL LOAF WITH ASPARAGUS AND MUSHROOMS

TIP

Use a sharp knife to cut through the asparagus.

Substitute ground chicken, beef or turkey for the veal.

Great as leftovers.

MAKE AHEAD

Prepare loaf up to a day ahead. Bake just before serving.

Preheat oven to 375° F (190° C)

9- by 5-inch (2 L) loaf pan sprayed with vegetable spray

6	medium asparagus spears	6
1 tsp	vegetable oil	5 mL
1 tsp	minced garlic	5 mL
3/4 cup	chopped onions	175 mL
1 cup	sliced mushrooms	250 mL

Loaf

1 lb	ground veal	500 g
1/3 cup	bread crumbs	75 mL
3 tbsp	tomato pasta sauce	45 mL
3 tbsp	chopped green onions (about 2 medium)	45 mL
1 1/2 tsp	minced garlic	7 mL
1 tsp	dried basil	5 mL
1	egg	1
1/4 cup	grated Parmesan cheese	50 mL
1/4 cup	tomato pasta sauce	50 mL

1. Steam asparagus spears over boiling water for 4 minutes or until tender-crisp; drain.

2. In nonstick saucepan, heat oil over medium-high heat. Add garlic and onions; sauté until softened and browned, approximately 6 minutes. Add mushrooms and sauté for 3 minutes until softened. Set aside.

3. In bowl, combine ground veal, bread crumbs, 3 tbsp (45 mL) tomato pasta sauce, green onions, garlic, basil and egg until well mixed.

PER SERVING

Calories	195
Protein	19 g
Fat, total	9 g
Fat, saturated	3 g
Carbohydrates	10 g
Sodium	262 mg
Cholesterol	98 mg
Fiber	1 g

4. Lay a 12-inch (30-cm) piece of waxed paper on work surface. Spread meat mixture into a rectangle; spread mushroom mixture on top. Sprinkle with Parmesan and lay asparagus spears crosswise on top, distributing them evenly. Using the waxed paper to help you, tightly roll up into a log. Gently drop the rolled meat loaf into the prepared pan, letting the waxed paper guide you. Toss out waxed paper. Pour 1/4 cup (50 mL) tomato sauce over top and bake, uncovered, for 35 minutes. Let stand for 10 minutes before cutting into slices.

VEAL WITH PINEAPPLE LIME SAUCE AND PECANS

TIP

Use chicken, pork or turkey scallopini to replace veal.

Use frozen juice concentrate and replace remainder in freezer. Orange juice can also be used.

If limes are unavailable, use lemons.

MAKE AHEAD

Prepare sauce earlier in the day and reheat gently before serving. Add more water if too thick.

1 lb	veal scallopini	500 g
2 tsp	oil	10 mL
3 tbsp	flour	45 mL

Sauce

1/4 cup	chopped green onions (about 2 medium)	50 mL
2 tbsp	chopped pecans	25 mL
1/4 cup	pineapple juice concentrate	50 mL
1/4 cup	water	50 mL
1 tbsp	honey	15 mL
1 tbsp	fresh lime juice	15 mL
1 tsp	grated lime zest	5 mL

1. Between sheets of waxed paper pound veal to 1/4-inch (5-mm) thickness. In large nonstick skillet sprayed with vegetable spray, heat oil over medium-high heat. Dredge veal in flour and cook for 2 minutes per side or until just done at center. Place on a serving dish and cover.

2. Add green onions and pecans to skillet. Cook for 2 minutes. Add pineapple juice concentrate, water, honey, lime juice and lime zest. Bring to a boil for 1 minute, or until slightly syrupy and thickened. Serve sauce over veal.

PER SERVING	
Calories	217
Protein	24 g
Fat, total	6 g
Fat, saturated	1 g
Carbohydrates	16 g
Sodium	71 mg
Cholesterol	84 mg
Fiber	1 g

VEGETABLES

VEGETABLE TIPS

1. Use fresh vegetables that are in season. If out of season vegetables are needed, use frozen, never canned. Canned vegetables have a high salt content and lack good color and texture. Keep vegetables in refrigerator in designated section.

2. If vegetables are to be cooked in advance, they can be steamed, microwaved, blanched or boiled. Stop cooking vegetables when they are tender-crisp and still retain their color. Drain and rinse with cold water to prevent overcooking. Overcooked vegetables are dull and soft, and most of the nutrients are lost.

3. Leaving the skin on vegetables, if it's not discolored or bruised, increases the fiber content.

4. A 10-oz (300-g) bag of fresh spinach yields the same amount as a 10-oz (300-g) frozen package. After cooking, squeeze out excess moisture from spinach.

5. When sautéeing vegetables, use a nonstick skillet sprayed with vegetable spray, and only the amount of fat in recipe. If the vegetables begin to burn and stick, respray or add a little water to skillet. Do not add extra oil or butter.

6. Most of the vegetable dishes should be cooked or baked just before serving to retain freshness.

ASPARAGUS WITH OYSTER SAUCE AND SESAME SEEDS

Serves 4

TIP

Substitute broccoli, green beans or snow peas for the asparagus. If using snow peas, cook for only 2 minutes.

Toast sesame seeds in a non-stick skillet on top of stove for 2 minutes or until brown.

MAKE AHEAD

Prepare sauce up to a day ahead. Reheat gently, adding more stock if too thick.

1/2 cup	chicken stock	125 mL
4 tsp	oyster sauce	20 mL
4 tsp	brown sugar	20 mL
2 tsp	rice wine vinegar	10 mL
1 1/2 tsp	cornstarch	7 mL
1 tsp	sesame oil	5 mL
1 tsp	minced garlic	5 mL
1/2 tsp	minced ginger root	2 mL
1 1/2 lbs	asparagus, cut into 1-inch (2.5 cm) pieces	750 g
2 tsp	toasted sesame seeds	10 mL

1. In small saucepan, combine stock, oyster sauce, brown sugar, vinegar, cornstarch, sesame oil, garlic and ginger; mix well. Cook over medium heat, stirring, for 2 minutes, or until sauce thickens; set aside.

2. Cook asparagus in boiling water, or in microwave, for 4 minutes or until tender. Drain and place in serving dish. Pour sauce over and sprinkle with sesame seeds.

PER SERVING	
Calories	85
Protein	6 g
Fat, total	2 g
Fat, saturated	0.4 g
Carbohydrates	13 g
Sodium	451 mg
Cholesterol	0 mg
Fiber	3 g

ASPARAGUS, RED PEPPER AND GOAT CHEESE PHYLLO ROLL

TIP

If goat cheese is not available, use grated mozzarella or Cheddar cheese.

Substitute thinly sliced ham (preferably smoked) for prosciutto.

When cutting this magnificent-looking vegetable dish, be sure to use a sharp knife.

MAKE AHEAD

Cook asparagus and rinse with cold water. Prepare cheese filling and cook vegetables before baking.

PER SERVING

Calories	139
Protein	7 g
Fat, total	7 g
Fat, saturated	1 g
Carbohydrates	12 g
Sodium	203 mg
Cholesterol	33 mg
Fiber	1 g

Preheat oven to 375° F (190° C)
Baking sheet sprayed with vegetable spray

6 oz	asparagus spears, trimmed	175 g

Filling

1 tsp	oil	5 mL
1 1/2 tsp	minced garlic	7 mL
1 1/2 cups	chopped red peppers	375 mL
1/4 cup	chopped green onions	50 mL
1/3 cup	5% ricotta cheese	75 mL
3 oz	goat cheese	75 g
1	egg	1
2 tbsp	grated Parmesan cheese	25 mL
1/4 tsp	coarsely grated pepper	1 mL
5	sheets phyllo pastry	5
2 tsp	margarine or butter, melted	10 mL
1 oz	sliced prosciutto	25 g

1. In saucepan of boiling water or in microwave, cook asparagus for 3 minutes or until tender; drain and set aside.

2. In nonstick skillet over medium heat, add oil and cook garlic and red peppers for 5 minutes or until tender; add green onions and cook for 1 minute more. Remove from heat.

3. In bowl, combine ricotta and goat cheeses, egg, Parmesan and pepper; mix until smooth.

4. Keeping remaining phyllo covered with a cloth to prevent drying out, layer two sheets of phyllo one on top of the other; brush with melted margarine. Layer two more sheets of phyllo on top; brush with melted margarine. Put last phyllo sheet on top. Spread cheese mixture evenly over top. Spread the prosciutto slices along one of the long sides, top it with the sweet pepper mixture, and put the asparagus spears on top. Starting from the long edge where the filling is, roll the phyllo and filling jelly roll fashion. Tuck the ends under and place on prepared baking sheet. Brush with remaining melted margarine and bake for 20 to 25 minutes, or until golden brown. Cut into slices and serve.

MUSHROOMS WITH CREAMY FETA CHEESE AND DILL STUFFING

Serves 4 to 6

TIP

If desired, use 8 jumbo mushrooms, but add 1/4 cup (50 mL) water to baking pan so they do not dry out.

Goat cheese can replace feta.

MAKE AHEAD

Stuff mushrooms up to a day ahead. Keep refrigerated. Bake just before serving.

Preheat oven to 425° F (220° C)

16	medium mushrooms	16
1 tsp	vegetable oil	5 mL
1 1/2 tsp	minced garlic	7 mL
1/3 cup	finely chopped onions	75 mL
1/3 cup	finely chopped red or green peppers	75 mL
1/3 cup	crumbled feta cheese	75 mL
3 tbsp	5% ricotta cheese	45 mL
2 tbsp	chopped fresh dill (or 1 tsp [5 mL] dried)	25 mL
2 tbsp	finely chopped green onions (about 1 medium)	25 mL

1. Remove stems from mushrooms; set caps aside and dice stems.

2. In small nonstick saucepan sprayed with vegetable spray, heat oil over medium heat; add diced mushroom stems, garlic, onions and peppers. Cook for 5 minutes, or until softened. Remove from heat.

3. Add feta and ricotta cheeses, dill and green onions; mix well. Carefully stuff mixture into mushroom caps. Place in a baking dish and bake for 15 to 20 minutes or just until mushrooms release their liquid.

PER SERVING (6)	
Calories	67
Protein	4 g
Fat, total	4 g
Fat, saturated	2 g
Carbohydrates	4 g
Sodium	162 mg
Cholesterol	14 mg
Fiber	1 g

CHEESY PESTO STUFFED MUSHROOMS

Serves 6

TIP

Use fresh parsley or spinach to replace basil, or use a combination.

Toast pine nuts in a nonstick skillet for 2 minutes until browned.

MAKE AHEAD

Prepare filling up to a day ahead. Fill mushrooms early in the day. Bake just before serving.

Preheat oven to 425° F (220° C)

Baking sheet sprayed with vegetable spray

14 oz	large stuffing mushrooms (approximately 16)	350 g
3/4 cup	packed basil leaves	175 mL
1 1/2 tbsp	olive oil	20 mL
1 1/2 tbsp	toasted pine nuts	20 mL
1 tbsp	grated Parmesan cheese	15 mL
1/2 tsp	minced garlic	2 mL
2 tbsp	chicken stock or water	25 mL
1/4 cup	5% ricotta cheese	50 mL

1. Wipe mushrooms clean and gently remove stems; reserve for another purpose. Put caps on baking sheet.

2. Put basil, olive oil, pine nuts, Parmesan and garlic in food processor; process until finely chopped, scraping down sides of bowl once. Add stock through the feed tube and process until smooth. Add ricotta and process until mixed.

3. Divide mixture evenly among mushroom caps. Bake for 10 to 15 minutes or until hot.

PER SERVING

Calories	75
Protein	4 g
Fat, total	6 g
Fat, saturated	1 g
Carbohydrates	4 g
Sodium	49 mg
Cholesterol	4 mg
Fiber	1 g

BAKED POTATOES STUFFED WITH SMOKED SALMON AND BROCCOLI

TIP

Smoked salmon freezes well for up to 4 weeks. Use as needed.

Red onions or sweet Vidalia onions can replace green onions.

★

If in a hurry, microwave potatoes. Each potato cooks in approximately 8 minutes at high power.

MAKE AHEAD

Prepare filling up to a day ahead and fill potatoes. Bake just before serving.

Preheat oven to 425° F (220° C)

4	medium baking potatoes	4
1 cup	chopped broccoli florets	250 mL
2/3 cup	light sour cream	150 mL
1/4 cup	2% milk	50 mL
1/4 cup	grated Parmesan cheese	50 mL
2 tbsp	chopped fresh dill (or 2 tsp [10 mL] dried)	25 mL
1/4 cup	chopped green onions (about 2 medium)	50 mL
3 oz	smoked salmon, chopped	75 g

1. Bake the potatoes for 1 hour or until easily pierced with a fork; let cool slightly. Meanwhile, in a saucepan of boiling water or in microwave, cook the broccoli for 1 minute or until tender-crisp. Drain and set aside.

2. Cut potatoes in half lengthwise, and carefully scoop out flesh, leaving skins intact. Mash potato with sour cream and milk; stir in 2 tbsp (25 mL) of the Parmesan, the dill, green onions, smoked salmon and broccoli. Spoon mixture back into potato skin shells; sprinkle with remaining 2 tbsp (25 mL) Parmesan. Bake for 10 to 15 minutes, or until heated through.

PER SERVING

Calories	102
Protein	7 g
Fat, total	2 g
Fat, saturated	1 g
Carbohydrates	16 g
Sodium	168 mg
Cholesterol	12 mg
Fiber	1 g

GREEK BAKED STUFFED POTATOES WITH TOMATO, OLIVES AND CHEESE

Serves 6

TIP

Use plum tomatoes if available — they have less liquid. Or you can remove the seeds from regular tomatoes.

★

If in a hurry, microwave potatoes. Each potato cooks in approximately 8 minutes at high power.

★

Goat cheese or another sharp cheese can replace feta.

MAKE AHEAD

Prepare entire filling and stuff potatoes early in the day. Bake an extra 5 minutes or until hot.

Preheat oven to 425° F (220° C)

3	medium baking potatoes	3
2 tsp	vegetable oil	10 mL
1 1/2 tsp	minced garlic	7 mL
2/3 cup	chopped green peppers	150 mL
1/2 cup	chopped red onions	125 mL
1 1/2 tsp	dried oregano	7 mL
2/3 cup	chopped fresh tomatoes	150 mL
1/3 cup	sliced black olives	75 mL
1/4 cup	chopped green onions (about 2 medium)	50 mL
1/4 cup	2% yogurt	50 mL
1/4 cup	2% milk	50 mL
1 1/2 oz	feta cheese, crumbled	40 g

1. Bake the potatoes for 45 minutes to 1 hour, or until easily pierced with the tip of a sharp knife.

2. Meanwhile, in a nonstick skillet, heat oil over medium heat. Add garlic, green peppers, red onions and oregano and cook for 7 minutes or until softened, stirring occasionally. Stir in tomatoes, black olives and green onions and cook 1 minute more. Remove from heat.

3. When potatoes are cool enough to handle, cut in half lengthwise and scoop out flesh, leaving shells intact. Place shells on baking sheet. Mash potato and add yogurt, milk and 1 oz (25 g) of the feta. Stir in vegetable mixture. Divide among potato skin shells, sprinkle with remaining feta and bake for 15 minutes, or until heated through.

PER SERVING

Calories	143
Protein	4 g
Fat, total	6 g
Fat, saturated	2 g
Carbohydrates	19 g
Sodium	349 mg
Cholesterol	8 mg
Fiber	2 g

CORN, LEEK AND RED PEPPER CASSEROLE

Serves 6

TIP

Be sure to use evaporated milk — it's what gives this dish its creaminess.

Leeks can have a lot of hidden dirt — to clean thoroughly, slice in half lengthwise and wash under cold running water, getting between the layers where dirt hides.

Use fresh parsley, basil or coriander instead of dill.

Reheat leftovers gently.

MAKE AHEAD

Cook vegetables early in day. Bake dish just before serving.

PER SERVING

Calories	194
Protein	11 g
Fat, total	5 g
Fat, saturated	1 g
Carbohydrates	30 g
Sodium	340 mg
Cholesterol	76 mg
Fiber	2 g

Preheat oven to 350° F (180° C)

2-quart (2 L) casserole dish sprayed with vegetable spray

1 tsp	vegetable oil	5 mL
1 tsp	minced garlic	5 mL
1 cup	sliced leeks	250 mL
1 cup	chopped red peppers	250 mL
2 cups	corn kernels	500 mL
2 1/2 tbsp	all-purpose flour	35 mL
2	whole eggs	2
2	egg whites	2
1 1/3 cups	2% evaporated milk	325 mL
1/4 cup	chopped fresh dill (or 2 tsp [10 mL] dried)	50 mL
1/4 cup	bread crumbs	50 mL
1/2 tsp	margarine or butter	2 mL

1. In nonstick skillet sprayed with vegetable spray, heat oil over medium heat. Add garlic, leeks and red peppers and cook for 7 minutes, or until tender, stirring occasionally; set aside.

2. Put 1 cup (250 mL) of corn in food processor with flour; purée. Add whole eggs, egg whites, evaporated milk and dill; process until smooth.

3. In large bowl, combine sautéed vegetables, corn purée and remaining 1 cup (250 mL) corn. Pour into prepared dish. Combine bread crumbs and margarine until crumbly. Sprinkle over top casserole and bake for 30 minutes or until set at center.

CREAMY EGGPLANT ZUCCHINI MOUSSAKA

TIP

Leaving the skin on vegetables increases the fiber.

Replace feta with goat cheese, Cheddar or another strong-tasting cheese.

Great reheated the next day.

MAKE AHEAD

Prepare vegetable mixture and milk sauce early in the day. Assemble and bake just before serving.

Preheat oven to 350° F (180° C)

8-Inch (2 L) square baking dish

2 tsp	vegetable oil	10 mL
2 tsp	minced garlic	10 mL
1 3/4 cups	chopped onions	425 mL
1 3/4 cups	unpeeled zucchini cut into 1/2-inch (1-cm) cubes	425 mL
1 3/4 cups	unpeeled eggplant cut into 1/2-inch (1-cm) cubes	425 mL
1 3/4 cups	sliced mushrooms	425 mL
1 1/2 tsp	dried basil	7 mL
1 tsp	dried oregano	5 mL
2 tsp	margarine or butter	10 mL
1 tbsp	flour	15 mL
1 cup	2% milk	250 mL
1	egg	1
1 cup	5% ricotta cheese	250 mL
1 cup	tomato pasta sauce	250 mL
3 oz	feta cheese, crumbled	75 g

1. In nonstick skillet sprayed with vegetable spray, heat oil over medium heat. Cook garlic, onions, zucchini and eggplant for 10 minutes or until softened, stirring occasionally. Add mushrooms, basil and oregano and cook for 4 minutes longer, or until vegetables are tender.

2. In small saucepan, melt margarine over medium heat; add flour and cook, stirring, for 1 minute. Gradually add milk and cook, stirring, for 4 minutes or until sauce begins to simmer. Remove from heat and let cool for 5 minutes. Whisk in egg and ricotta.

3. Spread tomato sauce over bottom of baking dish. Add vegetable mixture and top with milk sauce. Sprinkle with crumbled feta. Bake uncovered for 20 minutes or until heated through, and edges are set. Let rest 5 minutes before serving.

PER SERVING

Calories	235
Protein	13 g
Fat, total	12 g
Fat, saturated	5 g
Carbohydrates	20 g
Sodium	488 mg
Cholesterol	66 mg
Fiber	2 g

EGGPLANT WITH GOAT CHEESE AND ROASTED SWEET PEPPERS

TIP

Feta cheese, grated Cheddar or Swiss can replace goat cheese. A stronger tasting cheese suits this dish.

Either use bottled-in-water roasted red peppers or, under a broiler, roast a small pepper for 15 to 20 minutes or until charred. Cool, then peel, deseed and chop. Use remainder for another purpose.

MAKE AHEAD

Prepare entire dish early in the day. Bake just before serving.

Preheat oven to 350° F (180° C)

Baking sheet sprayed with vegetable spray

1	egg	1
1/4 cup	2% milk	50 mL
3/4 cup	seasoned bread crumbs	175 mL
2 tbsp	vegetable oil	25 mL
10	1/2-inch (1-cm) slices eggplant, skin on	10
3 oz	goat cheese	75 g
3 tbsp	2% milk	45 mL
3 tbsp	chopped roasted red peppers	45 mL
1/4 cup	chopped green onions (about 2 medium)	50 mL
1/2 tsp	minced garlic	2 mL

1. Beat egg and milk together in small bowl. Put bread crumbs on plate. Dip the eggplant slices in egg wash then press into bread crumbs. In large nonstick skillet sprayed with vegetable spray, heat 1 tbsp (15 mL) of the oil over medium heat. Add half of the breaded eggplant slices and cook for 4 minutes or until golden brown on both sides. Add remaining 1 tbsp (15 mL) oil and respray skillet with vegetable spray. Repeat with remaining eggplant slices. Place on prepared baking sheet.

2. In small bowl, stir together goat cheese, milk, red peppers, green onions and garlic. Put a spoonful of topping on top of each eggplant slice. Bake for 10 minutes or until heated through.

PER SERVING (6)

Calories	150
Protein	5 g
Fat, total	8 g
Fat, saturated	1 g
Carbohydrates	14 g
Sodium	399 mg
Cholesterol	37 mg
Fiber	1 g

CRUSTLESS DILL SPINACH QUICHE WITH MUSHROOMS AND CHEESE

Serves 6

Preheat oven to 350° F (180° C)

8-inch (2 L) springform pan sprayed with vegetable spray

10 oz	fresh spinach	300 g
2 tsp	vegetable oil	10 mL
1 tsp	minced garlic	5 mL
3/4 cup	chopped onions	175 mL
3/4 cup	chopped mushrooms	175 mL
2/3 cup	5% ricotta cheese	150 mL
2/3 cup	2% cottage cheese	150 mL
1/3 cup	grated Cheddar cheese	75 mL
2 tbsp	grated Parmesan cheese	25 mL
1	whole egg	1
1	egg white	1
3 tbsp	chopped fresh dill (or 2 tsp [10 mL] dried)	45 mL
1/4 tsp	ground black pepper	1 mL

TIP

Use a 10-oz (300-g) package of frozen spinach instead of fresh spinach.

★

All ricotta or all cottage cheese can be used, but ricotta gives a creamy texture.

MAKE AHEAD

Prepare mixture early in the day. Bake just before serving. Great reheated gently the next day.

1. Wash spinach and shake off excess water. In the water clinging to the leaves, cook the spinach over high heat just until it wilts. Squeeze out excess moisture, chop and set aside.

2. In large nonstick skillet, heat oil over medium heat; add garlic, onions and mushrooms and cook for 5 minutes or until softened. Remove from heat and add chopped spinach, ricotta, cottage, Cheddar and Parmesan cheeses, whole egg, egg white, dill and pepper; mix well. Pour into prepared pan and bake for 35 to 40 minutes or until knife inserted in center comes out clean.

PER SERVING

Calories	134
Protein	13 g
Fat, total	7 g
Fat, saturated	3 g
Carbohydrates	6 g
Sodium	259 mg
Cholesterol	54 mg
Fiber	2 g

SPINACH WITH CHEDDAR CHEESE SAUCE AND CRUNCHY TOPPING

Serves 6

TIP

Use 2 packages (10 oz [300 g]) of fresh spinach instead of frozen. Wash leaves and cook in the water clinging to leaves. Drain, squeeze out excess moisture and chop.

Swiss cheese or another strong cheese can replace Cheddar. Try to use an aged Cheddar.

MAKE AHEAD

Prepare spinach, cheese sauce and topping up to a day ahead. Reheat cheese sauce, adding more milk if too thick. Broil just before serving.

Preheat broiler

8- by 4-inch (1.5 L) baking dish sprayed with vegetable spray

2	packages (10 oz [300 g]) frozen spinach	2
1 tsp	vegetable oil	5 mL
1 1/2 tsp	minced garlic	7 mL
3/4 cup	chopped onions	175 mL

Sauce

2 tsp	margarine or butter	10 mL
1 tbsp	all-purpose flour	15 mL
1/2 cup	chicken stock	125 mL
3/4 cup	2% milk	175 mL
2/3 cup	grated Cheddar cheese (2 1/2 oz [65 g])	150 mL

Topping

3 tbsp	seasoned bread crumbs	45 mL
1 tsp	minced garlic	5 mL
1 tsp	margarine or butter	5 mL

1. Cook spinach according to package directions; drain well and chop. Heat oil in nonstick skillet over medium heat; add garlic and onions and cook for 4 minutes or until softened. Toss with spinach and put in prepared baking dish.

2. Melt margarine in saucepan over medium heat; add flour and cook, stirring, for 1 minute. Gradually add stock and milk, stirring constantly. Cook until sauce begins to simmer and thickens slightly, approximately 5 minutes. Stir in cheese and cook 1 minute until cheese melts. Pour over spinach.

3. In small bowl, combine bread crumbs, garlic and margarine; sprinkle over sauce. Broil for 3 minutes or until browned.

PER SERVING	
Calories	136
Protein	8 g
Fat, total	8 g
Fat, saturated	3 g
Carbohydrates	11 g
Sodium	519 mg
Cholesterol	15 mg
Fiber	3 g

SWEET POTATO AND CARROT CASSEROLE WITH MOLASSES AND PECANS

Serves 6

Preheat oven to 350° F (180° C)

8-inch square (2 L) baking dish sprayed with vegetable spray

1 lb	sweet potatoes, peeled and cut into 1/2-inch (1-cm) cubes	500 g
1 lb	carrots, peeled and thinly sliced	500 g
1 1/4 cups	canned pineapple chunks, drained	300 mL
1/2 cup	raisins	125 mL
1/3 cup	packed brown sugar	75 mL
2 tbsp	orange juice	25 mL
1 tbsp	margarine or butter	15 mL
1 tbsp	molasses	15 mL
1 1/2 tsp	cinnamon	7 mL
3 tbsp	chopped pecans	45 mL

1. In a saucepan of boiling water, cook sweet potatoes and carrots for approximately 7 minutes or until tender. Drain. Toss sweet potatoes and carrots together along with pineapple and raisins; put in prepared baking dish.

2. In saucepan, heat brown sugar, orange juice, margarine, molasses and cinnamon over medium heat, stirring, for 1 minute, or until melted and smooth. Pour syrup over vegetables and sprinkle pecans on top. Bake for 15 minutes or until heated through.

PER SERVING	
Calories	288
Protein	3 g
Fat, total	5 g
Fat, saturated	1 g
Carbohydrates	62 g
Sodium	67 mg
Cholesterol	0 mg
Fiber	5 g

MASHED WHITE AND SWEET POTATO CASSEROLE

Serves 8

TIP

To soften sun-dried tomatoes, pour boiling water over them and let rest 15 minutes. Drain and chop.

Serve this beautiful potato dish with grilled fish or chicken.

Great as leftovers.

MAKE AHEAD

Prepare up to a day ahead. Bake just before serving.

Preheat oven to 400° F (200° C)

8-inch square (2 L) casserole dish sprayed with vegetable spray

2 tsp	vegetable oil	10 mL
2 tsp	minced garlic	10 mL
1 cup	chopped onions	250 mL
1 lb	potatoes, peeled and quartered	500 g
2/3 cup	5% ricotta cheese	150 mL
1/4 cup	light sour cream	50 mL
1/4 cup	2% milk	50 mL
1/4 cup	finely chopped red or green peppers	50 mL
3 tbsp	fresh chopped dill (or 1 tsp [5 mL] dried)	45 mL
1 lb	sweet potatoes, peeled and quartered	500 g
1/2 cup	2% milk	125 mL
1/4 cup	chopped sun-dried tomatoes	50 mL
1/4 cup	chopped green onions (about 2 medium)	50 mL
3 tbsp	bread crumbs	45 mL
1 oz	goat cheese	25 g
1 tsp	margarine or butter	5 mL

1. In small nonstick skillet, heat oil over medium heat. Cook garlic and onions for 4 minutes, or until softened. Divide mixture in half.

2. Put potatoes in saucepan with cold water to cover; bring to a boil and cook for 15 minutes, or until tender when pierced with the tip of a knife. Drain and mash with ricotta, sour cream and milk; stir in red peppers, dill and half of onion mixture.

3. Put sweet potatoes in saucepan with cold water to cover; bring to a boil and cook for 10 minutes or until tender when pierced with the tip of a knife.

PER SERVING

Calories	182
Protein	7 g
Fat, total	3 g
Fat, saturated	1 g
Carbohydrates	32 g
Sodium	128 mg
Cholesterol	10 mg
Fiber	3 g

Drain and mash with milk; stir in sun-dried tomatoes, green onions, and remaining onion-garlic mixture. Place sweet potato mixture to one side of casserole dish, and put mashed white potato mixture to the other side.

4. In small bowl combine bread crumbs, goat cheese and margarine; sprinkle over top of casserole. Bake for 15 minutes, uncovered, or until heated through.

SWEET POTATO FRIES WITH CINNAMON AND MAPLE SYRUP

Serves 4

TIP

The maple syrup gives an unusual sweet taste. For a stronger flavor, use half molasses and half maple syrup. Honey can also be used.

MAKE AHEAD

Cut and brush potatoes with maple syrup mixture early in the day. Bake just before serving.

Preheat oven to 375° F (190° C)

Baking sheet sprayed with vegetable spray

2	large sweet potatoes, unpeeled	2
1 1/2 tbsp	melted margarine or butter	20 mL
3 tsp	maple syrup	15 mL
3/4 tsp	cinnamon	4 mL
1/4 tsp	ginger	1 mL
pinch	nutmeg	pinch

1. Scrub sweet potatoes and cut lengthwise into 8 wedges. Place on prepared baking sheet.

2. In small bowl, combine margarine, maple syrup, cinnamon, ginger and nutmeg; brush half over the potato wedges. Bake for 20 minutes. Turn wedges over and brush with remaining mixture. Bake for 20 minutes longer, or until tender.

PER SERVING	
Calories	125
Protein	1 g
Fat, total	4 g
Fat, saturated	1 g
Carbohydrates	22 g
Sodium	60 mg
Cholesterol	0 mg
Fiber	2 g

LAMB VEGETABLE STEW OVER GARLIC MASHED POTATOES (PAGE 134) ➤

Broccoli, Carrot and Dill Vegetable Strudel

Serves 4

TIP

This is a delicious, almost sweet strudel. Sweet potatoes can replace carrots, but cook in boiling water for 3 minutes to soften slightly.

Parsley or basil can replace dill.

Cheddar or mozzarella can replace Swiss cheese, but a stronger cheese tastes best.

When working with phyllo, work quickly so the sheets do not dry. Keep open phyllo covered with a slightly damp towel. Unused phyllo refreezes well — cover tightly.

MAKE AHEAD

Prepare filling up to a day before. Bake just before serving.

PER SERVING

Calories	173
Protein	7 g
Fat, total	7 g
Fat, saturated	2 g
Carbohydrates	22 g
Sodium	327 mg
Cholesterol	34 mg
Fiber	3 g

Preheat oven to 375° F (190° C)

Baking sheet sprayed with vegetable spray

1 tsp	vegetable oil	5 mL
1 tbsp	margarine or butter	15 mL
1 1/2 tsp	minced garlic	7 mL
1 1/2 cups	chopped onions	375 mL
3 cups	finely chopped broccoli	750 mL
2 cups	finely chopped carrots	500 mL
1/3 cup	chopped fresh dill (or 2 tsp [10 mL] dried)	75 mL
1	egg	1
1/4 cup	seasoned bread crumbs	50 mL
1/2 cup	grated Swiss cheese (2 oz [50 g])	125 mL
6	sheets phyllo pastry	6
2 tsp	melted margarine or butter	10 mL

1. In large nonstick pan sprayed with vegetable spray, heat oil and margarine over medium heat; cook garlic, onions, broccoli and carrots for 10 minutes or until tender-crisp, stirring occasionally. Stir in dill. Let cool for 10 minutes and stir in egg, bread crumbs and cheese.

2. Lay 2 phyllo sheets on work surface and brush with melted margarine. Top with 2 more phyllo sheets and brush with margarine. Lay last 2 phyllo sheets on top. Spread vegetable mixture over surface leaving a 1-inch (2.5 cm) border on all sides. Roll up tightly and tuck ends under. Brush with remaining margarine. Place on prepared baking sheet and bake for 25 minutes or until golden brown.

◄ Asparagus, Red Pepper and Goat Cheese Phyllo Roll (page 146)

VEGETABLE DILL LATKES
(PANCAKES)

Serves 4

Makes 10 latkes.

TIP

Although these vegetable patties are delicious on their own, a simple sauce can be made for them by whisking together 1/2 cup (125 mL) light sour cream and 1 tbsp (15 mL) chopped fresh dill.

★

These latkes taste great the next day reheated.

★

Prepare in 2 batches if necessary.

MAKE AHEAD

Prepare mixture early in the day, make into patties and refrigerate until ready to bake.

PER SERVING

Calories	225
Protein	8 g
Fat, total	3 g
Fat, saturated	1 g
Carbohydrates	41 g
Sodium	166 mg
Cholesterol	108 mg
Fiber	4 g

Preheat oven to 375° F (190° C)

Baking sheet sprayed with vegetable spray

1 1/4 cups	diced zucchini, unpeeled	300 mL
1 1/4 cups	diced peeled sweet potatoes	300 mL
3/4 cup	diced peeled carrots	175 mL
1/3 cup	diced onions	75 mL
2	eggs	2
1/3 cup	chopped fresh dill (or 2 tsp [10 mL] dried)	75 mL
1 tsp	minced garlic	5 mL
1 cup	all-purpose flour	250 mL
1/2 tsp	baking powder	2 mL
1/4 tsp	salt	1 mL
1/4 tsp	ground black pepper	1 mL

1. In food processor, combine zucchini, sweet potatoes, carrots, onions, eggs, dill and garlic; process on and off until well combined. In small bowl, stir together flour, baking powder, salt and pepper. Add flour mixture to vegetable mixture, process on and off just until combined.

2. Scoop 1/4 cup (50 mL) of batter into your hands and shape into a patty; put on prepared baking sheet. Repeat until all batter has been used. Bake for 10 minutes, turn over and bake for 10 minutes more.

PASTA AND GRAINS

PASTA AND GRAINS TIPS

1. Cook pasta in a large pot of boiling water. Use 12 to 16 cups (3 to 4 L) water for each pound (500 g) of pasta. Add a little oil to prevent pasta from sticking. Stir pasta occasionally while cooking.

2. Cook pasta "al dente," or firm to the bite. Never overcook or it will become soft and lose all its texture. When cooked, drain in colander, then transfer to a serving dish. Add sauce immediately and toss. Do not add sauce to pasta until just ready to serve, or pasta will absorb the sauce, leaving the appearance of not enough.

3. Prepare the sauce while the pasta is cooking. Plan ahead so the sauce will be completed at the same time the pasta is cooked.

4. For these recipes, approximately 1/2 lb (250 g) dry pasta serves 4 people, 3/4 lb (375 g) serves 6 people, and 1 lb (500 g) serves 8 people.

5. You can prepare the pasta early in the day if necessary. Drain cooked pasta, rinse with cold water and add 3 tbsp (45 mL) of stock or 3 tbsp (45 mL) of the sauce to be used, or 3 tbsp (45 mL) of the water in which the pasta was cooked. (This will ensure that pasta strands do not stick.) Let sit at room temperature. Before serving, either warm slightly in a microwave for 1 minute at High (be careful not to overcook the pasta), or heat sauce thoroughly in saucepan and pour over pasta immediately.

6. Heavier pasta such as rigatoni or jumbo shells needs a heavier, more robust sauce. Lighter pasta such as fettuccine, linguine or spaghetti needs a finer sauce and more finely diced vegetables. Sauces for rotini or penne should be somewhere between fine and robust.

7. Homemade pastas can be delicious, but most of the time I use dried pasta. There are several reasons for this:

    - It is easier to find and store, and it costs much less than fresh.
    - It lacks the fat and cholesterol of the fresh types, which have eggs added.
    - There are more varieties of dry pasta readily available.
    - Dried pastas have consistent flavor and texture. Fresh pasta can stick, even if cooked properly, and is best only if cooked immediately after the pasta is made.
    - It can be stored at room temperature for up to 1 year.

8. If reheating leftover pasta, add more stock or tomato sauce to provide extra moisture.

9. After cooking manicotti or cannelloni pasta shells, drain, rinse with cold water and cover until ready to use. To stuff easily, slice shell to open and lay flat. Place some filling over top shell, close and place seam side down in baking dish. These filled shells can be refrigerated up to 1 day ahead, then baked.

10. Filling for manicotti and cannelloni can also be used in jumbo pasta shells. Less filling is needed. Filling for 12 manicotti is sufficient for about 24 shells.

11. Lasagna sheets can be prepared early in day, rinsed with cold water, and covered. Rinse again with cold water before using if pasta sticks. Lasagna dishes can be prepared up to a day ahead. After baking, let rest for 10 minutes to make the lasagna easier to cut. Reheat lasagna at 350° F (180° C) just until warm.

12. Do not overcook rice or it becomes too soft. Wild rice begins to fall apart if overcooked.

13. Grains are wonderfully versatile. By adding vegetables, cheese, meat, fish or poultry, these foods can become an entire meal. They can be served as salads, appetizers, main entrees or as side dishes and can be eaten warm or cold.

LINGUINE WITH PECAN ORIENTAL SAUCE AND SALMON

Serves 6

TIP

Great to serve warm, at room temperature, or cold.

If to be served cold, this dish can be prepared early in the day. Toss before serving.

Sauce can be used as a marinade or in a stir-fry, or over another pasta dish.

MAKE AHEAD

Prepare sauce up to 2 days ahead. Stir again before using.

Sauce

5 tbsp	packed brown sugar	75 mL
1/4 cup	chopped pecans	50 mL
3 tbsp	chicken stock or water	45 mL
2 1/2 tbsp	soya sauce	35 mL
2 1/2 tbsp	rice wine vinegar	35 mL
2 tbsp	lemon juice	25 mL
2 tbsp	sesame oil	25 mL
2 tsp	minced garlic	10 mL
1 1/2 tsp	minced ginger root	7 mL
1 1/2 cups	chopped baby corn cobs	375 mL
1 1/2 cups	thinly sliced red or green peppers	375 mL
1/4 cup	chopped green onions (about 2 medium)	50 mL
12 oz	linguine	375 g
8 oz	salmon cut into 1/2-inch (1-cm) cubes	250 g
2 cups	broccoli florets	500 mL

1. Put brown sugar, pecans, stock, soya sauce, vinegar, lemon juice, sesame oil, garlic and ginger in food processor; process until smooth and set aside. Put corn cobs, red peppers and green onions in large serving bowl.

2. In large pot of boiling water, cook pasta according to package directions or until tender but firm. Drain and add to vegetables in bowl.

3. Meanwhile, in nonstick skillet sprayed with vegetable spray, cook salmon over high heat for 4 minutes or until just done at center; put in serving bowl.

4. Cook broccoli in boiling water or microwave for 2 minutes or until tender-crisp; add to serving bowl. Pour sauce over and toss.

PER SERVING

Calories	392
Protein	18 g
Fat, total	10 g
Fat, saturated	1 g
Carbohydrates	58 g
Sodium	895 mg
Cholesterol	21 mg
Fiber	3 g

TUNA DRESSING OVER PASTA NIÇOISE

Serves 6

TIP

Use chopped plum tomatoes or deseed regular tomatoes to eliminate excess liquid.

Try green stuffed olives instead of black olives.

MAKE AHEAD

Prepare sauce up to a day ahead. Keep refrigerated.

The entire salad can be tossed early in the day, as long as pasta is not hot.

Sauce

1	can (6.5 oz [184 g]) flaked tuna, water-packed, drained	1
1/2 cup	chicken stock	125 mL
2 tbsp	light mayonnaise	25 mL
2 tbsp	vegetable oil	25 mL
1 tbsp	lemon juice	15 mL
1 tbsp	drained capers	15 mL
1 1/2 tsp	minced garlic	7 mL
12 oz	rotini	375 g
1 1/2 cups	chopped tomatoes	375 mL
1 1/4 cups	chopped cucumbers	300 mL
3/4 cup	chopped red onions	175 mL
1/3 cup	sliced black olives	75 mL
1/3 cup	chopped green onions	75 mL

1. Put tuna, stock, mayonnaise, oil, lemon juice, capers and garlic in food processor; process until smooth.

2. In large pot of boiling water cook pasta according to package directions or until tender but firm; rinse under cold water and drain. Put in large serving bowl, along with tomatoes, cucumbers, onions, olives, green onions and tuna sauce; toss well. Serve at room temperature or chilled.

PER SERVING

Calories	321
Protein	15 g
Fat, total	7 g
Fat, saturated	1 g
Carbohydrates	49 g
Sodium	321 mg
Cholesterol	4 mg
Fiber	3 g

SEAFOOD TETRAZZINI WITH SUN-DRIED TOMATOES AND GOAT CHEESE

Preheat oven to broil

9- × 13-inch (3 L) baking dish

16	mussels	16
6 oz	shrimp	150 g
6 oz	scallops	150 g
12 oz	fettuccine	375 g

Vegetable Mixture

2 tsp	vegetable oil	10 mL
2 tsp	minced garlic	10 mL
1/2 cup	chopped red onions	125 mL
1 cup	chopped red peppers	250 mL
1/2 cup	chopped green peppers	125 mL
1/2 cup	sun-dried tomatoes	125 mL
1/3 cup	chopped fresh dill (1 tbsp [15 mL] dried)	75 mL
1/3 cup	chopped green onions	75 mL

Sauce

1 2/3 cup	2% milk	400 mL
1 2/3 cup	fish or chicken stock	400 mL
1/4 cup	all-purpose flour	50 mL
4 oz	goat cheese	125 g
4 tbsp	grated Parmesan cheese	60 mL
	Pepper to taste	

1. Bring 1/4 cup (50 mL) water to a boil in a heavy saucepan; add mussels, cover and steam for 1 minute or just until mussels open. Shell mussels and set aside.

2. In nonstick skillet sprayed with vegetable spray, cook scallops and shrimp over high heat for 3 to 4 minutes, or just until done. Drain excess liquid. Put with mussels.

TIP

To soften sun-dried tomatoes, cover with boiling water and let rest for 1 minute. Drain and chop

★

Use any combination of fish or seafood. Chicken also works well.

★

Sauce will be runny but this is necessary to coat pasta.

★

Feta cheese can replace goat cheese.

MAKE AHEAD

Prepare vegetable mixture, sauce and seafood. Keep separate. Pour over pasta just before broiling.

PER SERVING

Calories	333
Protein	22 g
Fat, total	7 g
Fat, saturated	2 g
Carbohydrates	44 g
Sodium	497 mg
Cholesterol	51 mg
Fiber	1 g

3. In large pot of boiling water, cook fettuccine according to package directions or until tender but firm. Drain and place in baking dish.

4. Heat oil in saucepan over medium heat; add garlic, onions and peppers and cook for 4 minutes or until softened. Add sun-dried tomatoes, dill and green onions; set aside.

5. In a medium saucepan, combine milk, stock and flour until smooth. Cook over medium heat for 8 to 10 minutes, stirring constantly until slightly thickened. Add 3 oz (75 g) of the goat cheese and 2 tbsp (25 mL) of the Parmesan. Combine seafood with milk sauce and vegetable mixture. Pour over pasta, mix until well combined, sprinkle with remaining goat cheese and Parmesan. Broil for 2 or 3 minutes just until browned.

PENNE WITH STEAK, PLUM TOMATOES AND PESTO

TIP

Use a good quality beef cut, such as rib eye, sirloin or tenderloin.

If basil is unavailable, substitute fresh spinach or parsley leaves, or use a combination.

Wild mushrooms would be great in this recipe.

MAKE AHEAD

Prepare pesto up to a day ahead, or freeze up to 3 weeks.

6 oz	thinly sliced beef steak	150 g

Pesto Sauce

1 1/2 cups	packed fresh basil	375 mL
3 tbsp	olive oil	45 mL
3 tbsp	Parmesan cheese	45 mL
2 tbsp	toasted pine nuts	25 mL
1 1/2 tsp	minced garlic	7 mL
3 tbsp	chicken stock or water	45 mL
12 oz	penne	375 g
1 tsp	vegetable oil	5 mL
1 tsp	minced garlic	5 mL
1 1/3 cups	chopped onions	325 mL
1 3/4 cups	sliced mushrooms	425 mL
2 1/4 cups	chopped fresh plum tomatoes	550 mL
1/2 cup	green peas	125 mL

1. In nonstick skillet sprayed with vegetable spray, cook beef just until desired doneness. Drain and set aside.

2. Pesto: Put basil, olive oil, Parmesan, pine nuts and garlic in food processor; process until finely chopped. Gradually add the stock through the feed tube and process until smooth. Put pesto in serving bowl.

3. In large pot of boiling water, cook the penne until tender but firm. Meanwhile, heat oil in nonstick skillet over medium heat; cook garlic and onions for 4 minutes until brown. Add mushrooms and sauté for 4 minutes until tender. Add tomatoes and peas and cook for 2 minutes more to heat through.

4. Place drained pasta in serving bowl along with vegetables and steak; toss and serve.

PER SERVING	
Calories	399
Protein	18 g
Fat, total	12 g
Fat, saturated	2 g
Carbohydrates	55 g
Sodium	376 mg
Cholesterol	16 mg
Fiber	4 g

TERIYAKI CHICKEN STIR-FRY WITH ASPARAGUS AND RED PEPPERS

Serves 6

Sauce

1/2 cup	chicken stock or water	125 mL
1/4 cup	rice wine vinegar	50 mL
4 tbsp	honey	60 mL
3 tbsp	soya sauce	45 mL
1 tbsp	sesame oil	15 mL
2 tsp	minced garlic	10 mL
2 tsp	minced ginger	10 mL
2 1/2 tsp	cornstarch	12 mL
12 oz	penne	375 g
12 oz	boneless, skinless chicken breast, cut into thin strips	375 g
2 tsp	vegetable oil	10 mL
1 1/2 cups	sliced red peppers	375 mL
1 1/2 cups	asparagus cut into 1-inch (2.5 cm) pieces	375 mL

1. In small bowl, combine stock, vinegar, honey, soya sauce, sesame oil, garlic, ginger and cornstarch; mix well.

2. In large pot of boiling water, cook penne until tender but firm. Drain and place in serving bowl. Meanwhile, in wok or skillet sprayed with vegetable spray, stir-fry chicken for 2 1/2 minutes or until just cooked at center. Drain any excess liquid and remove chicken from wok.

3. Add oil to wok and stir-fry red peppers and asparagus for 4 minutes or until tender-crisp; stir sauce again and add to wok along with chicken. Cook for 1 minute or until slightly thickened. Toss with drained pasta.

BOW-TIE PASTA WITH CHICKEN ALFREDO SAUCE

Serves 6

TIP

Cooking the entire chicken breast before slicing gives a moister piece.

If using fresh tarragon, chop 1/3 cup (75 mL) and add just before tossing entire pasta dish. Basil can replace tarragon.

MAKE AHEAD

Prepare sauce up to a day ahead. Reheat gently, adding more stock if too thick.

12 oz	skinless, boneless chicken breasts	375 g

Sauce

1 tbsp	margarine or butter	15 mL
2 tbsp	all-purpose flour	25 mL
1 cup	2% milk	250 mL
1 cup	chicken stock	250 mL
2 tsp	dried tarragon	10 mL
1/4 cup	grated Parmesan cheese	50 mL
2 tsp	vegetable oil	10 mL
2 tsp	minced garlic	10 mL
1 cup	chopped onions	250 mL
1 cup	chopped red or green peppers	250 mL
12 oz	bow-tie pasta	375 g

1. In nonstick skillet sprayed with vegetable spray, cook whole chicken breasts over medium-high heat until browned; turn over and cook for 3 minutes more, or until just done at center. Let cool slightly and slice into thin strips. Set aside.

2. In small saucepan, melt margarine over medium heat; add flour and cook, stirring, for 1 minute. Gradually add milk and stock, stirring constantly, just until mixture thickens slightly (approximately 5 minutes). Add tarragon and cook for 2 more minutes. Add Parmesan and remove from heat.

3. Meanwhile, in saucepan, heat vegetable oil over medium heat; add garlic and onions and sauté for 4 minutes until browned. Add red peppers and sauté for 4 minutes or until softened. Set aside. In large pot of boiling water, cook pasta according to package directions or until tender but firm; drain. Put pasta, chicken and cooked vegetables in serving bowl. Add sauce, toss and serve.

PER SERVING	
Calories	365
Protein	24 g
Fat, total	7 g
Fat, saturated	2 g
Carbohydrates	50 g
Sodium	307 mg
Cholesterol	37 mg
Fiber	2 g

WARM CAESAR PASTA SALAD

TIP

Great variation on Caesar salad and a lot healthier.

Sauce is wonderful served over cooked vegetables, fish, chicken or meat.

★

If prosciutto is not available, use sliced ham or smoked salmon.

MAKE AHEAD

Prepare sauce up to a day ahead. Refrigerate. Toss just before serving.

Sauce

1	egg	1
3	anchovies, chopped	3
3 tbsp	olive oil	45 mL
2 tbsp	grated Parmesan cheese	25 mL
1 tbsp	lemon juice	15 mL
1 tbsp	red wine vinegar	15 mL
2 tsp	Dijon mustard	10 mL
1 1/2 tsp	minced garlic	7 mL
2 cups	washed, dried and torn romaine lettuce	500 mL
2 oz	prosciutto, shredded	50 g
12 oz	penne	375 g

1. Put egg, anchovies, olive oil, Parmesan, lemon juice, vinegar, mustard and garlic in food processor; process until smooth.

2. Put lettuce and prosciutto in large serving bowl. In large pot of boiling water, cook pasta according to package directions or until tender but firm; drain and add to serving bowl. Pour dressing over pasta and toss.

PER SERVING

Calories	353
Protein	14 g
Fat, total	11 g
Fat, saturated	3 g
Carbohydrates	48 g
Sodium	325 mg
Cholesterol	45 mg
Fiber	2 g

PASTA WITH CREAMY SZECHUAN DRESSING AND CRISP VEGETABLES

Serves 4

TIP

Great pasta that can be served either cold, warm, or at room temperature.

If coriander is not available (or isn't a family favorite), use basil, dill or parsley.

This sauce can be used for other pastas or vegetable dishes or over fish or chicken.

MAKE AHEAD

Prepare sauce up to a day ahead, keeping refrigerated.

Sauce

1/4 cup	light mayonnaise	50 mL
3 tbsp	soya sauce	45 mL
2 tbsp	chicken stock	25 mL
2 tbsp	sesame oil	25 mL
1 tbsp	honey	15 mL
2 tsp	minced garlic	10 mL
1 1/2 tsp	minced ginger	7 mL
1/2 cup	sliced carrots	125 mL
1 cup	halved snow peas	250 mL
3/4 cup	canned baby corn cobs, sliced	175 mL
3/4 cup	chopped red or green peppers	175 mL
1/2 cup	chopped fresh coriander	125 mL
2	green onions, chopped	2
8 oz	capellini	250 g

1. In food processor combine mayonnaise, soya sauce, stock, sesame oil, honey, garlic and ginger; process until smooth.

2. Cook the carrots in boiling water or in microwave for 3 minutes or until tender-crisp; rinse with cold water, drain and put in serving bowl. Repeat with snow peas, cooking for 1 minute or until tender-crisp. Drain and rinse with cold water.

3. Place vegetables in serving bowl, along with baby corn cobs, red peppers, coriander and green onions.

4. Cook capellini in large pot of boiling water according to package directions, or until tender but firm. Drain and add to serving bowl. Pour sauce over pasta, toss and serve.

PER SERVING

Calories	358
Protein	11 g
Fat, total	10 g
Fat, saturated	1 g
Carbohydrates	57 g
Sodium	1240 mg
Cholesterol	0 mg
Fiber	3 g

FETTUCCINE WITH SPRING VEGETABLES IN A GOAT CHEESE SAUCE

1 1/2 cups	halved snow peas or sugar snap peas	375 mL
1 cup	asparagus cut into 1-inch (2.5 cm) pieces	250 mL
1 cup	cherry tomatoes, cut in half	250 mL

Sauce

1 tbsp	margarine or butter	15 mL
2 tbsp	all-purpose flour	25 mL
1 cup	2% milk	250 mL
1 cup	chicken stock	250 mL
1/3 cup	sun-dried tomatoes	75 mL
3 tbsp	grated Parmesan cheese	45 mL
4 oz	goat cheese	125 g
1/4 tsp	ground black pepper	1 mL
12 oz	fettuccine	375 g

1. Pour boiling water over sun-dried tomatoes and allow to soften for 15 minutes. Drain and chop. Set aside.

2. In a saucepan of boiling water or in microwave, cook snow peas for 1 minute or until tender-crisp; refresh in cold water and drain. Repeat with asparagus for 2 minutes or until tender-crisp; refresh in cold water and drain. Put peas, asparagus and cherry tomatoes in large serving bowl.

3. In saucepan, melt margarine over medium heat; add flour and cook, stirring, for 1 minute. Gradually add milk and stock and cook, stirring, until sauce begins to thicken slightly, approximately 4 minutes. Reduce heat to low; add sun-dried tomatoes, Parmesan and goat cheeses and pepper. Stir until cheese melts. Remove from heat.

4. In large pot of boiling water, cook pasta according to package directions or until tender but firm; drain and add to serving bowl. Pour sauce over pasta and toss.

BROCCOLI PESTO FETTUCCINE

TIP

Great variation on pesto sauce.

Toast pine nuts on top of stove in a nonstick skillet for 2 minutes or until browned.

To make a complete meal, add 8 oz (250 g) sautéed chicken, fish or beef.

MAKE AHEAD

Prepare pesto early in the day, keeping covered. Pour over hot pasta just before serving.

2 cups	broccoli florets	500 mL
1/2 cup	chopped fresh basil or parsley	125 mL
3 tbsp	olive oil	45 mL
3 tbsp	grated Parmesan cheese	45 mL
3 tbsp	toasted pine nuts	45 mL
1 1/2 tsp	minced garlic	7 mL
1/2 cup	chicken stock	125 mL
12 oz	fettuccine	375 g

1. Cook broccoli in boiling water or in microwave for 4 minutes, or until tender. Drain and put in food processor along with basil, olive oil, Parmesan, pine nuts and garlic; process until finely chopped. With machine running, add stock through the feed tube; process until smooth.

2. In large pot of boiling water, cook pasta according to package directions, or until tender but firm; drain and place in serving bowl. Pour broccoli pesto over top and toss.

PER SERVING

Calories	322
Protein	11 g
Fat, total	11 g
Fat, saturated	2 g
Carbohydrates	45 g
Sodium	149 mg
Cholesterol	2 mg
Fiber	3 g

Manicotti Stuffed with Chick Peas and Cheese

TIP

As an alternative, use about 16 jumbo pasta shells, with 2 tbsp (25 mL) of stuffing per shell.

Substitute Swiss or mozzarella for Cheddar.

MAKE AHEAD

Stuff shells and make sauce up to a day ahead. Pour over just before baking. If sauce is too thick, add extra stock.

Preheat oven to 350° C (180° C)

9- by 13-inch baking dish (3 L) sprayed with vegetable spray

10	manicotti shells	10

Sauce

2 tsp	margarine or butter	10 mL
1 tbsp	all-purpose flour	15 mL
1/2 cup	2% milk	125 mL
1/2 cup	chicken stock	125 mL
2 tbsp	grated Parmesan cheese	25 mL
1 1/2 cups	canned chick peas, drained	375 mL
1 cup	5% ricotta cheese	250 mL
1/2 cup	chopped green onions (about 4 medium)	125 mL
1/3 cup	grated Cheddar cheese	75 mL
1	egg	1
2 tbsp	grated Parmesan cheese	25 mL
1 1/2 tsp	minced garlic	7 mL
1 tsp	dried basil	5 mL
1 tbsp	grated Parmesan cheese	15 mL

1. In large pot of boiling water, cook pasta according to package directions or until tender but firm; rinse under cold water and drain.

2. In saucepan, melt margarine over medium heat; add flour and cook, stirring, for 1 minute. Gradually add milk and stock, stirring constantly, until sauce begins to simmer and thicken slightly, about 7 minutes. Stir in Parmesan and remove from heat.

3. Put chick peas, ricotta, green onions, Cheddar cheese, egg, Parmesan, garlic and basil in food processor; pulse on and off until well mixed. Stuff 3 tbsp (45 mL) into each shell and put in prepared dish. Pour white sauce over, sprinkle with remaining Parmesan, cover and bake for 15 minutes or until heated through.

PER SERVING (5)	
Calories	378
Protein	23 g
Fat, total	12 g
Fat, saturated	6 g
Carbohydrates	45 g
Sodium	482 mg
Cholesterol	73 mg
Fiber	5 g

SHELLS STUFFED WITH SPICY SAUSAGE AND RICOTTA

Serves 4

TIP

Pasta shells sometimes break when you cook them; boil a few extra to make sure you end up with enough to stuff.

Instead of using jumbo shells, use about 8 manicotti shells; fill each with about 3 tbsp (45 mL) of filling.

Mild sausage can replace the spicy variety.

MAKE AHEAD

Prepare stuffed shells up to a day ahead. Bake until hot, just before serving.

If reheating for leftovers, add extra tomato sauce over top.

Preheat oven to 350° F (180° C)

9- by 13-inch baking dish (3 L) sprayed with vegetable spray

14-16	jumbo pasta shells	14-16
1 tsp	vegetable oil	5 mL
1 tsp	minced garlic	5 mL
1/2 cup	chopped onions	125 mL
1/2 cup	chopped green peppers	125 mL
6 oz	spicy Italian sausage, chopped, casings removed	150 g
1 1/2 cups	5% ricotta cheese	375 mL
1/4 cup	chopped fresh parsley	50 mL
2 tbsp	2% milk	25 mL
2 tbsp	grated Parmesan cheese	25 mL
1/2 cup	tomato pasta sauce	125 mL

1. In large pot of boiling water, cook the pasta according to package directions or until tender but firm; rinse under cold water and drain.

2. In nonstick saucepan sprayed with vegetable spray, heat oil over medium heat. Cook garlic, onions and green peppers for 4 minutes or until softened. Add sausage and cook, stirring to break it up, for 3 minutes or until it is no longer pink. Pour off any excess fat from sausage. Stir in ricotta, parsley, milk and Parmesan and remove from heat.

3. Stuff each shell with approximately 2 tbsp (25 mL) filling and put in prepared dish. Spoon sauce over top, cover and bake for 20 minutes, or until heated through.

PER SERVING

Calories	380
Protein	25 g
Fat, total	16 g
Fat, saturated	7 g
Carbohydrates	34 g
Sodium	595 mg
Cholesterol	54 mg
Fiber	2 g

JUMBO SHELLS STUFFED WITH PESTO AND RICOTTA CHEESE

Serves 6

TIP

Pasta shells sometimes break when you cook them; boil a few extra to make sure you end up with enough to stuff.

Instead of using jumbo shells, use about 9 manicotti shells; fill each with 3 tbsp (45 mL) of filling.

Use spinach or parsley if basil is unavailable.

MAKE AHEAD

Prepare and stuff these up to a day ahead. Pour sauce over and bake just before serving, until hot.

PER SERVING

Calories	259
Protein	16 g
Fat, total	11 g
Fat, saturated	4 g
Carbohydrates	25 g
Sodium	302 mg
Cholesterol	25 mg
Fiber	1 g

Preheat oven to 350° F (180° C)

9- by 13-inch baking dish (3 L) sprayed with vegetable spray

18	jumbo pasta shells	18

Pesto Sauce

1 cup	well-packed basil leaves	250 mL
2 tbsp	olive oil	25 mL
1 1/2 tbsp	grated Parmesan cheese	20 mL
1 1/2 tbsp	toasted pine nuts	20 mL
1 tsp	minced garlic	5 mL
1/4 cup	chicken stock	50 mL
1 3/4 cups	5% ricotta cheese	425 mL
2/3 cup	tomato pasta sauce	150 mL
1 tbsp	grated Parmesan cheese	15 mL

1. In large pot of boiling water, cook the pasta according to package directions, or until tender but firm; rinse under cold water and drain. Set aside.

2. Put basil, olive oil, Parmesan, pine nuts and garlic in food processor; process until finely chopped, scraping sides of bowl once. With machine running, gradually add stock through the feed tube; process until smooth. Stir together pesto and ricotta.

3. Stuff each shell with approximately 1 1/2 tbsp (20 mL) of pesto mixture and put in pan. Pour tomato sauce over top and sprinkle with Parmesan. Cover and bake for 15 minutes or until heated through.

CREAMY SUN-DRIED TOMATO AND GOAT CHEESE LASAGNA

Serves 8

TIP

Toast pine nuts in a nonstick skillet for 2 minutes until browned.

Sun-dried tomato sauce can be used for other pastas, or as a sauce for fish or chicken.

MAKE AHEAD

Prepare sun-dried tomato sauce up to 2 days ahead, or freeze for up to 6 weeks.

Prepare white sauce up to 1 day ahead, adding more stock if it becomes too thick.

PER SERVING

Calories	276
Protein	10 g
Fat, total	14 g
Fat, saturated	2 g
Carbohydrates	31 g
Sodium	751 mg
Cholesterol	4 mg
Fiber	1 g

Preheat oven to 350° F (180° C)

9- by 13-inch (3 L) baking dish

9	lasagna noodles	9
4 oz	goat cheese	125 g
1/2 cup	sliced black olives	125 mL

Sun-Dried Tomato Sauce

4 oz	sun-dried tomatoes	125 g
1/2 cup	chopped fresh parsley	125 mL
3 tbsp	olive oil	45 mL
3 tbsp	grated Parmesan cheese	45 mL
2 tbsp	toasted pine nuts	25 mL
2 tsp	minced garlic	10 mL
1 cup	chicken stock	250 mL

White Sauce

1 tbsp	margarine or butter	15 mL
2 1/2 tbsp	all-purpose flour	32 mL
1 cup	2% milk	250 mL
1 cup	chicken stock	250 mL

1. Pour boiling water over sun-dried tomatoes. Let soften for 15 minutes. Drain and chop.

2. In large pot of boiling water, cook the lasagna noodles according to package directions or until tender but firm; rinse under cold water, drain and set aside.

3. Tomato Sauce: Put sun-dried tomatoes, parsley, olive oil, Parmesan, pine nuts and garlic in food processor; process until finely chopped, scraping sides of bowl once. With machine running, gradually add stock through the feed tube; process until smooth. Set aside.

4. White Sauce: Melt margarine in saucepan over medium heat; add flour and cook, stirring, for 1 minute. Gradually add milk and stock, stirring constantly; cook until sauce begins to simmer and thicken slightly, about 7 minutes.

5. Spread one-third of white sauce over bottom of baking dish; top with 3 lasagna noodles. Spread one-third of sun-dried tomato sauce over noodles; top with one-third of goat cheese and one-third of olives. Repeat layers twice more. Cover and bake for 25 minutes or until heated through.

GNOCCHI WITH TOMATOES, OLIVES AND GOAT CHEESE

TIP

Replace gnocchi with tortellini or ravioli.

★

This recipe can be halved.

★

Green olives add a distinct flavor, but can be replaced with black olives.

★

Goat cheese can be replaced with feta or, if a milder taste is desired, use ricotta cheese.

MAKE AHEAD

Sauce can be prepared early in the day and reheated. If too thick, add a little water.

2 tsp	vegetable oil	10 mL
2 tsp	minced garlic	10 mL
3/4 cup	chopped onions	175 mL
1	can (19 oz [540 mL]) tomatoes, crushed	1
1/3 cup	sliced stuffed green olives	75 mL
1 tsp	dried basil	5 mL
1/2 tsp	dried oregano	2 mL
1	bay leaf	1
2 oz	goat cheese	50 g
1 1/2 lb	potato gnocchi	750 g

1. In nonstick saucepan, heat oil over medium heat. Add garlic and onions and cook for 4 minutes or until softened. Add tomatoes, olives, basil, oregano and bay leaf; bring to a boil, reduce heat to medium-low and cook uncovered for 15 minutes, or until thickened, stirring occasionally. Add goat cheese and stir until it melts. Set aside.

2. In large pot of boiling water, cook gnocchi according to package directions; drain. Serve sauce over gnocchi.

PER SERVING (6)

Calories	317
Protein	9 g
Fat, total	7 g
Fat, saturated	2 g
Carbohydrates	55 g
Sodium	504 mg
Cholesterol	5 mg
Fiber	4 g

VEGETABLE HOISIN FRIED RICE

Serves 4

TIP

Use 3 cups (750 mL) leftover plain boiled rice.

Other vegetables can be substituted.

MAKE AHEAD

Prepare early in the day and gently reheat before serving.

1 cup	white rice	250 mL
1/4 cup	chicken stock	50 mL
2 tbsp	soya sauce	25 mL
2 tbsp	hoisin sauce	25 mL
1/2 cup	chopped carrots	125 mL
1 tbsp	vegetable oil	15 mL
1 tsp	minced garlic	5 mL
1 tsp	minced ginger root	5 mL
3/4 cup	chopped red peppers	175 mL
3/4 cup	chopped snow peas	175 mL
2	green onions, chopped	2

1. Bring 2 cups (500 mL) water to a boil in a saucepan; stir in rice, cover, reduce heat to medium and cook for 20 minutes or until liquid is absorbed. Remove from heat.

2. In small bowl, whisk together stock, soya sauce and hoisin sauce; set aside.

3. Cook carrots in boiling water or microwave for 4 minutes or until tender-crisp. Drain. Heat oil in wok or skillet over high heat. Add garlic, ginger, red peppers, snow peas and carrots; cook, stirring, for 2 minutes. Add rice; cook, stirring, 2 minutes longer. Add hoisin-soya mixture and cook for 1 minute longer. Serve garnished with green onions.

PER SERVING	
Calories	261
Protein	5 g
Fat, total	4 g
Fat, saturated	0.4 g
Carbohydrates	50 g
Sodium	578 mg
Cholesterol	0 mg
Fiber	2 g

MIXED-RICE-CRUST PIZZA WITH CHICKEN CACCIATORE TOPPING

Serves 6

TIP

Use goat cheese, mozzarella or Cheddar instead of feta.

This recipe can be prepared using all wild rice or all white rice.

To reduce cooking time of the sauce, drain canned tomatoes, purée and cook sauce for 10 minutes.

MAKE AHEAD

Prepare crust up to a day ahead and keep covered. Prepare filling early in the day and bake an extra 5 minutes to heat thoroughly.

Preheat oven to 400° F (200° C)

10- or 11-inch (25- or 28-cm) springform pan sprayed with vegetable spray

Crust

2 cups	chicken stock	500 mL
1/2 cup	wild rice	125 mL
1/2 cup	white rice	125 mL
1	egg	1
1/3 cup	2% milk	75 mL
3 tbsp	grated Parmesan cheese	45 mL

Topping

1 tsp	vegetable oil	5 mL
1 1/2 tsp	minced garlic	7 mL
1 cup	chopped onions	250 mL
1 cup	chopped red or green peppers	250 mL
1 cup	sliced mushrooms	250 mL
1	can (19 oz [540 mL]) tomatoes, crushed	1
1/4 cup	sliced black olives	50 mL
2 tbsp	tomato paste	25 mL
2 tsp	dried basil	10 mL
1 1/2 tsp	dried oregano	7 mL
8 oz	skinless, boneless chicken breast, cut into 1/2-inch (1-cm) cubes	250 g
1 1/2 oz	feta cheese	40 g

1. Bring stock to a boil; stir in wild and white rice, lower heat to medium, cover and cook for 20 minutes, or until liquid is absorbed. Put in bowl and let cool for 5 minutes; stir in egg, milk and Parmesan. Press into bottom of prepared pan and bake for 12 minutes; set aside.

PER SERVING

Calories	275
Protein	18 g
Fat, total	6 g
Fat, saturated	3 g
Carbohydrates	38 g
Sodium	794 mg
Cholesterol	68 mg
Fiber	3 g

2. In nonstick saucepan sprayed with vegetable spray, heat oil over medium heat. Add garlic and onions; cook for 4 minutes or until softened. Add peppers and mushrooms; cook for 2 minutes longer. Add tomatoes, olives, tomato paste, basil and oregano; bring to a boil, reduce heat to medium-low, cover and cook for 20 to 25 minutes, or until excess liquid is absorbed. Stir occasionally.

3. Stir in cubed chicken, cover and cook for 2 minutes, or until no longer pink. Pour over rice crust, sprinkle with cheese and bake for 12 minutes or until heated through.

RICE PILAF WITH ESCARGOTS AND SQUID

TIP

Boost spiciness by increasing chili powder to 1 1/2 tsp (7 mL) and capers to 3 tsp (15 mL).

Squid can be replaced with other firm seafood such as scallops or shrimp.

Goat cheese can be replaced with another strong-tasting cheese, such as feta, Swiss or aged Cheddar.

MAKE AHEAD

Prepare early in the day, but do not add seafood until just ready to serve. Great as leftovers.

2 tsp	vegetable oil	10 mL
2 tsp	minced garlic	10 mL
1 cup	chopped onions	250 mL
1 cup	white rice	250 mL
1 1/2 cups	chicken stock	375 mL
1 1/2 cups	crushed canned tomatoes	375 mL
1/3 cup	sliced black olives	75 mL
2 tsp	drained capers	10 mL
1 1/2 tsp	dried basil	7 mL
1 tsp	dried oregano	5 mL
1 tsp	chili powder	5 mL
2	anchovies, chopped	2
8 oz	squid cut into rings	250 g
1	can escargots, drained (about 24 to 26 snails)	1
1/4 cup	chopped fresh parsley	50 mL
2 oz	goat cheese	50 g

1. In nonstick saucepan, heat oil over medium heat. Add garlic and onions; cook for 4 minutes or until softened. Add rice and cook, stirring, for 2 minutes. Add stock, tomatoes, olives, capers, basil, oregano, chili powder and anchovies; bring to a boil, reduce heat to medium-low, cover and cook for 20 minutes or until rice is tender.

2. Stir in squid and escargots; cover and cook for 2 minutes or until squid is just cooked. Pour into serving dish; sprinkle with parsley and goat cheese.

PER SERVING

Calories	257
Protein	14 g
Fat, total	6 g
Fat, saturated	1 g
Carbohydrates	38 g
Sodium	671 mg
Cholesterol	99 mg
Fiber	2 g

COUSCOUS SALAD WITH TOMATOES, FETA CHEESE AND OLIVES

Serves 4 to 6

TIP

Another strong cheese can be substituted for feta. Goat, Cheddar or Swiss are ideal.

To eliminate excess liquid, deseed tomatoes or use plum tomatoes.

Bulgur can replace couscous.

MAKE AHEAD

Prepare entire salad early in the day and toss well before serving.

1 3/4 cups	chicken stock	425 mL
1 1/4 cups	couscous	300 mL
2 cups	chopped tomatoes	500 mL
3/4 cup	chopped cucumbers	175 mL
3/4 cup	chopped red or green peppers	175 mL
1/2 cup	crumbled feta cheese	125 mL
1/3 cup	sliced red onions	75 mL
1/3 cup	sliced black olives	75 mL
1/4 cup	chopped green onions (about 2 medium)	50 mL
1/2 cup	chopped fresh parsley (or 1 tbsp [15 mL] dried)	125 mL
1/2 cup	chopped fresh basil (or 1 tbsp [15 mL] dried)	125 mL

Dressing

3 tbsp	lemon juice	45 mL
2 tbsp	vegetable oil	25 mL
2 tsp	minced garlic	10 mL
1/4 tsp	ground black pepper	1 mL

1. Bring stock to boil in a saucepan. Add couscous and stir; cover and remove from heat. Let stand for 5 minutes.

2. In large serving bowl, combine tomatoes, cucumbers, red peppers, feta cheese, onions, olives, green onions, parsley and basil.

3. In small bowl, whisk together lemon juice, oil, garlic and pepper. Add to bowl along with couscous and toss.

PER SERVING (6)	
Calories	283
Protein	10 g
Fat, total	10 g
Fat, saturated	4 g
Carbohydrates	39 g
Sodium	603 mg
Cholesterol	20 mg
Fiber	2 g

BARLEY, TOMATO AND OLIVE CASSEROLE

TIP

If you don't like the taste of coriander (chinese parsley), substitute basil or dill.

If plum tomatoes are unavailable, use field tomatoes – deseeded to eliminate excess liquid.

The combination of flavors is delicious and unusual.

MAKE AHEAD

Prepare early in the day and reheat gently before serving. Tastes great next day.

PER SERVING	
Calories	140
Protein	5 g
Fat, total	3 g
Fat, saturated	0.4 g
Carbohydrates	27 g
Sodium	761 mg
Cholesterol	0 mg
Fiber	6 g

1 tsp	vegetable oil	5 mL
2 tsp	minced garlic	10 mL
1 cup	chopped red peppers	250 mL
1 cup	chopped green peppers	250 mL
3 cups	chicken stock	750 mL
3/4 cup	barley	175 mL
1/3 cup	sliced black olives	75 mL
1 tbsp	drained capers	15 mL
1 1/2 tsp	dried basil	7 mL
3/4 tsp	dried oregano	4 mL
1	dried bay leaf	1
1 1/2 cups	chopped plum tomatoes	375 mL
1/4 cup	chopped fresh coriander	50 mL
1/4 cup	chopped green onions (about 2 medium)	50 mL

1. In large nonstick saucepan, heat oil over medium heat; add garlic and red and green peppers and cook for 5 minutes, or until softened. Add stock, barley, olives, capers, basil, oregano and bay leaf; bring to a boil and cover. Reduce heat to low and cook covered for 35 minutes or until barley is tender. Add tomatoes, coriander and green onions and cook for 5 minutes longer.

FALAFEL BURGERS WITH CREAMY SESAME SAUCE

TIP

Replace coriander with dill or parsley.

Peanut butter can replace tahini.

MAKE AHEAD

Prepare burgers early in the day and refrigerate until ready to cook. Prepare sauce to up a day ahead.

2 cups	drained canned chick peas	500 mL
1/4 cup	chopped green onions	50 mL
1/4 cup	chopped fresh coriander	50 mL
1/4 cup	finely chopped carrots	50 mL
1/4 cup	bread crumbs	50 mL
3 tbsp	lemon juice	45 mL
3 tbsp	water	45 mL
2 tbsp	tahini (puréed sesame seeds)	25 mL
2 tsp	minced garlic	10 mL
1/4 tsp	ground black pepper	1 mL
2 tsp	vegetable oil	10 mL

Sauce

1/4 cup	light sour cream	50 mL
2 tbsp	tahini	25 mL
2 tbsp	chopped fresh coriander	25 mL
2 tbsp	water	25 mL
2 tsp	lemon juice	10 mL
1/2 tsp	minced garlic	2 mL

1. Put chick peas, green onions, coriander, carrots, bread crumbs, lemon juice, water, tahini, garlic and black pepper in food processor; pulse on and off until finely chopped. With wet hands, form each 1/4 cup (50 mL) into a patty.

2. In small bowl, whisk together sour cream, tahini, coriander, water, lemon juice and garlic.

3. In nonstick skillet sprayed with vegetable spray, heat 1 tsp (5 mL) of oil over medium heat. Add 4 patties and cook for 3 1/2 minutes or until golden; turn and cook 3 1/2 minutes longer or until golden and hot inside. Remove from pan. Heat remaining 1 tsp (5 mL) oil and cook remaining patties. Serve with sesame sauce.

PER SERVING

Calories	285
Protein	12 g
Fat, total	12 g
Fat, saturated	2 g
Carbohydrates	35 g
Sodium	276 mg
Cholesterol	5 mg
Fiber	7 g

POLENTA PIZZA WITH MUSHROOMS, OLIVES AND GOAT CHEESE

Serves 6

TIP

For a change, use 3 tbsp (45 mL) pesto sauce instead of tomato sauce.

★

Oyster mushrooms or another wild type is a great substitute.

★

Use feta, mozzarella or Cheddar instead of goat cheese.

MAKE AHEAD

Prepare cornmeal early in the day; pour in baking dish and cover.

Preheat oven to 400° F (200° C)

8-inch square (2 L) baking dish sprayed with vegetable spray

2 1/4 cups	chicken stock	550 mL
3/4 cup	yellow cornmeal	175 mL
1 tsp	minced garlic	5 mL
1/3 cup	tomato pasta sauce	75 mL
1/2 cup	sliced mushrooms	125 mL
1/3 cup	sliced black olives	75 mL
2 tbsp	chopped green onions (about 1 medium)	25 mL
1 oz	goat cheese	25 g

1. Bring stock to a boil in small saucepan; gradually add cornmeal and garlic, stirring constantly. Reduce heat to low and cook for 10 minutes, stirring frequently. Pour into prepared pan and smooth with the back of a wet spoon. Let cool for 10 minutes.

2. Spread tomato sauce over top. Sprinkle with mushrooms, olives and green onions; dot with goat cheese. Bake for 12 to 15 minutes or until heated through.

PER SERVING

Calories	104
Protein	3 g
Fat, total	3 g
Fat, saturated	0.3 g
Carbohydrates	17 g
Sodium	497 mg
Cholesterol	0 mg
Fiber	1 g

KIDS' FAVORITES

TIPS ON COOKING FOR CHILDREN

1. Children like tasty yet simple food. Do not over-spice or use ingredients that are foreign to their taste buds.

2. Children have a natural sweet tooth. Satisfy it by giving them the dessert recipes in this book that have fewer calories and lower cholesterol. Over time they will crave fewer commercial baked goods.

3. Foods that represent "fast food" to children — such as tortillas, chili, macaroni and cheese and "beefa-roni-type" dishes — are always a sure way to get them to eat with a smile on their faces.

4. Converting children and teenagers to eating better is easier than you might think. Do it slowly by introducing healthier versions of "fast foods." Once they start to enjoy these home-prepared foods, gradually introduce more sophisticated dishes. Over time, their taste for fatty foods will diminish as these new tasty foods enter into their repertoire.

PENNE WITH STEAK, PLUM TOMATOES AND PESTO (PAGE 170) ➤

ITALIAN PIZZA EGG ROLLS

Makes 9

Preheat oven to 425° F (220° C)
Baking sheet sprayed with vegetable spray

1 tsp	vegetable oil	5 mL
1 tsp	minced garlic	5 mL
1/4 cup	finely chopped carrots	50 mL
1/4 cup	finely chopped onions	50 mL
1/4 cup	finely chopped green peppers	50 mL
3 oz	lean ground beef	75 g
1/2 cup	tomato pasta sauce	125 mL
1/2 cup	grated mozzarella cheese (1 1/2 oz [40g])	125 mL
1 tbsp	grated Parmesan cheese	15 mL
9	egg roll wrappers (5 1/2 inches [13 cm] square)	9

TIP

Children devour these tasty egg rolls. Double the recipe if necessary.

Ground chicken or veal can replace beef.

Cheddar cheese can replace mozzarella for a more intense flavor.

Roll the wrappers any way that's easy. Wetting the edges of the wrappers with water may help secure roll.

MAKE AHEAD

Prepare these up to a day ahead and keep refrigerated. Bake an extra 5 minutes. These can also be prepared and frozen for up to a month.

1. In nonstick skillet sprayed with vegetable spray, heat oil over medium heat. Add garlic, carrots and onions; cook for 8 minutes, or until softened and browned. Add peppers and cook 2 minutes longer. Add beef and cook for 2 minutes, stirring to break it up, or until it is no longer pink. Remove from heat and stir in tomato sauce, mozzarella and Parmesan cheeses.

2. Keeping rest of wrappers covered with a cloth to prevent drying out, put one wrapper on work surface with a corner pointing towards you. Put 2 tbsp (25 mL) of the filling in the center. Fold the lower corner up over the filling, fold the 2 side corners in over the filling, and roll the bundle away from you. Put on prepared pan and repeat until all wrappers are filled. Bake for 14 minutes, until browned, turning the pizza rolls at the halfway mark.

PER SERVING

Calories	87
Protein	4 g
Fat, total	4 g
Fat, saturated	1 g
Carbohydrates	8 g
Sodium	138 mg
Cholesterol	9 mg
Fiber	0 g

◄ BANANA PEANUT BUTTER CHIP MUFFINS (PAGE 205); PEANUT BUTTER-COCONUT-RAISIN GRANOLA BARS (PAGE 206); OATMEAL DATE COOKIES (PAGE 237)

CREAMY BAKED BEEFARONI

Preheat oven to 450° F (230° C)

9- by 13-inch (3 L) baking dish sprayed with vegetable spray

Meat Sauce

1 tsp	vegetable oil	5 mL
2 tsp	minced garlic	10 mL
1 cup	chopped onions	250 mL
12 oz	lean ground beef	375 g
1 3/4 cups	tomato pasta sauce	425 mL
1/2 cup	beef or chicken stock	125 mL

Cheese Sauce

1 1/2 tbsp	margarine or butter	20 mL
1/4 cup	all-purpose flour	50 mL
2 cups	2% milk	500 mL
1 3/4 cups	beef or chicken stock	425 mL
1 cup	grated Cheddar cheese (3 1/2 oz [90 g])	250 mL
1 lb	penne	500 g
1/2 cup	grated mozzarella cheese	125 mL
2 tbsp	grated Parmesan cheese	25 mL

1. In nonstick saucepan, heat oil over medium heat. Cook garlic and onions for 4 minutes or until softened. Add beef, and cook, stirring to break it up, for 4 minutes or until no longer pink. Add tomato sauce and stock; simmer, covered, for 10 minutes or until thickened. Set aside.

2. In saucepan, melt margarine over medium-low heat. Add flour and cook, stirring, for 1 minute. Gradually add milk and stock. Cook, stirring constantly, until sauce begins to boil. Reduce heat to low and cook for 5 minutes, stirring occasionally, until slightly thickened. Stir in Cheddar cheese and remove from heat. Combine cheese sauce and meat sauce and set aside.

3. In large pot of boiling water, cook pasta according to package directions or until tender but firm; drain. Toss pasta with sauce and pour into prepared dish. Sprinkle with mozzarella and Parmesan cheeses and bake for 10 minutes or just until bubbly on top.

BEEF AND SAUSAGE SLOPPY JOES

Serves 6 to 8

TIP

Children often prefer this sauce smoother. If too chunky, run through the food processor.

★

If a livelier taste is desired, use spicy sausage.

★

This recipe can also be used as a pasta sauce.

MAKE AHEAD

Can be made up to 2 days ahead or frozen for up to 3 weeks. Great as leftovers.

2 tsp	vegetable oil	10 mL
1 cup	chopped onions	250 mL
2 tsp	minced garlic	10 mL
8 oz	lean ground beef	250 g
8 oz	mild Italian sausage, chopped, casings removed	250 g
4 cups	chopped fresh tomatoes (or 28 oz [796 mL] can, drained, chopped tomatoes)	1 L
1 1/2 tsp	dried basil	7 mL
1 tsp	chili powder	5 mL
1/2 tsp	dried oregano	2 mL
2 tbsp	grated Parmesan cheese (optional)	25 mL

1. In large nonstick skillet, heat oil over medium heat; add onions and garlic and cook for 4 minutes or until softened. Add ground beef and sausage and cook for 5 minutes, breaking up meat with a spoon, or until no longer pink. Drain off excess fat.

2. Add tomatoes, basil, chili powder and oregano; bring to a boil, reduce heat to low and simmer uncovered for 30 minutes, stirring occasionally. Serve over toasted hamburger buns. Sprinkle with Parmesan cheese if desired.

PER SERVING (8)	
Calories	230
Protein	12 g
Fat, total	16 g
Fat, saturated	6 g
Carbohydrates	10 g
Sodium	268 mg
Cholesterol	41 mg
Fiber	3 g

Spicy Meatball and Pasta Stew

Meatballs

8 oz	lean ground beef	250 g
1	egg	1
2 tbsp	ketchup or chili sauce	25 mL
2 tbsp	seasoned bread crumbs	25 mL
1 tsp	minced garlic	5 mL
1/2 tsp	chili powder	2 mL

Stew

2 tsp	vegetable oil	10 mL
1 tsp	minced garlic	5 mL
1 1/4 cups	chopped onions	300 mL
3/4 cup	chopped carrots	175 mL
3 1/2 cups	beef stock	875 mL
1	can (19 oz [540 mL]) tomatoes, crushed	1
3/4 cup	canned chick peas, drained	175 mL
1 tbsp	tomato paste	15 mL
2 tsp	granulated sugar	10 mL
2 tsp	chili powder	10 mL
1 tsp	dried oregano	5 mL
1 1/4 tsp	dried basil	6 mL
2/3 cup	small shell pasta	150 mL

1. In large bowl, combine ground beef, egg, ketchup, bread crumbs, garlic and chili powder; mix well. Form each 1/2 tbsp (7 mL) into a meatball and place on a baking sheet; cover and set aside.

2. In large nonstick saucepan, heat oil over medium heat. Add garlic, onions and carrots and cook for 5 minutes or until onions are softened. Stir in stock, tomatoes, chick peas, tomato paste, sugar, chili powder, oregano and basil; bring to a boil, reduce heat to medium-low, cover and let cook for 20 minutes. Bring to a boil again and stir in pasta and meatballs; let simmer for 10 minutes or until pasta is tender but firm, and meatballs are cooked.

CHICKEN TORTILLAS

TIP

Boneless turkey breast, pork or veal scallopini can replace chicken.

The cheese adds a creamy texture to the tortillas. Mozzarella can also be used.

MAKE AHEAD

Prepare filling early in the day and gently reheat before stuffing tortillas. Add extra stock if sauce is too thick.

Preheat oven to 375° F (190° C)

Baking sheet sprayed with vegetable spray

6 oz	skinless, boneless chicken breast, diced	150 g
1 tsp	vegetable oil	5 mL
1 tsp	crushed garlic	5 mL
1 cup	chopped onions	250 mL
1/2 cup	finely chopped carrots	125 mL
1 cup	tomato pasta sauce	250 mL
1 cup	canned red kidney beans, drained	250 mL
1/2 cup	chicken stock	125 mL
1 tsp	chili powder	5 mL
8	small 6-inch (15-cm) flour tortillas	8
1/2 cup	shredded Cheddar cheese (optional)	125 mL

1. In nonstick skillet sprayed with vegetable spray, cook chicken over high heat for 2 minutes, or until done at center. Remove from skillet and set aside.

2. Reduce heat to medium and add oil to pan. Respray with vegetable spray and cook garlic, onions, and carrots for 10 minutes, or until browned and softened, stirring often. Add some water if vegetables start to burn. Add tomato sauce, beans, stock and chili powder and cook for 10 to 12 minutes or until carrots are tender, mixture has thickened and most of the liquid is absorbed. Stir in chicken and remove from heat.

3. Put 1/3 cup (75 mL) of mixture on each tortilla, sprinkle with cheese (if using) and roll up. Put on prepared baking sheet and bake for 10 minutes or until heated through.

PER SERVING

Calories	438
Protein	21 g
Fat, total	10 g
Fat, saturated	2 g
Carbohydrates	65 g
Sodium	884 mg
Cholesterol	25 mg
Fiber	7 g

SWEET AND SOUR CHICKEN MEATBALLS OVER RICE

Serves 8

TIP

If your kids don't like rice, serve this dish over 1 lb (500 g) of spaghetti.

You can omit onions.

If children like pineapple, add 1 cup (250 mL) pineapple cubes (canned or fresh) at the end of the cooking time.

MAKE AHEAD

Make up to 2 days ahead and reheat. Can be frozen for up to 6 weeks. Great for leftovers.

PER SERVING

Calories	351
Protein	15 g
Fat, total	6 g
Fat, saturated	2 g
Carbohydrates	58 g
Sodium	558 mg
Cholesterol	54 mg
Fiber	2 g

Meatballs

12 oz	ground chicken	375 g
1/4 cup	finely chopped onions	50 mL
2 tbsp	ketchup	25 mL
2 tbsp	bread crumbs	25 mL
1	egg	1
2 tsp	olive oil	10 mL
2 tsp	minced garlic	10 mL
1/3 cup	chopped onions	75 mL
2 cups	tomato juice	500 mL
2 cups	pineapple juice	500 mL
1/2 cup	chili sauce	125 mL
2 cups	white rice	500 mL

1. In bowl, combine chicken, onions, ketchup, bread crumbs and egg; mix well. Form each 1 tbsp (15 mL) into a meatball and place on plate; set aside.

2. In large saucepan, heat oil over medium heat. Add garlic and onions and cook just until softened, approximately 3 minutes. Add tomato and pineapple juices, chili sauce and meatballs. Simmer uncovered for 30 to 40 minutes just until meatballs are tender.

3. Meanwhile, bring 4 cups (1 L) of water to a boil. Stir in rice, reduce heat, cover and simmer for 20 minutes or until liquid is absorbed. Remove from heat and let stand for 5 minutes, covered. Serve meatballs and sauce over rice.

CRUNCHY CHEESE AND HERB DRUMSTICKS

TIP

Use bran flakes, not All-Bran, bran buds or natural bran. Bran flakes have a sweetness that children love.

MAKE AHEAD

Coat these drumsticks up to a day ahead. These can be baked a few hours in advance and gently reheated. Great for leftovers.

Preheat oven to 400° F (200° C)

Baking sheet sprayed with vegetable spray

1 1/2 cups	bran flakes cereal or corn flakes	375 mL
1 1/2 tbsp	fresh chopped parsley	20 mL
2 1/2 tbsp	grated Parmesan cheese	35 mL
1 tsp	minced garlic	5 mL
3/4 tsp	dried basil	4 mL
1/2 tsp	chili powder	2 mL
1/8 tsp	ground black pepper	0.5 mL
1	egg	1
2 tbsp	milk or water	25 mL
8	chicken drumsticks, skin removed	8

1. Put bran flakes, parsley, Parmesan, garlic, basil, chili powder and pepper in food processor; process until bran flakes are fine crumbs. Place on plate.

2. In small bowl whisk together egg and milk. Dip each drumstick in egg wash, then roll in crumbs; place on prepared baking sheet. Bake for 35 minutes, turning halfway, until browned and chicken is cooked through.

PER SERVING

Calories	230
Protein	30 g
Fat, total	7 g
Fat, saturated	2 g
Carbohydrates	11 g
Sodium	345 mg
Cholesterol	153 mg
Fiber	1 g

POTATO WEDGE FRIES

TIP

Serve these fries with Drumsticks (page 199).

If children like spicier fries, use chili powder instead of paprika.

MAKE AHEAD

Cut potatoes early in the day and leave in cold water so they don't discolor.

Preheat oven to 375° F(190° C)

Baking sheet sprayed with vegetable spray

3	large potatoes	3
2 tbsp	melted margarine or butter	25 mL
1 tsp	minced garlic	5 mL
2 tbsp	grated Parmesan cheese	25 mL
1/4 tsp	paprika	1 mL

1. Scrub potatoes and cut lengthwise into 8 wedges. Put on prepared baking sheet. Combine margarine and garlic in a small bowl. Combine Parmesan and paprika in another small bowl.

2. Brush potato wedges with half of the margarine and cheese mixture. Bake for 20 minutes, turn the wedges, brush with remaining margarine mixture (reheat if necessary). Sprinkle on remaining Parmesan mixture, and bake for another 20 minutes or just until potatoes are tender and crisp.

PER SERVING

Calories	87
Protein	2 g
Fat, total	4 g
Fat, saturated	1 g
Carbohydrates	12 g
Sodium	78 mg
Cholesterol	1 mg
Fiber	1 g

HONEY COATED CRUNCHY CHICKEN FINGERS

Serves 6

TIP

Use a firm-fleshed white fish, cut into strips, instead of chicken.

About 3 cups (750 mL) corn flakes equals 1 cup (250 mL) crushed flakes.

MAKE AHEAD

These "fingers" can be coated early in the day and refrigerated. Bake before serving. Also excellent if gently reheated. These can be frozen and reheated for children's meals.

Preheat oven to 425° F (220° C)

Baking sheet sprayed with vegetable spray

1 lb	skinless, boneless chicken breasts	500 g
1/4 cup	honey (slightly warmed)	50 mL
1/4 cup	water	50 mL
1 cup	crushed corn flakes	250 mL

1. Cut chicken breasts crosswise into strips 3/4 inch (2 cm) wide. In small bowl combine honey and water. Put corn flakes on a plate.

2. Dip chicken strips in honey mixture then coat with corn flake crumbs. Put on prepared baking sheet. Bake for 10 minutes, or until cooked at center, turning chicken over at halfway point.

PER SERVING

Calories	174
Protein	18 g
Fat, total	1 g
Fat, saturated	0.3 g
Carbohydrates	23 g
Sodium	196 mg
Cholesterol	44 mg
Fiber	0 g

TURKEY MACARONI CHILI

Serves 8

TIP

Great mild-tasting chili that children love. Can be served as a soup or alongside rice or pasta.

Ground turkey can be replaced with ground chicken, beef or veal.

Red kidney beans can be replaced with white beans or chick peas.

MAKE AHEAD

Can be prepared up to 2 days ahead and reheated. Can be frozen for up to 3 weeks. Great for leftovers.

1 1/2 tsp	vegetable oil	7 mL
1 tsp	minced garlic	5 mL
1/2 cup	finely chopped carrots	125 mL
1 cup	chopped onions	250 mL
8 oz	ground turkey	250 g
1	can (19 oz [540 mL]) tomatoes, crushed	1
2 cups	chicken stock	500 mL
1 1/2 cups	peeled, diced potatoes	375 mL
3/4 cup	canned red kidney beans, drained	175 mL
3/4 cup	corn kernels	175 mL
2 tbsp	tomato paste	25 mL
1 1/2 tsp	chili powder	7 mL
1 1/2 tsp	dried oregano	7 mL
1 1/2 tsp	dried basil	7 mL
1/3 cup	elbow macaroni	75 mL

1. In large nonstick saucepan, heat oil over medium heat; add garlic, carrots and onions and cook for 8 minutes or until softened, stirring occasionally. Add turkey and cook, stirring to break it up, for 2 minutes or until no longer pink. Add tomatoes, stock, potatoes, beans, corn, tomato paste, chili, oregano and basil; bring to a boil, reduce heat to low, cover and simmer for 20 minutes.

2. Bring to a boil and add macaroni; cook for 12 minutes or until pasta is tender but firm.

PER SERVING	
Calories	161
Protein	10 g
Fat, total	4 g
Fat, saturated	1 g
Carbohydrates	23 g
Sodium	483 mg
Cholesterol	18 mg
Fiber	4 g

CRUNCHY BAKED MACARONI AND CHEESE CASSEROLE

TIP

If using whole corn flakes, use 1 1/2 cups (375 mL) to equal 1/2 cup (125 mL) crumbs.

Bran flakes are also a delicious substitute for corn flakes.

MAKE AHEAD

Can be prepared a day ahead and gently reheated in 350° F (180° C) oven.

Can be frozen in portions for up to 6 weeks. Great as leftovers.

Preheat oven to 450° F (230° C)

2-quart (2 L) casserole dish sprayed with vegetable spray

1 tbsp	margarine or butter	15 mL
3 tbsp	all-purpose flour	45 mL
1 1/4 cups	2% milk	300 mL
1 1/3 cups	chicken stock	325 mL
1 1/4 cup	grated Cheddar cheese (3 1/2 oz [90 g])	300 mL
12 oz	macaroni	375 g

Topping
1/2 cup	corn flake crumbs	125 mL
3 tbsp	grated Parmesan cheese	45 mL
1 tsp	margarine or butter	5 mL

1. In saucepan over medium heat, melt margarine; add flour and cook, stirring, for 1 minute (mixture will be crumbly). Gradually add milk and stock, stirring constantly; let simmer for 5 to 8 minutes or until slightly thickened, stirring constantly. Stir in cheese and cook until melted, approximately 1 minute. Remove from heat.

2. In pot of boiling water cook the pasta according to package directions or until tender but firm; drain. Toss with cheese sauce and pour into prepared casserole dish.

3. In small bowl, combine corn flake crumbs, Parmesan and margarine. Sprinkle over casserole and bake just until top is browned, approximately 10 minutes.

PER SERVING

Calories	288
Protein	12 g
Fat, total	8 g
Fat, saturated	4 g
Carbohydrates	41 g
Sodium	375 mg
Cholesterol	18 mg
Fiber	1 g

RIGATONI WITH TOMATO BEAN SAUCE

Serves 8

TIP

Red kidney beans or small white navy beans can replace white beans.

Mashing the beans gives more texture to sauce.

Great as leftovers the next day. Add more stock if too dry.

MAKE AHEAD

Sauce can be made up to 2 days ahead or frozen for up to 6 weeks.

PER SERVING	
Calories	361
Protein	18 g
Fat, total	7 g
Fat, saturated	2 g
Carbohydrates	57 g
Sodium	452 mg
Cholesterol	18 mg
Fiber	7 g

1 tsp	vegetable oil	5 mL
2 tsp	minced garlic	10 mL
1/2 cup	chopped carrots	125 mL
1 cup	chopped zucchini	250 mL
1 cup	chopped onions	250 mL
8 oz	lean ground beef	250 g
1	can (19 oz [540 mL]) tomatoes, crushed	1
1 cup	chicken stock	250 mL
1 1/2 cups	canned white kidney beans, drained and mashed	375 mL
2 tsp	dried basil	10 mL
2 tsp	chili powder	10 mL
1 tsp	dried oregano	5 mL
1	bay leaf	1
1 lb	rigatoni	500 g
1/4 cup	grated Parmesan cheese	50 mL

1. In large nonstick saucepan sprayed with vegetable spray, heat oil over medium-high heat. Add garlic, carrots, zucchini and onions; cook for 8 minutes or until softened and browned, stirring occasionally. Add a little water if vegetables begin to burn. Add beef and cook, stirring to break it up, for 2 minutes or until no longer pink. Add tomatoes, stock, beans, basil, chili powder, oregano and bay leaf; bring to a boil, reduce heat to medium-low and simmer for 30 minutes, covered, stirring occasionally, or until carrots are tender and sauce is thickened.

2. Meanwhile, in large pot of boiling water, cook pasta according to package directions or until tender but firm; drain and place on serving platter. Pour sauce over pasta and sprinkle with Parmesan.

BANANA PEANUT BUTTER CHIP MUFFINS

Preheat oven to 375° F (190° C)

12 muffin cups sprayed with vegetable spray

2/3 cup	granulated sugar	150 mL
3 tbsp	vegetable oil	45 mL
3 tbsp	peanut butter	45 mL
1	large banana, mashed	1
1	egg	1
1 tsp	vanilla	5 mL
3/4 cup	all-purpose flour	175 mL
3/4 tsp	baking powder	4 mL
3/4 tsp	baking soda	4 mL
1/4 cup	2% yogurt	50 mL
3 tbsp	semi-sweet chocolate chips	45 mL

1. In large bowl or food processor, combine sugar, oil, peanut butter, banana, egg and vanilla; mix until well blended. In another bowl combine flour, baking powder and baking soda; add to batter and mix just until blended. Stir in yogurt and chocolate chips.

2. Fill muffin cups half-full. Bake for 15 to 18 minutes, or until tops are firm to the touch and cake tester inserted in the center comes out dry.

Peanut Butter-Coconut-Raisin Granola Bars

Makes 25 bars

TIP

Corn flakes can replace bran flakes. Don't worry if you only have raisin bran on hand.

★

Chopped dates can replace raisins.

★

Use a natural smooth or chunky peanut butter.

★

Do not overcook the peanut butter mixture.

MAKE AHEAD

Prepare these up to 2 days ahead and keep tightly closed in a cookie tin. These freeze for up to 2 weeks.

Preheat oven to 350° F (180° C)

9-inch square (2.5 L) pan sprayed with vegetable spray

1 1/3 cups	rolled oats	325 mL
2/3 cup	raisins	150 mL
1/2 cup	bran flakes	125 mL
1/3 cup	unsweetened coconut	75 mL
3 tbsp	chocolate chips	45 mL
2 tbsp	chopped pecans	25 mL
1 tsp	baking soda	5 mL
1/4 cup	peanut butter	50 mL
1/4 cup	brown sugar	50 mL
3 tbsp	margarine or butter	45 mL
3 tbsp	honey	45 mL
1 tsp	vanilla	5 mL

1. Put oats, raisins, bran flakes, coconut, chocolate chips, pecans and baking soda in bowl. Combine until well mixed.

2. In small saucepan, whisk together peanut butter, brown sugar, margarine, honey and vanilla over medium heat for approximately 30 seconds or just until sugar dissolves and mixture is smooth. Pour over dry ingredients and stir to combine. Press into prepared pan and bake for 15 to 20 minutes or until browned. Let cool completely before cutting into bars.

PER BAR

Calories	88
Protein	2 g
Fat, total	4 g
Fat, saturated	1 g
Carbohydrates	12 g
Sodium	77 mg
Cholesterol	0 mg
Fiber	1 g

PEANUT BUTTER FUDGE COOKIES

Makes 40 cookies

TIP

Chopped dates can replace raisins.

Use a natural peanut butter, smooth or chunky.

MAKE AHEAD

Cookies never last long, but these can be made up to a day ahead, kept tightly covered in a cookie jar or tin.

Prepare cookie dough and freeze up to 2 weeks, then bake.

Preheat oven to 350° F (180° C)

Baking sheets sprayed with vegetable spray

1/4 cup	softened margarine or butter	50 mL
1/3 cup	peanut butter	75 mL
3/4 cup	granulated sugar	175 mL
1/4 cup	brown sugar	50 mL
1	egg	1
1 tsp	vanilla	5 mL
1 cup	all-purpose flour	250 mL
1/4 cup	cocoa	50 mL
1 tsp	baking powder	5 mL
1/4 cup	2% yogurt	50 mL
3/4 cup	raisins	175 mL
3 tbsp	chocolate chips	45 mL

1. In large bowl, cream together margarine, peanut butter, sugar and brown sugar. Add egg and vanilla and beat well.

2. In another bowl, combine flour, cocoa and baking powder; add to peanut butter mixture and stir just until combined. Stir in yogurt, raisins and chocolate chips. Drop by heaping teaspoonful (15 mL) onto prepared sheets 2 inches (5 cm) apart, and press down slightly with back of fork. Bake approximately 12 minutes, or until firm to the touch and slightly browned.

PER COOKIE

Calories	67
Protein	1 g
Fat, total	2 g
Fat, saturated	0.6 g
Carbohydrates	11 g
Sodium	20 mg
Cholesterol	5 mg
Fiber	1 g

TRIPLE CHOCOLATE BROWNIES

Makes 16 brownies.

Preheat oven to 350° F (180° C)

8-inch square (2 L) cake pan sprayed with vegetable spray

1/2 cup	granulated sugar	125 mL
1/3 cup	margarine or butter	75 mL
1	egg	1
1 tsp	vanilla	5 mL
1/2 cup	all-purpose flour	125 mL
1/3 cup	cocoa	75 mL
1 tsp	baking powder	5 mL
1/4 cup	2% milk	50 mL
1/4 cup	chocolate chips	50 mL

Icing

1/4 cup	icing sugar	50 mL
1 1/2 tbsp	cocoa	20 mL
1 tbsp	milk	15 mL

TIP

Children love chocolate, but 1 oz (25 g) of chocolate has 140 calories and 9 g of fat. One ounce (25 g) of cocoa has 90 calories and 3 g of fat. Even though children should not be on "low-fat" diets, lowering excess fat is recommended.

MAKE AHEAD

Prepare up to a day ahead. These freeze well for up to 4 weeks. Great for lunch bags.

1. In bowl, beat together sugar and margarine. Beat in egg and vanilla, mixing well.

2. In another bowl, combine flour, cocoa and baking powder; stir into sugar and butter mixture just until blended. Stir in milk and chocolate chips. Pour into prepared pan and bake approximately 18 minutes or until edges start to pull away from pan and center is still a little wet. Let cool slightly before glazing.

3. In small bowl, whisk together icing sugar, cocoa and milk; pour over brownies in pan.

PER BROWNIE

Calories	102
Protein	2 g
Fat, total	5 g
Fat, saturated	1 g
Carbohydrates	14 g
Sodium	69 mg
Cholesterol	14 mg
Fiber	1 g

DESSERTS

DESSERT TIPS

1. Different types of ovens and utensils can affect baking times. To be on the safe side, 5 to 10 minutes before the baking time is up, check cakes, muffins and loaves. Stick a toothpick in several different points in the cake. If it comes out wet, continue baking. Brownies are the exception; their center should be wet when ready.

2. When mixing liquid and dry ingredients together for a cake batter, blend just until incorporated. Do not overmix.

3. Cheesecakes should appear a little loose before removing from oven to ensure moistness. Do not bake until set—that is, until they appear firm—or cheesecake can dry out.

4. Cookies can be baked longer than the recommended time to give them a crispy texture. Less baking time makes a softer, chewier cookie. Cookie dough can be frozen and used frozen on cookie sheets. Bake frozen cookie dough a few minutes longer than given in the recipe.

5. Cakes, cheesecakes, brownies, muffins and loaves can be frozen for up to 3 months if wrapped tightly. Do not freeze cakes with fruit garnishes. Add the garnish before serving.

6. Whole wheat flour can replace up to half the flour in a recipe. Do not add more or the cake will be heavy and dense.

7. Sifted icing sugar and cocoa can be sprinkled over cake tops for decoration. For a patterned effect, place a doily over the cake before sprinkling, then carefully remove it.

8. Desserts taste delicious and look great with puréed fruit sauce over top or alongside. Purée fresh or frozen strawberries or raspberries until smooth. Add

a little water for desired consistency. Raspberries may need a little icing sugar added.

9. Muffins and loaf recipes can be interchanged. The loaf recipes will need to bake approximately 10 minutes longer or until tester comes out dry.

10. Dessert batters can be mixed in a bowl with a whisk, in an electric mixer or in a food processor. If using a food processor, be careful to use on-and-off motion so as not to over-process.

MARBLE MOCHA CHEESECAKE

Serves 12

Preheat oven to 350° F (180° C)

8-inch (2 L) springform pan sprayed with vegetable spray

TIP

Serve with chocolate-dipped strawberries. Melt 2 oz (50 g) chocolate with 1 tsp (5 mL) vegetable oil. Dip the bottom half of the berry in chocolate.

Graham crackers or other cookie crumbs can be used for the crust.

Melt chocolate in microwave on defrost or in a double boiler.

If instant coffee is unavailable, use 2 tsp (10 mL) prepared strong coffee.

MAKE AHEAD

Bake up to 2 days ahead and keep refrigerated.

Freeze for up to 6 weeks.

Crust

1 1/2 cups	chocolate wafer crumbs	375 mL
2 tbsp	granulated sugar	25 mL
2 tbsp	water	25 mL
1 tbsp	margarine or butter	15 mL

Filling

1 2/3 cups	5% ricotta cheese	400 mL
1/3 cup	softened light cream cheese	75 mL
3/4 cup	granulated sugar	175 mL
1	egg	1
1/3 cup	light sour cream or 2% yogurt	75 mL
1 tbsp	all-purpose flour	15 mL
1 tsp	vanilla	5 mL
1 1/2 tsp	instant coffee granules	7 mL
1 1/2 tsp	hot water	7 mL
3 tbsp	semi-sweet chocolate chips, melted	45 mL

1. Combine chocolate crumbs, sugar, water and margarine; mix thoroughly. Press into bottom and up sides of springform pan.

2. In large bowl or food processor, beat together ricotta cheese, cream cheese, sugar, egg, sour cream, flour and vanilla until well blended. Dissolve coffee granules in hot water; add to batter and mix until incorporated.

3. Pour batter into springform pan and smooth top. Drizzle melted chocolate on top. Draw knife or spatula through the chocolate and batter several times to create marbling. Bake for 35 to 40 minutes; center will be slightly loose. Let cool, and refrigerate several hours before serving.

PER SERVING

Calories	210
Protein	8 g
Fat, total	7 g
Fat, saturated	4 g
Carbohydrates	29 g
Sodium	178 mg
Cholesterol	34 mg
Fiber	1 g

LEMON POPPY SEED CHEESECAKE

TIP

An electric mixer or electric hand-held beater can be used. Be certain that the cottage cheese is well blended.

MAKE AHEAD

Bake up to 2 days ahead, keeping refrigerated. Freeze for up to 4 weeks.

Preheat oven to 350° F (180° C)
8-inch (2 L) springform pan sprayed with vegetable spray

Crust

1 1/2 cups	vanilla wafer or graham cracker crumbs	375 mL
2 tbsp	granulated sugar	25 mL
1 1/2 tbsp	water	22 mL
1 tbsp	melted margarine or butter	15 mL

Filling

1 1/4 cups	5% ricotta cheese	300 mL
3/4 cup	2% cottage cheese	175 mL
3/4 cup	granulated sugar	175 mL
1	egg	1
1 tbsp	grated lemon zest	15 mL
3 tbsp	fresh lemon juice	45 mL
1 tbsp	poppy seeds	15 mL
3 tbsp	all-purpose flour	45 mL
1/4 cup	light sour cream	50 mL

Topping

1 cup	light sour cream	250 mL
3 tbsp	granulated sugar	45 mL
1 tsp	grated lemon zest	5 mL
1 tbsp	fresh lemon juice	15 mL

PER SERVING

Calories	220
Protein	9 g
Fat, total	7 g
Fat, saturated	4 g
Carbohydrates	33 g
Sodium	187 mg
Cholesterol	37 mg
Fiber	0 g

1. In bowl, combine crumbs, sugar, water and margarine; mix well. Press onto bottom and sides of springform pan. Set aside.

2. In food processor, combine ricotta cheese, cottage cheese, sugar, egg, lemon zest, lemon juice, poppy seeds, flour and sour cream; process until smooth. Pour into prepared crust; bake for 30 minutes.

3. Meanwhile, in small bowl, combine sour cream, sugar, lemon zest and lemon juice; mix well and pour over cake at end of 30 minutes and bake for 10 minutes longer. Let cool; chill before serving.

APPLE CINNAMON CHEESECAKE

Serves 12

TIP

Use vanilla wafer crumbs, or any dry cookie of your choice for the crust. Use food processor to break up whole cookies until they are crumbly.

Toast almonds in nonstick skillet on top of stove for 2 minutes until browned.

MAKE AHEAD

Bake up to 2 days ahead or freeze for up to 6 weeks. Tastes great even after 2 days in the refrigerator.

PER SERVING

Calories	241
Protein	10 g
Fat, total	6 g
Fat, saturated	4 g
Carbohydrates	37 g
Sodium	278 mg
Cholesterol	34 mg
Fiber	1 g

Preheat oven to 350° F (180° C)

8-inch (2 L) springform pan sprayed with vegetable spray

Crust

1 1/2 cups	graham cracker crumbs	375 mL
2 tbsp	granulated sugar	25 mL
2 tbsp	water	25 mL
1 tbsp	melted margarine or butter	15 mL
1/2 tsp	cinnamon	2 mL

Cake

1 cup	5% ricotta cheese	250 mL
1 cup	2% cottage cheese	250 mL
3/4 cup	granulated sugar	175 mL
3 tbsp	all-purpose flour	45 mL
1	egg	1
2 tsp	cinnamon	10 mL
1 1/2 tsp	vanilla	7 mL
1/4 tsp	almond extract	1 mL
1/2 cup	peeled, diced apples	125 mL

Topping

1 cup	light (1%) sour cream	250 mL
2 tbsp	granulated sugar	25 mL
1 tsp	vanilla	5 mL
1 tbsp	sliced toasted almonds	15 mL

1. In bowl, combine graham cracker crumbs, sugar, water, margarine and cinnamon; mix well. Press onto bottom and sides of springform pan; refrigerate.

2. Put ricotta cheese, cottage cheese, sugar, 2 tbsp (25 mL) of the flour, egg, 1 tsp (5 mL) of the cinnamon, vanilla and almond extract in food processor; process until smooth. In small bowl, combine remaining 1 tbsp (15 mL) flour and remaining 1 tsp (5 mL)

cinnamon with apples. Stir apple mixture into batter. Pour into pan and bake for 25 minutes or until set around edges but still slightly loose at center.

3. Meanwhile, in small bowl, stir together sour cream, sugar and vanilla; pour over cheesecake and sprinkle with nuts. Return to oven and bake for 10 minutes longer. Topping will be loose. Let cool and refrigerate for 3 hours or overnight.

PHYLLO CHEESECAKE WITH CHOCOLATE SAUCE

Serves 10

TIP

One-third cup (75 mL) chocolate chips can replace raisins. This will add slightly to calories and fat.

When working with phyllo, work quickly, and cover the phyllo not being used with a slightly damp towel.

★

The chocolate sauce can be made and refrigerated for several days.
Reheat before using.

MAKE AHEAD

Best if baked right before serving, but can be prepared early in the day. Cover tightly and keep refrigerated until ready to bake.

PER SERVING

Calories	200
Protein	6 g
Fat, total	3 g
Fat, saturated	1 g
Carbohydrates	38 g
Sodium	96 mg
Cholesterol	32 mg
Fiber	1 g

Preheat oven to 375° F (190° C)

Baking sheet sprayed with vegetable spray

Cheesecake

4 oz	light cream cheese	125 g
6 oz	5% ricotta cheese	150 g
3/4 cup	granulated sugar	175 mL
1	egg	1
1 tsp	vanilla	5 mL
1/2 cup	raisins	125 mL
5	sheets phyllo pastry	5
2 tsp	melted margarine or butter	10 mL

Chocolate Sauce

1/3 cup	granulated sugar	75 mL
1/4 cup	2% milk	50 mL
2 tbsp	cocoa	25 mL

1. In food processor, combine cream cheese, ricotta cheese, sugar, egg and vanilla; process until smooth. Stir in raisins.

2. Lay two phyllo sheets one on top of the other; brush with melted margarine. Layer another two phyllo sheets on top and brush with melted margarine. Lay last sheet on top. Put cheese filling over top of phyllo; fold sides in, and roll. Put on prepared baking sheet, brush with remaining margarine and bake for 25 to 30 minutes or until golden.

3. Combine sugar, milk and cocoa in saucepan; cook over medium heat, stirring, for 5 minutes or until smooth. Serve cheesecake with chocolate sauce.

SOUR CREAM CINNAMON COFFEE CAKE

Serves 12

TIP

This can be made in a 9-inch (3 L) bundt pan. Bake for 30 to 35 minutes or until tester comes out dry.

★

Raisins can be replaced with chopped dates.

MAKE AHEAD

Prepare up to a day ahead or freeze for up to 6 weeks.

Preheat oven to 350° F (180° C)

8.5-inch (2.25 L) springform pan sprayed with vegetable spray

Cake

1/3 cup	margarine or butter	75 mL
2/3 cup	granulated sugar	150 mL
2	eggs	2
1 tsp	vanilla	5 mL
1 1/4 cups	all purpose flour	300 mL
1 1/2 tsp	baking powder	7 mL
1 1/4 tsp	cinnamon	6 mL
1/2 tsp	baking soda	2 mL
1 cup	light sour cream or 2% yogurt	250 mL

Filling

2/3 cup	brown sugar	150 mL
1/2 cup	raisins	125 mL
3 tbsp	semi-sweet chocolate chips	45 mL
4 1/2 tsp	cocoa	22 mL
1/2 tsp	cinnamon	2 mL

1. In large bowl, cream together margarine and sugar; add eggs and vanilla and mix well. In bowl combine flour, baking powder, cinnamon and baking soda; stir into wet ingredients alternately with sour cream just until mixed.

2. Put brown sugar, raisins, chocolate chips, cocoa and cinnamon in food processor; process until crumbly.

3. Put half of batter into prepared pan; top with half of filling. Repeat layers. Bake for approximately 40 minutes or until cake tester inserted in the center comes out clean.

PER SERVING

Calories	235
Protein	5 g
Fat, total	7 g
Fat, saturated	3 g
Carbohydrates	41 g
Sodium	149 mg
Cholesterol	44 mg
Fiber	1 g

CHOCOLATE CHIP CRUMB CAKE

TIP

A 9-inch (3 L) springform pan can be used. Check baking at 30 to 40 minutes to see if it needs a few minutes longer.

Even though chocolate is higher in fat and cholesterol than cocoa, 1/2 cup (125 mL) when spread over 16 slices is acceptable. Here's proof you don't have to eliminate chocolate when you eat light.

MAKE AHEAD

Prepare up to a day ahead or freeze for up to 6 weeks.

PER SERVING	
Calories	226
Protein	5 g
Fat, total	7 g
Fat, saturated	4 g
Carbohydrates	36 g
Sodium	111 mg
Cholesterol	42 mg
Fiber	2 g

Preheat oven to 350° F (180° C).

Bundt pan (9-inch [3 L]) sprayed with vegetable spray

8 oz	5% ricotta cheese	250 g
1/3 cup	margarine or butter	75 mL
1 1/4 cups	granulated sugar	300 mL
2	eggs	2
2 tsp	vanilla	10 mL
1 1/2 cups	all-purpose flour	375 mL
2 tsp	baking powder	10 mL
1/2 tsp	baking soda	2 mL
3/4 cup	2% yogurt or light sour cream	175 mL
1/2 cup	semi-sweet chocolate chips	125 mL

Filling

1/2 cup	brown sugar	125 mL
4 tsp	cocoa	20 mL
1/2 tsp	cinnamon	2 mL

1. In large bowl or food processor, beat together ricotta cheese, margarine and sugar, mixing well. Add eggs and vanilla, mixing well.

2. Combine flour, baking powder and baking soda; add to bowl alternately with yogurt, mixing just until incorporated. Stir in chocolate chips. Pour half of batter into pan.

3. Combine brown sugar, cocoa and cinnamon in small bowl. Sprinkle half over batter in pan. Add remaining batter to pan and top with remaining filling. Bake for 35 to 40 minutes or until tester inserted in the center comes out dry. Sprinkle with icing sugar if desired.

MANGO BLUEBERRY STRUDEL

Serves 8

TIP

Mango can be replaced with ripe peaches or even pears.

Phyllo pastry is located in the freezer section of store. Handle quickly so the sheets do not dry out. Cover those not being used with a slightly damp cloth.

MAKE AHEAD

Prepare filling early in the day. For best results, do not fill until just ready to bake. If in a hurry, fill phyllo, cover and refrigerate. Bake just ahead serving.

Preheat oven to 375° F (190° C)

Baking sheet sprayed with vegetable spray

2 cups	fresh blueberries (or frozen, thawed and drained)	500 mL
1 tbsp	all-purpose flour	15 mL
2 1/2 cups	peeled chopped ripe mango	625 mL
1/4 cup	granulated sugar	50 mL
1 tbsp	lemon juice	15 mL
1/2 tsp	cinnamon	2 mL
6	sheets phyllo pastry	6
2 tsp	melted margarine or butter	10 mL

1. Toss blueberries with flour. In large bowl, combine mango, blueberries, sugar, lemon juice and cinnamon.

2. Lay 2 phyllo sheets one on top of the other; brush with melted margarine. Layer another 2 phyllo sheets on top and brush with melted margarine. Layer last 2 sheets on top. Put fruit filling along long end of phyllo; gently roll over until all of filling is enclosed, fold sides in, and continue to roll. Put on prepared baking sheet, brush with remaining margarine and bake for 20 to 25 minutes or until golden. Sprinkle with icing sugar.

PER SERVING	
Calories	146
Protein	2 g
Fat, total	2 g
Fat, saturated	0.4 g
Carbohydrates	31 g
Sodium	65 mg
Cholesterol	0 mg
Fiber	3 g

BANANA CHOCOLATE FUDGE LAYER CAKE

Serves 12

PER SERVING

Calories	265
Protein	8 g
Fat, total	9 g
Fat, saturated	3 g
Carbohydrates	39 g
Sodium	241 mg
Cholesterol	42 mg
Fiber	2 g

Preheat oven to 350° F (180° C)

Two 8-inch (2 L) round cake pans sprayed with vegetable spray

Banana Cake

3 tbsp	margarine or butter	45 mL
1/3 cup	granulated sugar	75 mL
1	egg	1
1	large ripe banana, mashed	1
1 tsp	vanilla	5 mL
3/4 cup	all-purpose flour	175 mL
1/2 tsp	baking soda	2 mL
1/4 cup	2% yogurt	50 mL

Chocolate Fudge Cake

3 tbsp	margarine or butter	45 mL
3/4 cup	brown sugar	175 mL
1	egg	1
3 tbsp	cocoa	45 mL
1/2 cup	all-purpose flour	125 mL
1/2 tsp	baking soda	2 mL
1/2 tsp	baking powder	2 mL
1/3 cup	2% yogurt	75 mL

Frosting

1 1/2 cups	5% ricotta cheese	375 mL
3/4 cup	icing sugar	175 mL
1/4 cup	cocoa	50 mL
half	banana, sliced thinly	half

1. Banana Cake: Combine margarine and sugar in large bowl or food processor; mix until smooth. Add egg, banana and vanilla; mix until well-combined. In small bowl, stir together flour and baking soda; add flour mixture to banana mixture alternately with

yogurt and mix just until combined. Pour into pre-pared pan and bake for 15 to 20 minutes or until cake tester inserted in the center comes out clean.

2. Chocolate Fudge Cake: Combine margarine, sugar and egg in large bowl; mix until well combined (mix-ture may look curdled). In small bowl, stir together cocoa, flour, baking soda and baking powder; add to the batter alternately with the yogurt. Mix just until combined. Pour into prepared pan and bake for 15 to 20 minutes or until cake tester inserted in the center comes out clean.

3. Frosting: Put ricotta cheese, icing sugar and cocoa in food processor; process until smooth, or beat with electric mixer.

4. Assembly: Put banana cake on serving plate; top with one-quarter of the frosting. Place banana slices over top. Put chocolate cake on top and use remain-ing frosting to frost sides and top.

LEMON AND LIME MERINGUE PIE

Serves 12

PER SERVING

Calories	243
Protein	3 g
Fat, total	6 g
Fat, saturated	1 g
Carbohydrates	46 g
Sodium	109 mg
Cholesterol	18 mg
Fiber	0 g

Preheat oven to 375° F (190° C)

8- or 8.5-inch (2 or 2.25 L) springform pan sprayed with vegetable spray

Crust

1 cup	all-purpose flour	250 mL
1/3 cup	granulated sugar	75 mL
1/3 cup	cold margarine or butter	75 mL
2 tbsp	2% yogurt	25 mL
1 to 2 tbsp	cold water	15 to 25 mL

Filling

1/4 cup	freshly squeezed lime juice	50 mL
1/4 cup	freshly squeezed lemon juice	50 mL
1 1/2 tsp	grated lime zest (about 2 limes)	7 mL
1 1/2 tsp	grated lemon zest (about 1 lemon)	7 mL
1	egg	1
1	egg white	1
1 1/3 cups	granulated sugar	325 mL
1 1/4 cups	water	300 mL
1/3 cup	cornstarch	75 mL
2 tsp	margarine or butter	10 mL

Topping

3	egg whites	3
1/2 tsp	cream of tartar	2 mL
1/3 cup	granulated sugar	75 mL

1. In bowl or food processor, combine flour and sugar; cut in margarine just until crumbly. With fork, gradually stir in yogurt and just enough of the cold water so dough comes together. Pat onto bottom and sides of pan. Bake approximately 18 minutes or until light brown. Raise heat to 425° F (220° C).

2. Meanwhile, in small bowl, combine lime and lemon juices, lime and lemon zest, egg and egg white; set aside.

3. In saucepan, combine sugar, water and cornstarch. Bring to a boil; reduce heat to low and simmer for approximately 1 minute, stirring constantly until mixture is smooth and thick. Pour a bit of the cornstarch mixture into the lemon-lime mixture and whisk together. Pour all back into saucepan and simmer, stirring constantly, for 5 minutes, or until thickened and smooth. Remove from heat. Stir in margarine. Pour into crust.

4. In bowl, beat egg whites with cream of tartar until foamy; continue to beat, gradually adding sugar. Beat until stiff peaks form. Spread over filling. Bake approximately 5 minutes, or until golden brown. Let cool.

BLUEBERRY COFFEE CAKE WITH ALMOND TOPPING

TIP

Almonds can be replaced with pecans. Toast almonds in skillet for 2 minutes until browned.

MAKE AHEAD

Prepare up to a day ahead or freeze up to 3 weeks.

Preheat oven to 350° F (180° C)

9-inch (2.5 L) square baking pan sprayed with vegetable spray

1 cup	granulated sugar	250 mL
1/3 cup	margarine or butter	75 mL
2	eggs	2
1 tsp	almond extract	5 mL
1 2/3 cups	all-purpose flour	400 mL
1 1/2 tsp	baking powder	7 mL
1 1/2 tsp	baking soda	7 mL
3/4 cup	2% yogurt	175 mL
1 1/2 cups	fresh blueberries (or frozen, thawed and drained)	375 mL
2 tsp	all-purpose flour	10 mL

Topping

1/3 cup	toasted chopped almonds	75 mL
1/3 cup	all-purpose flour	75 mL
1/4 cup	packed brown sugar	50 mL
1 tbsp	margarine or butter	15 mL
1/2 tsp	cinnamon	2 mL

1. Topping: In small bowl, combine almonds, flour, brown sugar, margarine and cinnamon until mixed; set aside.

2. In large bowl, beat together sugar, margarine, eggs and almond extract, mixing well.

3. Combine flour, baking powder and baking soda; stir into bowl just until blended. Stir in yogurt. Stir together blueberries and flour; fold into batter. Pour into pan. Sprinkle with topping. Bake for 35 to 40 minutes or until cake tester inserted into center comes out clean.

MARBLE MOCHA CHEESECAKE (PAGE 212) ➤

PER SQUARE	
Calories	198
Protein	4 g
Fat, total	7 g
Fat, saturated	1 g
Carbohydrates	31 g
Sodium	181 mg
Cholesterol	28 mg
Fiber	1 g

CARROT CAKE WITH CREAM CHEESE FROSTING

Serves 16

Preheat oven to 350° F (180° C)

9-inch (3 L) Bundt pan sprayed with vegetable spray

1/3 cup	margarine or butter	75 mL
1 cup	granulated sugar	250 mL
2	eggs	2
1 tsp	vanilla	5 mL
1	large ripe banana, mashed	1
2 cups	grated carrots	500 mL
2/3 cup	raisins	150 mL
1/2 cup	canned pineapple, drained and crushed	125 mL
1/2 cup	2% yogurt	125 mL
2 cups	all-purpose flour	500 mL
1 1/2 tsp	baking powder	7 mL
1 1/2 tsp	baking soda	7 mL
1 1/2 tsp	cinnamon	7 mL
1/4 tsp	nutmeg	1 mL

Icing

1/3 cup	light cream cheese, softened	75 mL
2/3 cup	icing sugar	150 mL
1 tbsp	2% milk	15 mL

1. In large bowl, cream together margarine and sugar until smooth; add eggs and vanilla and beat well (mixture may look curdled). Add mashed banana, carrots, raisins, pineapple and yogurt; stir until well combined.

2. In bowl, stir together flour, baking powder, baking soda, cinnamon and nutmeg. Add to the carrot mixture; stir just until combined. Pour into prepared pan and bake for 40 to 45 minutes or until cake tester inserted in the center comes out clean. Let cool for 10 minutes before inverting onto serving plate.

3. In bowl or food processor, beat together cream cheese, icing sugar and milk until smooth; drizzle over top of cake. Decorate with grated carrots if desired.

≺ CARROT CAKE WITH CREAM CHEESE FROSTING (THIS PAGE)

FRUIT PIE IN SHORTBREAD CRUST WITH CRUNCHY TOPPING

Serves 12

Preheat oven to 375° F (190° C)

9-inch (2.5 L) springform pan sprayed with vegetable spray

TIP

Other fruits can be used, such as peaches, mangoes, nectarines, or a combination. Even fresh blueberries or sliced strawberries can be used.

MAKE AHEAD

Bake crust up to a day ahead. Bake pie earlier in the day. Tastes great out of the oven.

Crust

1 cup	all-purpose flour	250 mL
1/2 cup	granulated sugar	125 mL
1/2 tsp	cinnamon	2 mL
1/4 cup	cold margarine or butter	50 mL
1	egg	1
1 tbsp	water	15 mL

Filling

1 1/2 cups	peeled chopped pears	375 mL
1 1/2 cups	peeled chopped apples	375 mL
1 cup	canned mandarin oranges, drained	250 mL
2/3 cup	raisins	150 mL
1/2 cup	granulated sugar	125 mL
2 tbsp	all-purpose flour	25 mL
1 tsp	cinnamon	5 mL

Topping

1/2 cup	brown sugar	125 mL
1/3 cup	all-purpose flour	75 mL
1/4 cup	rolled oats	50 mL
3/4 tsp	cinnamon	4 mL
2 tbsp	cold margarine or butter	25 mL

1. In bowl, combine flour, sugar and cinnamon. Cut in margarine until crumbly. In small bowl, whisk together egg and water. Gradually add to flour mixture, stirring gently with a fork, until mixture forms a ball. Press into bottom and sides of pan. Bake for 20 to 25 minutes, or until browned. Let cool. Reduce oven to 350° F (180° C).

PER SERVING	
Calories	266
Protein	3 g
Fat, total	5 g
Fat, saturated	1 g
Carbohydrates	54 g
Sodium	71 mg
Cholesterol	18 mg
Fiber	2 g

2. In bowl, combine pears, apples, mandarin oranges, raisins, sugar, flour and cinnamon. Pour into cooled crust.

3. In small bowl, combine brown sugar, flour, oats and cinnamon; cut in margarine until crumbly. Sprinkle on top of fruit. Bake for 30 to 35 minutes or until fruit is tender and top is browned.

BLUEBERRY STRAWBERRY PEAR CRISP

TIP

Other fruits can be substituted, such as peaches, apples or mangoes.

Serve with frozen yogurt.

MAKE AHEAD

Bake earlier in the day, but best if baked just ahead serving.

Preheat oven to 350° F (180° C)

9-inch square (2.5 L) cake pan sprayed with vegetable spray

1 1/2 cups	fresh blueberries (or frozen, thawed and drained)	375 mL
1 1/2 cups	sliced strawberries	375 mL
1 1/2 cups	chopped peeled pears	375 mL
1/2 cup	granulated sugar	125 mL
2 tbsp	all-purpose flour	25 mL
2 tsp	orange juice	10 mL
1 tsp	grated orange zest	5 mL
1/2 tsp	cinnamon	2 mL

Topping

3/4 cup	brown sugar	175 mL
3/4 cup	all-purpose flour	175 mL
1/2 cup	rolled oats	125 mL
1/2 tsp	cinnamon	2 mL
1/4 cup	cold margarine or butter	50 mL

1. In large bowl, combine blueberries, strawberries, pears, sugar, flour, orange juice, orange zest and cinnamon; toss gently to mix. Spread in cake pan.

2. In small bowl, combine brown sugar, flour, oats and cinnamon; cut margarine in until crumbly. Sprinkle over fruit mixture. Bake for 30 to 35 minutes or until topping is browned and fruit is tender.

PER SERVING

Calories	267
Protein	3 g
Fat, total	5 g
Fat, saturated	1 g
Carbohydrates	54 g
Sodium	69 mg
Cholesterol	0 mg
Fiber	3 g

DATE CAKE WITH COCONUT TOPPING

TIP

To chop dates easily, use kitchen shears. Whole pitted dates can be used, but then use food processor to finely chop dates after they are cooked.

Chopped pitted prunes can replace dates.

MAKE AHEAD

Prepare up to 2 days ahead, or freeze for up to 6 weeks. The dates keep this cake moist.

Preheat oven to 350° F (180° C)
9-inch square (2.5 L) cake pan sprayed with vegetable spray

Cake

12 oz	chopped, pitted dried dates	300 g
1 3/4 cups	water	425 mL
1/4 cup	margarine or butter	50 mL
1 cup	granulated sugar	250 mL
2	eggs	2
1 1/2 cups	all-purpose flour	375 mL
1 1/2 tsp	baking powder	7 mL
1 tsp	baking soda	5 mL

Topping

1/3 cup	unsweetened coconut	75 mL
1/4 cup	brown sugar	50 mL
3 tbsp	2% milk	45 mL
2 tbsp	margarine or butter	25 mL

1. Put dates and water in saucepan; bring to a boil, cover and reduce heat to low. Cook for 10 minutes, stirring often, or until dates are soft and most of the liquid has been absorbed. Set aside to cool for 10 minutes.

2. In large bowl or food processor, beat together margarine and sugar. Add eggs and mix well. Add cooled date mixture and mix well.

3. In bowl, combine flour, baking powder and baking soda. Stir into date mixture just until blended. Pour into cake pan and bake for 35 to 40 minutes or until cake tester inserted in center comes out dry.

4. In small saucepan, combine coconut, brown sugar, milk and margarine; cook over medium heat, stirring, for 2 minutes, or until sugar dissolves. Pour over cake.

PER SERVING

Calories	217
Protein	3 g
Fat, total	5 g
Fat, saturated	2 g
Carbohydrates	41 g
Sodium	136 mg
Cholesterol	27 mg
Fiber	2 g

PRUNE ORANGE SPICE CAKE

TIP

To cut prunes easily, use kitchen shears, or you can use whole pitted prunes, but you'll need to finely chop prunes in food processor after they are cooked.

Chopped dried dates can replace prunes.

MAKE AHEAD

Bake up to 2 days ahead or freeze for up to 6 weeks. The dried fruit keeps this cake very moist.

PER SERVING

Calories	179
Protein	3 g
Fat, total	4 g
Fat, saturated	1 g
Carbohydrates	33 g
Sodium	90 mg
Cholesterol	27 mg
Fiber	2 g

Preheat oven to 350° F (180° C)

9-inch square (2.5 L) baking dish sprayed with vegetable spray

8 oz	chopped pitted prunes	250 g
1 cup	orange juice	250 mL
1/3 cup	margarine or butter	75 mL
3/4 cup	granulated sugar	175 mL
2	eggs	2
2 tsp	grated orange zest	10 mL
1 tsp	vanilla	5 mL
1 cup	all-purpose flour	250 mL
1/2 cup	whole wheat flour	125 mL
1 tsp	baking powder	5 mL
3/4 tsp	cinnamon	4 mL
1/2 tsp	baking soda	2 mL
1/8 tsp	nutmeg	0.5 mL
1/3 cup	2% yogurt	75 mL

Icing

4 tsp	orange juice	20 mL
1/2 cup	icing sugar	125 mL

1. Put prunes and orange juice in saucepan; bring to a boil, cover and reduce heat to low. Cook for 10 to 12 minutes, stirring often, or until prunes are soft and most of the liquid has been absorbed. Set aside.

2. In large bowl, cream together margarine and sugar; add eggs, orange zest and vanilla and mix well. Stir in prune mixture and mix well.

3. In bowl, combine flour, whole wheat flour, baking powder, cinnamon, baking soda and nutmeg. Add to wet ingredients alternately with yogurt. Pour into cake pan and bake for 30 to 35 minutes or until cake tester inserted in center comes out clean.

4. In small bowl, combine orange juice and icing sugar until well mixed. Pour over cake.

PUMPKIN MOLASSES RAISIN LOAF

Makes 20 half-slices

TIP

In season, fresh cooked pumpkin can be used.

★

Raisins can be replaced with chopped dried dates, apricots or prunes.

MAKE AHEAD

Can be prepared up to 2 days ahead. Keep tightly covered, or freeze loaf for up to 6 weeks.

Preheat oven to 350° F (180° C)

9- by 5-inch (2 L) loaf pan sprayed with vegetable spray

1 1/4 cups	brown sugar	300 mL
1/3 cup	margarine or butter	75 mL
2	eggs	2
2 tbsp	molasses	25 mL
1 tsp	vanilla	5 mL
1 cup	canned pumpkin purée	250 mL
1 cup	raisins	250 mL
1 1/3 cups	all-purpose flour	325 mL
2/3 cup	whole wheat flour	150 mL
2 1/4 tsp	cinnamon	11 mL
1 1/2 tsp	baking powder	7 mL
1/2 tsp	baking soda	2 mL
1/4 tsp	ginger	1 mL
1/2 cup	2% yogurt	125 mL

1. In large bowl, beat sugar and margarine together until crumbly. Add eggs and mix until smooth. Beat in molasses, vanilla and pumpkin. (Mixture may appear curdled.) Stir in raisins.

2. In bowl, combine flour, whole wheat flour, cinnamon, baking powder, baking soda and ginger. Add to wet ingredients alternately with the yogurt; stir just until combined. Pour into pan and bake for 55 to 60 minutes or until cake tester inserted in center comes out clean.

PER HALF-SLICE

Calories	160
Protein	3 g
Fat, total	4 g
Fat, saturated	1 g
Carbohydrates	31 g
Sodium	79 mg
Cholesterol	22 mg
Fiber	1 g

CARROT, APPLE AND COCONUT LOAF

TIP

Grate carrots or chop and process them in food processor just until finely diced.

Chopped, pitted dates can replace raisins.

MAKE AHEAD

Prepare up to a day ahead, or freeze up to 4 weeks.

Preheat oven to 350 F (180 C)

9- by 5-inch (2 L) loaf pan sprayed with vegetable spray

2/3 cup	granulated sugar	150 mL
1/4 cup	margarine or butter	50 mL
2	eggs	2
1 1/2 tsp	cinnamon	7 mL
1/4 tsp	nutmeg	1 mL
1 tsp	vanilla	5 mL
1 1/4 cup	grated carrots	300 mL
2/3 cup	peeled, finely chopped apples	150 mL
1/3 cup	unsweetened shredded coconut	75 mL
1/3 cup	raisins	75 mL
2/3 cup	all-purpose flour	150 mL
1/2 cup	whole wheat flour	125 mL
1 tsp	baking powder	5 mL
1 tsp	baking soda	5 mL
1/3 cup	2% yogurt	75 mL

1. In large bowl or food processor, cream together sugar and margarine. Add eggs, cinnamon, nutmeg and vanilla; beat well. Stir in carrots, apples, coconut and raisins.

2. In bowl, combine flour, whole wheat flour, baking powder and baking soda; add to batter alternately with yogurt, mixing until just combined. Pour batter into loaf pan; bake for 40 to 45 minutes or until tester inserted in center comes out clean.

PER HALF-SLICE

Calories	101
Protein	2 g
Fat, total	3 g
Fat, saturated	1 g
Carbohydrates	16 g
Sodium	99 mg
Cholesterol	22 mg
Fiber	1 g

PINEAPPLE CARROT DATE MUFFINS

Makes 12 muffins

TIP

By using vegetable oil, not butter, you cut down on the total cholesterol.

★

Raisins, prunes or apricots can replace dates.

★

This can be made in 9- by 5-inch (2 L) loaf pan. Bake for approximately 30 minutes or until tester comes out dry.

MAKE AHEAD

Prepare up to a day ahead. Freeze for up to 6 weeks.

Preheat oven to 375° F (190° C)

12 muffin cups sprayed with vegetable spray

3/4 cup	granulated sugar	175 mL
1/3 cup	vegetable oil	75 mL
1	egg	1
1 tsp	vanilla	5 mL
1/2 cup	grated carrots	75 mL
1/2 cup	canned pineapple, drained and crushed	125 mL
1/3 cup	finely chopped dates	75 mL
1/3 cup	light sour cream or 2% yogurt	75 mL
1 cup	all-purpose flour	250 mL
2/3 cup	rolled oats	150 mL
1 tsp	baking powder	5 mL
1 tsp	baking soda	5 mL
1 tsp	cinnamon	5 mL
1/4 tsp	nutmeg	1 mL

1. In large bowl, combine sugar, oil, egg and vanilla; mix well.

2. Stir in carrots, pineapple, dates and sour cream.

3. In bowl, combine flour, oats, baking powder, baking soda, cinnamon and nutmeg. Add to wet ingredients and mix just until combined. Spoon into prepared muffin cups and bake for 15 to 18 minutes or until tops are firm to the touch and tester inserted in center comes out clean.

PER MUFFIN

Calories	189
Protein	3 g
Fat, total	7 g
Fat, saturated	1 g
Carbohydrates	30 g
Sodium	118 mg
Cholesterol	20 mg
Fiber	1 g

BANANA DATE MUFFINS

TIP

These muffins will be fairly flat due to the weight of the dates.

A food processor can be used. Do not overmix flour mixture.

If using bran flakes cereal, be sure not to use All-Bran or raw bran. The flakes give a crunchy texture.

Dates can be replaced with dried apricots, prunes or raisins.

MAKE AHEAD

Prepare up to a day ahead, or freeze up to 3 weeks.

Preheat oven to 375° F (190° C)

12 muffin cups sprayed with vegetable spray

1/4 cup	margarine or butter	50 mL
1	medium banana, mashed	1
3/4 cup	granulated sugar	175 mL
1	egg	1
1 tsp	vanilla	5 mL
3/4 cup	all-purpose flour	175 mL
1/2 cup	bran or corn flakes cereal	125 mL
1 tsp	baking powder	5 mL
1 tsp	baking soda	5 mL
3/4 cup	pitted, dried and chopped dates	175 mL
1/2 cup	2% yogurt	125 mL

1. In large bowl, combine margarine, banana, sugar, egg and vanilla; mix well.

2. In bowl, combine flour, bran flakes cereal, baking powder and baking soda. Add to wet ingredients and stir just until mixed. Stir in dates and yogurt, just until smooth.

3. Spoon batter into prepared muffin cups and bake for 15 to 20 minutes, or until tops are firm and tester inserted in center comes out clean.

PER MUFFIN	
Calories	158
Protein	2 g
Fat, total	4 g
Fat, saturated	1 g
Carbohydrates	30 g
Sodium	176 mg
Cholesterol	19 mg
Fiber	1 g

RUGELACH
(CINNAMON CHOCOLATE TWIST COOKIES)

TIP

These traditionally high-fat cookies are lower in fat and calories because we've used yogurt, and cocoa instead of chocolate.

 ★

These are best eaten the day they are made; any leftover cookies are best eaten biscotti-fashion, dipped in coffee.

MAKE AHEAD

Prepare dough and freeze for up to 2 weeks. Bake cookies up to a day ahead, keeping tightly covered.

PER COOKIE

Calories	117
Protein	2 g
Fat, total	4 g
Fat, saturated	1 g
Carbohydrates	19 g
Sodium	53 mg
Cholesterol	0 mg
Fiber	1 g

Preheat oven to 350° F (180° C)

Baking sheets sprayed with vegetable spray

Dough

2 1/4 cups	all-purpose flour	550 mL
2/3 cup	granulated sugar	150 mL
1/2 cup	cold margarine or butter	125 mL
1/3 cup	2% yogurt	75 mL
3 to 4 tbsp	water	45 to 50 mL
1/2 cup	brown sugar	125 mL
1/3 cup	raisins	75 mL
2 tbsp	semi-sweet chocolate chips	25 mL
1 tbsp	cocoa	15 mL
1/2 tsp	cinnamon	2 mL

1. In bowl, combine flour and sugar. Cut in margarine until crumbly. Add yogurt and water, and mix until combined. Roll into a smooth ball, wrap and place in refrigerator for 30 minutes.

2. Put brown sugar, raisins, chocolate chips, cocoa and cinnamon in food processor; process until crumbly, approximately 20 seconds.

3. Divide dough in half. Roll one portion into a rectangle of 1/4-inch (5 mm) thickness on a well-floured surface. Sprinkle half of the filling on top of the dough rectangle. Roll up tightly, long end to long end, jelly-roll fashion; pinch ends together. Cut into 1-inch (2.5 cm) thick pieces; some filling will fall out. Place on baking sheets cut side up. Repeat with remaining dough and filling.

4. With the back of a spoon or your fingers, gently flatten each cookie. Bake for 25 minutes, turning the cookies over at the halfway mark (12 1/2 minutes).

OATMEAL ORANGE COCONUT COOKIES

Preheat oven to 350° F (180° C)

Baking sheets sprayed with vegetable spray

1/4 cup	margarine or butter	50 mL
1/4 cup	brown sugar	50 mL
1/2 cup	granulated sugar	125 mL
1	egg	1
1 tsp	vanilla	5 mL
2 tbsp	orange juice concentrate, thawed	25 mL
1/2 tsp	grated orange zest	2 mL
2/3 cup	all-purpose flour	150 mL
1/2 tsp	baking powder	2 mL
1/2 tsp	baking soda	2 mL
1/2 tsp	cinnamon	2 mL
1 cup	corn flakes or bran flakes cereal	250 mL
2/3 cup	raisins	150 mL
1/2 cup	rolled oats	125 mL
1/4 cup	coconut	50 mL

TIP

The orange juice concentrate gives a more intense flavor than just orange juice. Remove some from package in freezer, then refreeze remainder.

If using bran flakes cereal, do not use All-Bran or raw bran.

Replace raisins with dried chopped dates, apricots or prunes.

MAKE AHEAD

Bake cookies up to a day ahead, keeping tightly covered in a cookie tin. Freeze cookie dough for up to 2 weeks.

1. In large bowl, cream together margarine, brown sugar and granulated sugar. Add egg, vanilla, orange juice concentrate and orange zest and mix well.

2. In another bowl, combine flour, baking powder, baking soda, cinnamon, corn flakes, raisins, rolled oats and coconut just until combined. Add to sugar mixture and mix until just combined

3. Drop by heaping teaspoons (5 mL) onto prepared baking sheets 2 inches (5 cm) apart and press down with back of fork; bake approximately 10 minutes or until browned.

PER COOKIE

Calories	51
Protein	1 g
Fat, total	1 g
Fat, saturated	1 g
Carbohydrates	9 g
Sodium	34 mg
Cholesterol	5 mg
Fiber	0 g

Oatmeal Date Cookies

Preheat oven to 350° F (180° C)

Baking sheets sprayed with vegetable spray

1/3 cup	margarine or butter	75 mL
1/3 cup	granulated sugar	75 mL
1	egg	1
1 tsp	vanilla	5 mL
2/3 cup	all-purpose flour	150 mL
1 tsp	baking powder	5 mL
3/4 tsp	cinnamon	4 mL
3/4 cup	rolled oats	175 mL
3/4 cup	bran flakes cereal or corn flakes	175 mL
2/3 cup	chopped, pitted and dried dates	150 mL

1. In large bowl, cream together margarine and sugar. Add egg and vanilla and mix well.

2. In another bowl, combine flour, baking powder, cinnamon, rolled oats, cereal and dates. Add to sugar mixture and mix until just combined.

3. Drop by heaping teaspoonfuls (5 mL) onto prepared baking sheets 2 inches (5 cm) apart and press down with back of fork; bake for approximately 10 minutes or until browned.

APRICOT DATE BISCOTTI

TIP

Use a serrated knife to cut the logs into slices.

Dried prunes or raisins can replace, or be used in combination, with the apricots and dates.

Orange juice concentrate gives a more intense flavor than just orange juice. Use frozen concentrate, then refreeze the remainder.

MAKE AHEAD

Bake cookies up to 2 days ahead for best flavor, keeping tightly covered in cookie tin. Freeze cookie dough for up to 2 weeks.

PER COOKIE

Calories	62
Protein	1 g
Fat, total	1 g
Fat, saturated	0.3 g
Carbohydrates	11 g
Sodium	19 mg
Cholesterol	9 mg
Fiber	1 g

Preheat oven to 350° F (180° C)

Baking sheet sprayed with vegetable spray

1/3 cup	margarine or butter	75 mL
3/4 cup	granulated sugar	175 mL
2	eggs	2
2 tbsp	orange juice concentrate, thawed	25 mL
2 tbsp	water	25 mL
2 tsp	grated orange zest	10 mL
1 tsp	vanilla	5 mL
2 2/3 cups	all-purpose flour	650 mL
2 1/4 tsp	baking powder	11 mL
1 tsp	cinnamon	5 mL
2/3 cup	pitted, dried and chopped dates	150 mL
2/3 cup	chopped dried apricots	150 mL

1. In large bowl, cream together margarine and sugar; add eggs, orange juice concentrate, water, orange zest and vanilla and mix well.

2. In bowl, combine flour, baking powder, cinnamon, dates and apricots; add to wet ingredients and stir just until mixed. Divide dough into 3 portions; shape each portion into a 12-inch (30-cm) long log, 2 inches wide (5 cm), and put on prepared baking sheet. Bake for 20 minutes. Let cool for 10 minutes.

3. Cut logs on an angle into 1/2-inch (1-cm) thick slices. Put slices flat on baking sheet and bake for another 20 minutes or until lightly browned.

MOCHA BROWNIES WITH CREAM CHEESE ICING

Makes 16 squares

TIP

These brownies are rather moist, not dry, and they're sensational. Remember not to eat all 16 pieces yourself!

One tablespoon (15 mL) prepared strong coffee can be used instead of instant.

Icing can be eliminated if desired.

MAKE AHEAD

Prepare up to 2 days ahead, keeping refrigerated or at room temperature. Freeze for up to 4 weeks.

PER SQUARE

Calories	122
Protein	2 g
Fat, total	5 g
Fat, saturated	2 g
Carbohydrates	18 g
Sodium	127 mg
Cholesterol	16 mg
Fiber	2 g

Preheat oven to 350° F (180° C)

8-inch (2 L) square cake pan sprayed with vegetable spray

1/3 cup	margarine or butter	75 mL
3/4 cup	granulated sugar	175 mL
1	egg	1
2 tsp	instant coffee granules	10 mL
1 tbsp	warm water	15 mL
1/3 cup	unsweetened cocoa	75 mL
1/3 cup	all-purpose flour	75 mL
1 tsp	baking powder	5 mL
1/4 cup	2% yogurt	50 mL

Icing

1/4 cup	light cream cheese, softened	50 mL
1/2 cup	icing sugar	125 mL

1. In bowl, cream together margarine and sugar until smooth. Add egg and mix well. Dissolve coffee granules in the warm water; add to batter and beat until well combined. (Mixture may look curdled.)

2. In small bowl, stir together cocoa, flour and baking powder; add to batter alternately with yogurt, stirring just until blended. Pour batter into prepared pan and bake for 20 minutes, or until edges begin to pull away from pan (center will be still slightly soft). Let cool.

3. Icing: In small bowl, beat together cream cheese and icing sugar until smooth. Spread over top of brownies.

CHOCOLATE COFFEE TIRAMISU

Serves 16

TIP

Sift some icing sugar or cocoa on top of each portion just before serving.

This tiramisu tastes so decadent, you'll never believe it hasn't the same calories and fat as the one made with mascarpone.

Spongy or harder lady fingers can be used.

The longer this chills, the better it is. The liqueur-coffee mixture penetrates the cookies.

MAKE AHEAD

Prepare up to 2 days ahead. It tastes best after 8 hours of refrigeration.

PER SERVING

Calories	133
Protein	5 g
Fat, total	3 g
Fat, saturated	2 g
Carbohydrates	18 g
Sodium	121 mg
Cholesterol	26 mg
Fiber	0 g

9-inch (2.5 L) square baking dish sprayed with vegetable spray

1 1/2 cups	5% ricotta cheese	375 mL
1/2 cup	light cream cheese	125 mL
1/2 cup	granulated sugar	125 mL
3 tbsp	cocoa	45 mL
1	egg yolk	1
1 tsp	vanilla	5 mL
3	egg whites	3
1/3 cup	granulated sugar	75 mL
3/4 cup	strong, prepared coffee	175 mL
3 tbsp	chocolate or coffee-flavored liqueur	45 mL
16	lady finger cookies	16

1. In food processor, combine ricotta cheese, cream cheese, sugar, cocoa, egg yolk and vanilla until smooth; transfer to a bowl.

2. In bowl, beat egg whites until soft peaks form. Gradually add sugar and continue to beat until stiff peaks form. Gently fold the whites into the ricotta mixture.

3. Combine coffee and liqueur in a small bowl.

4. Put half of lady fingers in bottom of dish. Sprinkle with half of coffee-liqueur mixture. Spread half of ricotta mixture on top. Repeat layers. Cover and chill for at least 3 hours, or overnight.

MENUS FOR EVERYONE

With over 175 recipes ranging from soups right through to desserts, finding the right courses to make a complete meal is not always easy. At the end, whatever you enjoy eating is the right choice. But there will be times when finding the right soup to fit the chicken entrée and finding the appropriate dessert is not easy. Here are some suggested menus so that you can enjoy certain foods that go better with each other.

FAMILY DINNERS

Potato Cheddar Cheese Soup
Tuna Dressing over Pasta Niçoise
Sour Cream Cinnamon Coffee Cake

★

English Muffin Tomato Olive Bruschetta
Chicken Fagioli
Vegetable Dill Latkes
Fresh Fruit

★

Spinach Salad with Oranges and Mushrooms
Crunchy Fish with Cucumber Dill Relish
Carrot Cake with Cream Cheese Frosting

★

Four-Tomato Salad
Hoisin Garlic Burgers
Broccoli Pesto Fettuccine

★

Mini Pesto Shrimp Tortilla Pizzas
Lamb Vegetable Stew over Garlic Mashed Potatoes
Date Cake with Coconut Topping

REHEATABLE FAMILY CASSEROLES

Ratatouille Meatloaf Casserole with Cheese Topping
Seafood Tetrazzini with Sun-Dried Tomatoes and Goat Cheese
Lamb Vegetable Stew over Garlic Mashed Potatoes
Spicy Meatball and Pasta Stew
Creamy Baked Beefaroni
Turkey Macaroni Chili
Pesto Seafood Paella

ASIAN EVENINGS

Oriental Egg Rolls
Pork Stir-Fry with Sweet & Sour Sauce, Snow Peas and Red Peppers over Rice Noodles

★

Oriental Coleslaw
Chicken Satay with Peanut Sauce
Pasta with Creamy Szechuan Dressing and Crisp Vegetables

★

Hoisin Cocktail Meatballs
Oriental Chicken Salad with Mandarin Oranges, Snow Peas and Asparagus

★

Oriental Eggrolls
Chicken Stir-Fry with Asparagus, Bok Choy and Oyster Sauce over Pasta

★

Chinese Chicken with Garlic Ginger Sauce
Vegetable Hoisin Fried Rice

★

Chinese Lemon Chicken on a Bed of Red Pepper and Snow Peas
Asparagus with Oyster Sauce and Sesame Sauce

★

Polynesian Wild Rice Salad
Salmon Fillets with Black Bean Sauce

★

Oriental Beef Bundles in Lettuce
Asparagus with Oyster Sauce & Sesame Seeds

SUMMER BARBECUE MEALS

Seafood Kebabs with Pineapple and Green Pepper in Apricot Glaze
Couscous Salad with Tomato, Feta Cheese and Olives

★

Red and Yellow Bell Pepper Soup
Avocado Tomato Salsa
Salmon over Black-and-White-Bean Salsa

★

Creamy Pesto Dip
Lamb Kebabs with Pecan Oriental Sauce
Pasta with Creamy Szechuan Dressing and Crisp Vegetables

★

Pesto Potato Salad
Hoisin Garlic Burgers

★

Oriental Coleslaw
Fish Fillets with Corn and Red Pepper Salsa

SEAFOOD EXTRAVAGANZAS

Creamy Salmon Dill Bisque
Pesto Seafood Paella
★
Squid Rings with Creamy Tomato Dip
Fish with Sun-Dried Tomato Pesto, Feta and Black Olives
★
Clam and Scallop Chowder
Mussels with Pesto
french bread for dipping
★
Seafood Garlic Antipasto
Salmon Salad with Peanut Lime Dressing
★
Mussel and Sweet Pepper Salad
Seafood Tetrazzini with Sun-dried Tomatoes and Goat Cheese
★
Clam Minestrone
Rice Pilaf with Escargots and Squid
★
Sautéed Crab Cakes with Chunky Dill Tarter Sauce
Linguine with Pecan Oriental Sauce and Salmon

HOT BUFFET MEALS

English Muffin Tomato Olive Bruschetta/ Mini Pesto Shrimp Tortilla Pizzas
Creamy Sun-dried Tomatoes and Goat Cheese Lasagna
Shells stuffed with Spicy Sausage and Ricotta
Fish with Cornbread and Dill Stuffing/ Chicken and Eggplant Parmesan
Greek Baked Stuffed Potatoes
Chocolate Coffee Tiramisu/ Blueberry Coffee Cake with Almond Topping
★
Chicken Satay with Peanut Sauce/ Smoked Salmon Quiche Bites
Manicotti Stuffed with Chick peas and Cheese
Gnocchi with Tomatoes, Olives and Goat Cheese
Leg of Lamb with Pesto and Wild Rice/ Phyllo Chicken and Spinach Bake
Sweet Potato and Carrot Casserole with Molasses and Pecans/ Banana
Chocolate Fudge Layer Cake/ Rugelach

CHILDREN'S & TEENAGER'S GET-TOGETHERS

Veggies & Dip
Spicy Meatballs and Pasta Stew
Banana Peanut Butter Chip Muffins
★

Beef and Sausage Sloppy Joes over Hamburger Buns
Corn on the Cob
Triple Chocolate Brownies
★

Three Bean Soup
Honey Coated Chicken Fingers with Potato Wedge Fries
Peanut Butter Fudge Cookies
★

Vegetable Bean Chicken Soup
Crunchy Baked Macaroni and Cheese/ or Crunchy Cheese and Herb Drumsticks
Oatmeal Date Cookies
★

Sweet & Sour Chicken Meatballs over Rice
Peanut Butter-Coconut-Raisin Granola Bars
★

Beef and Bean Couscous Minestrone
Creamy Baked Beefaroni/ or Chicken Tortillas
Oatmeal Orange Coconut Cookies

COLD BUFFET MEALS

Creamy Pesto Dip/ Seafood Tortilla Pinwheels
Swordfish with Mango Coriander Salsa
Fish with Corn and Red Pepper Salsa
Greek Barley Salad
Turkey Pesto Salad
Pasta with Creamy Szechuan Dressing and Crisp Vegetables
Apple Cinnamon Cheesecake
Apricot Date Biscotti
★

Double Salmon and Dill Pâté/ Seafood Garlic Antipasto
Salmon over Black and White Bean Salsa
Chinese Chicken with Garlic Ginger Sauce
Polynesian Wild Rice Salad
Tuna Dressing over Pasta Niçoise
Sour Cream Cinnamon Coffee Cake
Oatmeal Orange Coconut Cookies

EXTRAVAGANT "IMPRESSIVE" DINNERS

Double Salmon and Dill Pâté/ Goat Cheese and Spinach Phyllo Triangles
Mussel and Sweet Pepper Salad
Roasted Chicken with Apricot Orange Glaze and Couscous Stuffing
Mushrooms with Creamy Feta Cheese and Dill Stuffing
Banana Chocolate Fudge Layer Cake
★
Mini Pesto Shrimp Tortilla Pizza
Red and Yellow Bell Pepper Soup
Leg of Lamb with Pesto and Wild Rice
Eggplant with Goat Cheese and Roasted Sweet Peppers
Lemon Poppy Seed Cheesecake
★

Seafood Tortilla Pinwheels
Four-Tomato Salad
Salmon Fillets with Black Bean Sauce
Asparagus, Red Pepper and Goat Cheese Phyllo Roll
Marble Mocha Cheesecake
★
Chicken Satay with Peanut Sauce or Hoisin Cocktail Meatballs
Warm Caesar Pasta Salad
Fish with Smoked Salmon and Green Peas
Broccoli, Carrot and Dill Vegetable Strudel
Chocolate Coffee Tiramisu
★

Greek Egg Rolls with Spinach and Feta
Creamy Sun-dried Tomato and Goat Cheese Lasagna
Chicken Breast Stuffed with Brie Cheese, Red Pepper and Green Onions
Greek Baked Stuffed Potatoes with Tomato, Olives and Cheese
Lemon and Lime Meringue Pie

VEGETARIAN HEAVEN*

Black Bean Soup
Broccoli Pesto Fettuccine
Carrot, Apple and Coconut Loaf
★
Chunky Red Pepper and Tomato Soup
Polenta Pizza with Mushrooms, Olives and Goat Cheese
Falafel Burgers with Creamy Sesame Sauce
Pumpkin Molasses Raisin Loaf
★
Mushroom Phyllo Pizza
Barley, Tomato and Olive Casserole
Prune Orange Spice Cake
★
Rice Black Bean and Red Pepper Salad
Jumbo Shells filled with Pesto & Ricotta Cheese
Fruit Pie in Shortbread Crust with Crunchy Topping
★
Leek Split Pea Soup
Couscous Salad with Tomatoes, Feta Cheese and Olives
Mango Blueberry Strudel

Where chicken stock is called for in the above recipes, substitute vegetable stock.

INDEX